TO
MY WIFE, LINDA

BIBLIOTHECA «EPHEMERIDES LITURGICAE»
«SUBSIDIA»

Collectio cura A. Pistoia, C.M., et A.M. Triacca, S.D.B. recta

---- 33 ----

FROM THE LORD
AND "THE BEST REFORMED CHURCHES"

*A study of the eucharistic liturgy
in the English Puritan and Separatist traditions
1550-1633*

By
BRYAN D. SPINKS

Volume I

C.L.V. - EDIZIONI LITURGICHE — 00192 ROMA
Via Pompeo Magno, 21 - Tel. (06) 353.114
1984

The Author

The Reverend Bryan D. Spinks is a priest in the Church of England, and has specialised in the liturgy of the English Reformed tradition, and of the East Syrian tradition. At present he is Chaplain at Churchill College in the University of Cambridge, England, and also lectures in liturgy in the Divinity Faculty of the University.

The Companion volume to *From the Lord and 'the best Reformed Churches'* is *Freedom or Order?* The Eucharistic Liturgy in English Congregationalism, 1645-1980, (Pittsburgh Theological Monograph New Series 8) Pickwick Publications, Pittsburgh USA, 1984.

PREFACE

For far too long the liturgies of the English Reformed tradition have been regarded as merely a tiresome by-product in the history of Anglican liturgy. In fact, during the sixteenth and seventeenth centuries, there was a strong Reformed tradition within the English Church, and an equally strong desire to introduce into England a liturgy of the Continental Reformed pattern. This liturgical tradition is quite distinct from that of the *Book of Common Prayer*, and it is considered here in its own right. Thwarted in the reigns of Elizabeth I and James I, this tradition had its hour of glory under Cromwell, when in 1645 the Prayer Book was legally replaced by the *Westminster Directory*. This volume considers the liturgical background of this tradition, which set the scene for the making of the *Westminster Directory*, and forms a companion volume to my *Freedom or Order?*, published by Pickwick Publications, which examines the English Reformed tradition as it developed within Congregationalism, from 1645 to 1980.

I would like to acknowledge my debt to those who have previously considered some aspects of this study: W. D. Maxwell, *The Liturgical Portions of the Genevan Service Book*, 1931; Horton Davies, *The Worship of the English Puritans*, 1948, and his more general treatment in the volumes of *Worship and Theology in England*; and Stephen Mayor, *The Lord's Supper in Early English Dissent*, 1972. It will be evident that at times I, have found it necessary to dissent from some of their suggestions and findings.

I would like also to thank those who assisted my researches, particularly Dr. A.C. Honders and Professor Nijenhuis of Groningen University, and Rev. M. Den Dulk, minister of Austin Friars, who guided me through the complications surrounding John à Lasco and the Dutch liturgies. I am also grateful to Mr. David G. Lane for permission to include his translation of à Lasco's rite in this volume (Text B). I would also like to express my thanks to the Revs. Molinelli, Pistoia and Triacca of Centro Liturgico Vincenziano who have so kindly published this work in the distinguished series Bibliotheca "Ephemerides Liturgicae" Subsidia.

The book is dedicated to my wife Linda, without whose support these last two years this study would never have been published.

Bryan D. Spinks.
Churchill College,
University of Cambridge.
England.   16th July 1983

ABBREVIATIONS

AC	=	Alcuin Club.
CHST	=	*Congregational Historical Society Transactions.*
CQR	=	*Church Quarterly Review.*
DNB	=	*Dictionary of National Biography.*
ET	=	English Tanslation.
HSB	=	Henry Bradshaw Society.
JEH	=	*Journal of Ecclesiastical History.*
JTS	=	*Journal of Theological Studies.*
LACT	=	Library of Anglo-Catholic Theology.
LR	=	*Liturgical Review.*
n.d.	=	no date of publication.
n.p.	=	no place of publication.
N.S.	=	*New Series.*
PR	=	*A Parte of a Register*, Middleburg, 1953.
SL	=	*Studia Liturgica.*
SPR	=	A Seconde Parte of a Register. M.S.

INTRODUCTION: PURITANISM AND SEPARATISM

Since the name "Puritan" first emerged in Elizabethan England, there has been no agreement about who were the Puritans or what Puritanism was. The name originated as a term of abuse in the religious propaganda of the period; and from the beginning it was applied to all sorts of people for all sorts of reasons [1]. Indeed, it was often deliberately exploited to create confusion [2].

The terms "pure", "purify" and "purity" were in common use among the German and Swiss reformers — Philip Melanchthon, Martin Bucer, Peter Martyr, Henry Bullinger and John Calvin, and many others. This notion of "pure" refuted the charge that the reformers were innovators; instead it was their aim to cleanse the Church and restore it to its pristine state, and for their authority to do this the reformers appealed to Scripture. However, as to the extent of the purification demanded by Scripture, the reformers were sharply divided. Luther, while appealing to the Word of God, was of the opinion that such things of human invention such as ceremonial, unless actually forbidden by Scripture, were optional and left to individual choice. On the other hand, the Swiss school, represented by Calvin, with its emphasis on the depravity and helplessness of man, would only accept what the Bible specifically warranted. Such things as vestments, the sign of the cross in Baptism, and the oil in Confirmation, would be erased from a truly reformed church. This difference of opinion on the extent of Scriptural authority and purification was the cause of controversy over vestments during the German Interim (1547-55) [3].

In England the word "Puritan" came to be applied to those who followed the Swiss school of thought, represented by Donne's "Crantz", who

> ... loves her onely, who at Geneva is call'd
> Religion, plaine, simple, sullen, yong,
> Contemptuous, yet unhansome; As among
> Lecherous humors, there is one that judges
> No wenches wholsome, but coarse country drudges [4].

---

[1] L.J. TRINTERUD, *Elizabethan Puritanism*, New York, 1971, p. 3.
[2] C. HILL, *Society and Puritanism in Pre-Revolutionary England*, Panther Edition, London, 1969, P. 18.
[3] L.J. TRINTERUD, *Op. cit.*, pp. 5 ff.
[4] JOHN DONNE, "Satyre on Religion".

The Puritan believed that the sole authority and criterion for the Church was the literal text of the Bible:

> ... the Word is a rule of faith, a canon to direct our lives. The Word in the judge of controversies, the rock of infallibility. That only is to be received for truth which agrees with Scripture, as the transcript with the original. All maxims in divinity are to be brought to the touchstone of Scripture, as all measures are brought to the standard [5].

It has been pointed out, however, that Calvin had believed that the conjunction of Word and Spirit made the Scriptures normative through the way in which they created and nourished faith; for many Puritans the efficacy of Scripture rested upon the identification of the text and the Spirit, through a conception of the Bible as verbally inspired and inerrant. In this conception, the English Puritan went beyond Calvin [6].

Since the Elizabethan Church retained unscriptural names and offices such as "Archbishop", "Priest", "Canon", "Dean", unscriptural institutions such as the ecclesiastical courts, and unscriptural ceremonies such as the sign of the cross, the Puritan believed that the English Reformation remained incomplete. Furthermore, these reformers became alarmed at the Erastian nature of the English Church; the Queen's refusal to initiate further reform seemed to imply that the Royal Supremacy had more authority than Scripture. It was the aim of the Puritans to reform the English Church in accordance with the Word of God.

In his analysis of Elizabethan Puritan writings, Trinterud discerned three types of Puritanism: The Original, Anti-vestment Party; The Passive-Resistance Party; and the Presbyterian Party [7]. But since the boundaries between these parties are very faint, it is difficult to draw such sharp distinctions. It would probably be more accurate to suggest that the more the logical conclusions of obedience to Scripture were pressed, the more the Puritans found in the Established Church with which to be dissatisfied. The original dispute, imported from the Continent, was over vestments; the argument was later extended to ministry and worship. The ultimate extension of the Puritan protest was Separatism.

In the Edwardian Church the various continental schools of thought were well represented, though no one school ever dominated. The Swiss Puritan element asserted itself in 1550 when John Hooper, a pupil of the Zurich re-

---

[5] THOMAS WATSON, *A Body of Divinity*, (1692), Banner of Truth Trust edition, London, 1970, p. 30.
[6] PETER TOON, *Hyper-Calvinism*, London, 1967, P. 16.
[7] TRINTERUD, *op. cit.*

former, Henry Bullinger, was made Bishop of Gloucester. Hooper, "an opponent of Lutherans and Bucerians, but a constant defender and promoter of the true faith" [8], objected to the traditional vestments of his office, and the taking of oaths, citing Scripture to justify his complaint. This "independent" protest was renewed under Elizabeth by the Marian exiles returning from the Continent. After Edward's death, his sister Mary had restored the Roman Catholich faith to England, and many protestants had fled abroad. While in exile they had followed the custom of the more advanced continental Reformed Churches of the minister wearing a gown for worship rather than the surplice. Also, the size of their numbers, and the fact that they were exiles, had meant that church government had been centered upon the congregation itself. On their return after the accession of Elizabeth, they found that the Edwardian Church had been restored, with certain additions, and "frozen" by law. Vestments were retained, and so also was Episcopal church government, the latter being significantly different from the continental Reformed church government. Puritans such as Bishop Miles Coverdale, Thomas Sampson, Thomas Lever and William Whittingham, in defiance of the Queen, continued their continental practices in England, appealing to Scripture for the lawfulness of their actions. As Peter Toon says:

> The origin of Elizabethan Puritanism is thus be sought in the critical attitude of convinced Protestants to the Settlement of Religion. For their biblically-enlightened consciences the essential rock of offence was the large measure of continuity with the Roman Catholic past which persisted in the ministry and government of the Church as well as in its liturgy and church furnishings. Abroad they had seen the Reformed Churches of the Rhineland and Switzerland. They had become Bible Christians — that is they interpreted the Bible in the way that men like Calvin, Beza and Bullinger did [9].

Already by 1566 a number of clergymen had been suspended for "nonconformity" in matters of vesture.

By the 1570's a more radical Puritanism began to emerge. Its leaders included Thomas Cartwright, William Fulke, John Field and Thomas Wilcox. They demanded far-reaching structural changes in the Church, in its administration and finances, and in the relation between Church and State, as well as in doctrine and liturgy. They had their eyes on the organisation of the Reformed Churches — the Calvinistic Huguenots and protestants of the Palatinate and the Netherlands, as well as Scotland, and hoped to effect a similar

---

[8] *Original Letters relative to the English Reformation*, Parker Society, 2 vols., London, 1846-47; Vol. 2 p. 662. John Burcher to Henry Bullinger, April 20th, 1550.
[9] P. TOON, *Puritans and Calvinism*, Swengel, Pennsylvania, 1973, p. 12.

reform in England through Parliament and by theological argument. It was their belief that in the New Testament there was one ideal Church delineated which not only could be reconstructed in its essentials, but must as part of their generation's obedience to God, be reconstructed in Elizabethan England. In practice this meant replacing the Episcopal system of church government with that of a Presbyterian, or Classis, system. Thus, for example, William Fulke (1538-1589), the Puritan Master of Pembroke Hall and Vice-Chancellor of Cambridge University, wrote:

> The church of God is the house of God, and therefore ought to be directed in all things according to the order prescribed by the Householder himself; which order is not to be learned elsewhere but in his holy word [10].

Fulke argued for a church government of Doctors, Elders or Presbyters, and Deacons, with a Synod or General Council [11].

Some Puritan ministers organised themselves independently of the establishment, forming a Presbyterian Classis system and holding "Prophesyings" — a semi-public discussion of biblical passages, a practice originating in Zurich. They also held their own ordinations before sending ordinands to the bishops [12]. They hoped that since the Queen and bishops would not reform the Church, they could effect their own reform from the grass roots.

This demand for reformation was strongly put by Thomas Cartwright in his lectures on the Acts of the Apostles, at Cambridge University. On account of his views, Cartwright was forced to leave Cambridge, but a pamphleteer warfare followed, in which the *Admonitions to Parliament* and the *Martin Marprelate Tracts* represented the bitterness and frustration of the Puritan parties. However, it was the intention of the Puritans to effect a national reform of the Church, and to remain within it as the leaven in the lump. But in Cartwright's lectures the basis for Separatism was clearly to be seen; if the Church of England refused to conform its ministry to that laid down in the New Testament, could it in fact be regarded as a Church at all?

Although various sectarian congregations existed prior to Elizabeth's reign [13], B.R. White has recently argued that the origin of Separatism can be traced to Foxe's *Acts and Monuments*, recording the nonconformity and in-

---

[10] W. FULKE, *A Brief and Plain Declaration Concerning the Desires of All Those Faithful Ministers that Have and do Seek for the Discipline and Reformation of the Church of England*, (1584) in TRINTERUD, *op. cit.*, pp. 239-301; p. 243.
[11] *Ibid.*
[12] P. COLLINSON, *The Elizabethan Puritan Movement*, London 1967, for a detailed discussion.
[13] C. BURRAGE, *op. cit.*, Vol. 1, p. 69 ff.

dependency of protestant groups in Mary's reign [14]. Since the Elizabethan Church retained so many traditional elements of the Roman Catholic Church, the Separatists argued that, like Rome, the Church of England was no true Church at all. It was the duty of the faithful, therefore, in obedience to the Word of God, to separate from the false Church. While it was their general intention to restore the apostolic pattern of church life as they believed it to be recorded in the New Testament, their most urgent desire was to restore the practice of discipline [15]. Yet if the idea might be found in Foxe's work, the same conclusions could also be drawn from Cartwright's lectures.

An early example of Separation may be seen in the Plumber's Hall congregation in the city of London, discovered by the authorities in 1567. Their case was:

> ... there was a congregation of us in this city in Queen Mary's days; and a congregation at Geneva, which used a book and order of preaching, ministering of the sacraments and discipline, most agreeable to the word of God; which book is allowed by that godly and well learned man, Master Calvin, and the preachers there; which book and order we now hold. And if you can reprove this book, or anything we hold, by the word of God, we will yield to you, and do open penance at Paul's cross; if not we will stand to it by the grace of God [16].

This congregation was puritan and yet quite independent of the Church of England. Some of its members seceded to form a separate congregation under Richard Fitz. Their desire was to have:

> the Glorious worde and Evangell preached, not in bondage and subiection, but freely, and purelye. Secondly to have the Sacraments mynistred purely, onely and all together accordinge to the institution and good worde of the Lorde Iesus, without any tradicion or invention of man. And laste of all to have, not the fylthye Cannon lawe, but dissiplyne onelye, and all together agreable to the same heavenlye and allmighty worde of oure good Lorde, Iesus Chryste [17].

However, whereas the Puritans strove for a Reformed National Church, the Separatists sought to establish local churches that were independent of the State, restricted to the godly in membership and autonomous in polity. They rejected the idea of a regional Church, Episcopal or Presbyterian: a Church

---

[14] B.R. WHITE, *The English Separatist Tradition from the Marian Martyrs to the Pilgrim Fathers*, Oxford, 1971.
[15] *Ibid.*, p. 32.
[16] *The Remains of Edmund Grindal*, Parker Society, London, 1843, pp. 203-4.
[17] In C. BURRAGE, *op. cit.*, Vol. 2, p. 13.

was a gathered community of believers who convenanted together. From their members they elected the officers of pastor (bishop), teachers, elders and deacons. Each congregation of believers was a complete manifestation of the catholic Church, and though fellowship with other congregations was important, each congregation was autonomous. This doctrine, similar to that which was to become the hallmark of the Independents, and the point which separated them from their Reformed brethren, is usually associated with the names of Robert Browne, and Henry Barrow, John Greenwood and John Penry.

When Robert Browne graduated from Corpus Christi College, Cambridge, in 1572 (after the date of Cartwright's lectures) he was a Puritan and associated himself with a distinguished Puritan theologian, Richard Greenham [18].
But by 1580 he had become convinced of Separatist principles. After refusing a bishop's licence to preach, he left Cambridge to join Robert Harrison at Norwich, where they formed a Separatist Church. Later they removed to Middleburg in the Netherlands. In *A Treatise of Reformation without tarying for anie* (1582), Browne argued that believers must take the initiative and leave the false Church of England, and set up true Churches, as a means of provoking the State to reform the Church [19]. In his works, Browne made three points [20]:

1. Only in the covenanted community does Christ really rule, by Spirit and Word.
2. Discerning Christ's will is the priviledge of all members of the congregation.
3. The responsibility for guiding the people is shared by the more gifted and mature members.

The Congregational church polity was stated by Browne in *A Booke which Sheweth* (1582). A Church is a single congregation which is under the immediate leadership of Christ and by his direct guidance is able in general to regulate its own affairs, though in important matters it may consult the opinion of other congregations. In each congregation the wisest and most able are chosen by the people to be elders, and the elders of a particular congregation act in conjunction to form the Eldership. The people choose the other officers as

---

[18] C. BURRAGE, *The True Story of Robert Browne*, Oxford 1906, p. 3.
[19] Text in, ed. A. PEEL and L. H. CARLSON, *The writings of Robert Harrison and Robert Browne*, London, 1953, pp. 151-170.
[20] B.R. WHITE, *op. cit.*, p. 62.

well as the elders, but the elders ordain the pastor. The whole Church is ultimately responsible for discipline [21].

The Separatist, Henry Barrow, though disassociating himself from Browne, had similar principles. He attacked

1. The fals maner of worshiping the true God.
    Esaias 66:17; Deuteronomy 17:1.
2. The profane and ungodlie people receved
    into and retayned in the bozom and
    bodie of ther churches. Esaias 65:11, 12.
3. The false and antichristian ministrie
    imposed upone ther churches.
    Numbers 16:21, 35.
4. The false and antichristian government
    wherwith ther churches ar ruled [22].

According to Barrow, a true Church was

> a companie and fellowship of faithful and holie people gathered (togither) in the name of Christ Jesus, their only king, priest, and prophet, worshipping him aright, being peaceablie and quietlie governed by his officers and lawes, keeping the unitie of faith in the bonde of peace and love unfained [23].

For their attack on the Queen's supremacy in the Church, Barrow and his colleagues, Greenwood and Penry, were executed for sedition. Their congregation was taken over by Francis Johnson, a Puritan minister converted by Barrow's writings.

Another group which dissented from the Established Church was made up of diverse persons whom Champlain Burrage called "Independent Puritans', such as Henry Jacob, William Bradshaw and the leader of those who were later to become the Pilgrim Fathers, John Robinson [24]; a number of groups in the Dutch Netherlands also seem to fit into this category. These Puritans, while organising themselves in covenanting communities similar to the Separatists, still recognised the Established Church as a true Church, and wished to remain in communion with it.

A precedent for such Churches was the existence of the "Stranger Chur-

---

[21] Text in PEEL and CARLSON, *op. cit.*, pp. 222-395; summary in BURRAGE, *The Early English Dissenters*, vol. 1, p. 103.
[22] Four Causes of Separation, 1587, in, ed. L.H. CARLSON, *The Writings of Henry Barrow 1587-1590*, London, 1962, p. 54.
[23] *A True Description out of the Worde of God, of the Visible Church*, 1589, in L.H. CARLSON, *op. cit.*, p. 214.
[24] C. BURRAGE, *op. cit.*, Vol. 1, pp. 281 ff.

ches" of London. In 1550 a congregation under the reformer John à Lasco had been given permission to organise itself independently of the English Church. In the Royal charter of 1550 which established a Lasco's Church, the Superintendent and Ministers were granted the right "to practise, enjoy, use and exercise their own rites and ceremonies and their own peculiar ecclesiastical discipline, notwithstanding that they do not conform with the rites and ceremonies in our Kingdom" [25]. À Lasco prepared his own order of Service and Discipline. Another similar congregation was to be found in Edward's reign at Glastonburny under Valerand Poullain. In Elizabeth's reign both the Dutch and French Churches were permitted to worship freely according to their own customs; indeed, the Dutch Church in London was rumoured to be a hot-bed for Puritanism.

The Plumbers Hall congregation of 1567 seem to have considered themselves in the same category as these "Stranger Churches". So did that of Henry Jacob; in *A Third Humble Supplication*, addressed to James I in 1605, corrected by Jacob, the plea was made that they might

> Assemble togeather somwhere publikly to the Service & Worship of God, to vse & enioye peaceably among our selves alone the wholl exercyse of Gods worship and of Church Government viz. by a Pastor Elder, & Deacons in our severall Assemblie(s) without any tradicion of men whatsoever, according only to the specification of God's written word and no otherwise, which hitherto as yet in this our present State we could never enjoye.
>
> ... And shall also afterwards keepe brotherly communion with the rest of our English Churches as they are now established, according as the French and Dutch Churches do; ... [26]

In this category we way also place John Cotton, minister at Boston, Lincolnshire, who in 1633 emigrated to New England. Cotton had become convinced that the visible Church consisted in "visible Saints"; that its form was "a mutuall Convenant, whether an explicite or implicite Profession of Faith, and subjection to the Gospel of Christ in the society of the Church or Presbytery thereof"; and that the "power of the keyes" belonged to each visible congregation. Cotton insisted that the Congregational Churches of New England were not Separatist Churches; they had indeed separated, but from the world, not the Church of England [27]. On the eve of his departure for New

---

[25] The Charter is given in, J. LINDEBOOM, *Austin Friars. History of the Dutch Reformed Church in London 1550-1950*, The Hague, 1950.
[26] C. BURRAGE, *op. cit.*, Vol. 1, p. 286.
[27] *The Way of Congregational Churches Cleared*, cited in C. BURRAGE, *op cit.*, Vol. 1, pp. 361-362.

England, Cotton had converted Thomas Goodwin, Philip Nye and John Davenport to his views, and through reading his work *Of the Keyes of the Kingdom of Heaven*, 1644, John Owen would later come to accept "the Congregational way". Cotton claimed to have learned his views from three Puritans — Robert Parker, Paul Baynes and Dr. William Ames [28].

By means of the magistrates and the ecclesiastical courts, the Monarchy and bishops attempted to stamp out the more extreme Puritan and Separatist disobedience. In April 1593, the Act to retain the Queen's subjects had been passed, making nonconformity punishable by exile. During the 1630's many Puritans were forced to flee from the attacks of Archbishop Laud and Bishop Wren. During this period therefore, many fled to Holland, on account of the tolerance shown to religious exiles by the Dutch States General. The Netherlands proved to be an ideal refuge for several Puritan and Separatist groups. Keith L. Sprunger draws attention to the fact that we find the Merchant Adventures' Churches of Antwerp and Middleburg, the garrison churches, and various types of Separatist Churches, all defying the English Church, together making up "Dutch Puritanism" [29]. The English Merchant Adventurers at Middleburg enjoyed the ministries of Puritan, Separatist and Independent Puritan leaders — Dudley Fenner, Francis Johnson, Matthew Holmes, Henry Jacob, Hugh Broughton, Lawrence Potts and John Forbes [30]. Cartwright had also been one of their chaplains. Francis Johnson and the Barrowist congregation set up first at Middleburg, and then moved to Amsterdam; John Robinson's congregation settled at Leiden.

The relations between the English Separatist Churches and the Dutch Reformed Church seem to have been strained, though many of the discontented and disheartened Separatists were later absorbed into the English Reformed Churches. These latter seem to have been English congregations organised into covenanting communities, but as Independent Puritan Churches, on good terms with the Dutch Reformed Church and being closely associated with it, yet still in theory retaining communion with the Curch of England. It is thus that we find the scholar, Dr. Ames, Henry Jacob and Hugh Goodyear at Leiden; John Paget at Amsterdam; Hugh Peters at Rotterdam; and the five "Dissenting Brethren" — Philip Nye, Thomas Goodwin, William Bridge, Jeremiah Burroughes and Sidrach Simpson (later to state the Congregational way as against Presbyterianism) — were connected with a gathered Church

---

[28] *Ibid.*
[29] KEITH L. SPRUNGER, *Dutch Puritanism. A History of English and Scottish Churches of the Netherlands in the Sixteenth and Seventeenth Centuries*, Leiden 1982.
[30] *Ibid.*, p. 23.

at Arnhem, which was in association with the English Reformed Church at Rotterdam [31].

The study which follows is concerned to investigate the nature of the eucharistic liturgies or forms used by these various Puritan and Separatist groups.

---

[31] B. GUSTAFSSON, *The Five Dissenting Brethren*, Lund, 1955, pp. 19-28; G.F. NUTTALL, *Visible Saints*, Oxford, 1957, p. 11.

CHAPTER 1

PURITANS, SEPARATISTS, AND LITURGICAL FORMS

The Book of Common Prayer

Although during the 1530's varoius unofficial liturgical reforms of a protestant nature had appeared in several English Primers [1], the official reformation of English public worship was almost entirely the work of Archbishop Thomas Cranmer. As early as 1538 Cranmer had been working on a revision of the Latin Breviary [2], and in 1544 his English Litany virtually replaced all those of the Latin Processional. In 1548 he prepared an English communion devotion entitled *The Order of the Communion*, which provided for communion in two kinds, and was to be inserted into the Mass. There is also some evidence which suggests that Cranmer had also been working on the reform of the Baptismal and Marriage liturgies [3]. Much of this earlier work was incorporated into the 1549 *Book of Common Prayer*, which together with the Ordinal of 1550, replaced all previous liturgical forms in use in the English Church. These official reforms of the liturgy were in turn replaced by a second *Book of Common Prayer* in 1552.

Cranmer, as indeed all other reformers, had inherited the forms of the Western liturgical tradition. These forms were collected into various books, the main ones being the Missal, the Breviary, the Manual, and the Processional [4]. Although these liturgical forms were fairly uniform across Western Europe, there were a great variety of local variations. The 1549 Act of Uniformity described the situation in England and Wales as consisting of "divers forms of common prayer, commonly called the service of the Church; that is to say, the Use of Sarum, of York, of Bangor, and of Lincoln" [5]. Yet

---

[1] C.C. BUTTERWORTH, *The English Primers (1529-1545)*, Philadelphia, 1963.
[2] Ed. J.W. LEGG, *Cranmer's Liturgical Projects*, HBS, London, 1915.
[3] G.J. CUMING, *A History of Anglican Liturgy*, London, 1969 [1], p. 68.
[4] For details, C. WORDSWORTH and H. LITTLEHALES, *The Old Service-Books of the English Church*, London, 1904.
[5] Text in H. GEE and W.J. HARDY, *Documents illustrative of English Church History*, 1896, pp. 358-366.

these differences were minimal: occasionally in the wording of a prayer or the choice of psalm or antiphon, and, more notceably, in the ceremonial which accompanied the liturgical forms. But overall, the Western tradition was one of "liturgical variety in detail, within the framework of a unity of rite" [6]; according to Dr. F.E. Brightman, that framework may be defined as a "broad Gregorian basis" [7]; that is, the liturgical forms attributed to St. Gregory, revised during the Carolingian reform and which generally prevailed in the West. These liturgical forms provided the basis for Cranmer's revision.

However, by the 1540's he was also in a position to consider the Latin rites in the light of reforms made on the Continent. His planned Breviary drew upon the reformed Breviary of the Catholic Cardinal Quignon; in 1532 he had attended Lutheran services at Nuremburg, and had married the niece of the Lutheran reformer, Osiander; his Litany drew on Luther's Litany. It is also known that in the 1548 *The Order of the Communion*, Cranmer drew upon Hermann's Lutheran order for Cologne. In addition, Cranmer seems to have been aware of the Greek Liturgy of John Chrysostom which he used in his Litany, and possibly he may have known a manuscript copy of the Liturgy of St. James [8].

However, in his programme of liturgical reform, Cranmer, backed by the Royal Supremacy, seems to have had a definite policy. The Greek liturgies may have been interesting, but they, no more than the work of any one continental reformer, were to provide the foundation of his liturgical work. Instead, Cranmer simply retained the basic framework of the Latin services, translating them into the vernacular, and transposing catholic phraseology into a protestant key. The reform was to be gradual over a period of time, and not a drastic once-and-for-all reform. Furthermore, the new reforms would not be optional; they would replace all previous liturgical books. At the same time there were to be no private or independent reforms.

This policy of moderation and uniformity was set out succinctly in the Royal Proclamation of the 1548 *The Order of the Communion*. The King's subjects were requested to receive the ordinance with such obedience and conformity:

> that we may be encouraged from time to tyme, further to travell for the reformation & setting furthe of suche godly orders, as maye bee moste to godes glory, the edifying of our subiectes, and for thadvan-

---

[6] T.M. PARKER, "The Problem of Uniformity, 1559-1604", in M. RAMSEY et al, *The English Prayer Book 1549-1662*, AC, London, 1966, p. 33.
[7] F.E. BRIGHTMAN, *The English Rite*, 2 Vols., London, 1915, Vol. 1, p. xiii.
[8] Miscel. graec. 134, Bodleian Library, Oxford. Apparently belonging to Henry VIII. F.E. BRIGHTMAN, *Liturgies Eastern and Western*, Vol. 1. Eastern Liturgies, Oxford, 1896, p. li.

cemente, of true religion. Whiche thing, wee (by the healpe of God) mooste earnestly entend to bring to effecte: Willyng all our loving subiectes in the meane tyme, to staye and quiet theim sealfes with this oure direction, as men content to folowe aucthoritie (according to the bounden duty of subiectes, & not enterprisyng to ronne afore, and so by their rashenes, become the greatest hynderers of suche thynges, as they more arrogantly then godly, wolde seme (by their awne private aucthoritie) moste hotly to set forwarde. Wee woulde not have oure subiectes so much to mislike oure Judgement, so much to mistruste our zeale, as though we wyther coulde not discerne what were to be done, or woulde not do all things in due tyme [9].

The emphasis here is on obedience to the Royal Supremacy, with a promise of further official reforms "in due tyme".

This policy was continued with the 1549 *Book of Common Prayer*, and the accompanying Act of Uniformity. The latter explained that a committee had been appointed consisting of "the archbishop of Canterbury and certain of the most learned and discreet bishops, and other learned men of this realm to consider and ponder the premises" of "a uniform, quiet, and godly order". The Committee's terms of reference were to "draw and make one convenient and meet order, rite, and fashion of common and open prayer and administration of the sacraments ... having as well eye and respect to the most sincere and pure Christian religion taught by the Scripture, as to the usage in the primitive Church". In practice this meant a moderate reform of the old services. Certain ceremonies and practices were abolished; certain doctrines were removed or made less explicit; but the traditional vestments were retained, the use of candles, the sign of the cross and chrism. These were enforced by law.

The new book was greeted with mixed feelings. On the question of the real presence in the Eucharist, the conservative Bishop Gardiner could urge that it was well expressed, and in his judgment, "not distant from the catholic faith" [10]. But other conservatives were not convinced; Edmund Bonner, Bishop of London, took no steps to introduce it into his diocese, and a rising in the West Country demanded the restoration of the old services. On the other hand, the Zurich-trained Hooper could write to Bullinger, "I am so much offended with that book ... that if it be not corrected, I neither can nor will communicate with the church in the administration of the supper" [11]. Hooper wished for a more radically reformed rite. But uniformity was insisted upon; Bonner was ordered to introduce the book into his diocese, and did so reluctantly; the West Country rebels were dealt with as rebels; and Hopper, when

---

[9] Text in, H.A. WILSON, *The Order of the Communion, 1548*, HBS, London, 1908.
[10] T. CRANMER, *On the Lord's Supper*, Parker Society, London, 1844, p. 92.
[11] *Original Letters*, Vol. 1, p. 79. March 27th, 1550.

refusing to wear the prescribed episcopal vesture, was imprisoned until he agreed to conform. Clearly there was no room for private opinion or diversity of usage.

The 1549 book was short lived; as it was coming off the Grafton Press, the Strasbourg reformer, Martin Bucer, wrote:

> We hear that some concessions have been made both to a respect of antiquity, and to the infirmity of the present age; such, for instance, as the vestments commonly used in the sacrament of the eucharist, and the use of candles: ... They affirm that there is no superstition in these things, and that they are only to be retained for a time, lest the people, not having yet learned Christ, should be deterred by too extensive innovations from embracing his religion, and that rather they may be won over [12].

"For a time" was in fact to be less than three years. In 1552 a new book was issued, which, with a new Act of Uniformity, replaced that of 1549. Once again in the new book conformity was stressed; the 1549 book was abolished because of "divers doubts" arising from the "curiosity of the minister and mistakers" [13]. The new book "explained and made fully perfect" the former book: this in fact meant that the new book was more protestant in character than that of 1549; the Eucharistic vestments were abolished, candles and crosses were to be removed, and chrism disappeared; various changes in the wording of the services and their structure gave the book a more protestant ethos. However, the derivation from the Latin rites was still clearly discernible, and the retention of the surplice, the use of the cross in Baptism, and the use of versicles, responses and canticles gave the book a rather different ethos as compared with the radical rites of Geneva and Zurich.

Whether or not Cranmer and his fellow English reformers had in mind further changes is not known. Edward VI died, Mary succeeded to the throne, and the Roman Catholic faith and the old Latin services were restored. But among the English exiles at Frankfurt there was a rumour that although

> Cranmer, Bishop of Canterbury, had drawn up a Book of Prayer a hundred times more perfect than this that we now have, the same could not take place; for that he was matched with such a wicked clergy and convocation [14].

---

[12] *Ibid.*, Vol. 2, pp. 535-6. April 26th, 1549.
[13] Act of Uniformity 1552. Text, GEE and HARDY, *op. cit.*, pp. 369-372.
[14] Ed. E. ARBER, *A Brief Discourse of the Troubles at Frankfort, 1554-1558 A.D.*, London, 1908, p. 75.

If there was any truth in this rumour, "a hundred times more perfect" would suggest a book of a more radical protestant character than that of 1552.

With the succession of Elizabeth in 1558 the English protestants returned from exile, bringing with them their first hand experience of the Reformed Churches of the Continent, and many expected and immediate return to a programme of protestant reform. But although the Roman Catholic faith and the Latin services were abrogated, Elizabeth certainly did not embark on a programme of reform of the Genevan or Zurich type. The 1552 *Book of Common Prayer* was re-enacted, with three minor but significant changes: the petition against the Pope was removed from the Litany; the "Black rubric" explaining kneeling for communion was removed; and the 1549 words of administration of communion were added to those of 1552. Elizabeth also included an Ornaments rubric, which, if carried into effect, would have retained all liturgical vesture in use in 1549. This "freezing" of the 1552 *Book of Common Prayer*, together with what some considered to be "catholic concessions", clearly did not please the more radical reformers; for them the process of reformation was far from complete: in the words of the eighteenth century Congregational historian, Daniel Neal:

> With good King *Edward* died all further advances of the reformation; for the alterations that were made afterwards by Queen *Elizabeth* hardly came up to his standard [15].

As with previous books of common prayer, that of 1559 was enforced by an Act of Uniformity:

> And that if any manner of parson, vicar, or other whatsoever minister, that ought or should sing or say common prayer mentioned in the said book, or minister the sacraments, from and after the feast of the Nativity of St. John Baptist next coming, refuse to use the said common prayers, or to minister the sacraments in such cathedral or parish church, or other places as he should use to minister the same, in such order and form as they be mentioned and set forth in the said book, or shall, wilfully or obstinately standing in the same, use any other rite, ceremony, order, form, or manner of celebrating of the Lord's Supper, openly or privily, or Matins, Evensong, administration of the sacraments, or other open prayers, than is mentioned and set forth in the said book ... shall lose and forfeit to the queen's highness, her heirs and successors, for his first offence, the profit of all his spiritual benefices or promotions coming or arising in the whole year next after his conviction; and also that the person so convicted shall for the same offence suffer imprisonment by the space of six months, without bail or mainprize [16].

---

[15] D. NEAL, *A History of the Puritans*, 4 vols., 1732-38, Vol. 1, p. 75.
[16] Text, GEE and HARDY, *op. cit.*, pp. 458-467.

CHAPTER 1

Puritans and Liturgical Criteria

It is against the background of the formation of the English Liturgy that the Puritan liturgical protest must be seen; this protest was concerned with the criteria for liturgical revision. The Prayer Books had been compiled using the old Latin rites as a basis, and these had been made scriptural as far as the Royal authority deemed it expedient. It may be repressed thus:

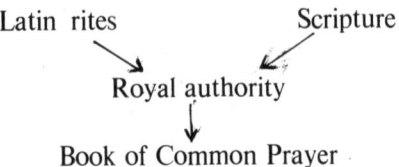

Since such things as vestments and the cross in Baptism were retained — for they were not actually forbidden by Scripture — the English reformation resembled a Lutheran approach to the authority of Scripture rather than a Calvinist approach. This approach was unacceptable to the Puritans, who looked to Geneva for their inspiration. In liturgical matters, as in all others, the Puritan's sole authority and criterion was the written word of God. William Bradshaw, giving a summary of Puritan beliefs, affirmed:

> IMPRIMIS, They hould and mainetaine that the word of God contained in the writings of the Prophets and Apostles, is of absolute perfection, given by Christ the head of the Churche, to bee unto the same, the sole Canon and rule of all matters of Religion, and the worship and service of God whatsoever. And that whatsoever done in the same service and worship cannot bee iustified by the said word, is unlawfull [17].

Bradshaw, writing in 1605, simply restated that principle found in Field and Wilcox's *An Admonition to Parliament*, 1572; they had demanded of Church and liturgy alike that:

> nothing be don in this or ani other thing, but that which you have the expresse warrant of Gods worde for [18].

In the same manner the great seventeenth century Puritan theologian Thomas Watson, wrote:

---

[17] W. BRADSHAW, *English Puritanism. Containing the main opinions of the rigidist sort of those that are called Puritans in the realme of England*, London, 1605.

[18] *An Admonition to Parliament*, 1572, in Ed. W.H. FRERE and C.E. DOUGLAS, *Puritan Manifestoes*, London, 1907, p. 15.

> Divine worship must be such as God himself has appointed, else it is offering strange fire. Lev. x 1. The Lord would have Moses make the tabernacle, "according to the pattern in the mount". Exod xxv 40. He must not leave out anything in the pattern, nor add to it. If God was so exact and curious about the place of worship, how exact will he be about the matter of his worship! Surely here everything must be according to the pattern prescribed in his word [19].

Professor Horton Davies, in his study of the worship of the English Puritans [20], has demonstrated that this attitude derives ultimately from two doctrines of Calvinism; the utter depravity of man, and the all-sufficiency of Scripture for salvation. The result was that the Puritans viewed the literal text of the Bible as a sufficient source for all matters liturgical, and diligently searched it to substantiate their belief. Professor Davies continues:

> The Scriptural citations warranting their main thesis are derived from both Testaments. Thus II Peter i 19-21 and II Timothy iii 15-17 urge the perfection of the Scriptures; while Matthew xv 9, 13, and Rev. xxii 19 are taken to forbid any man-made additions to the worship of God. Even more relevant and stronger proof-text are found in the Old Testament. Exodus xx 4-6 (the Second Commandment), Joshua i 7, Deut. iv 2, xii 32, and Proverbs xxx 6 assert that God will not tolerate any additions to his worship since he is a "jealous God" [21].

The Puritan approach to liturgical matters may be illustrated from William Fulke's *A Brief and Plaine Declaration* [22]. Fulke viewed worship as something inseparable from the Church and its ministry, both of which were dependent upon the Word of God. Worship in terms of Public prayer was dealt with as belonging to the office of the pastor. Thus the pastor was to teach and exhort - 2 Tim. 3:16 - 4:2; it was also his duty to make prayer, as in Acts 16:16. The congregation may join in the singing of psalms - I Cor. 14:15, 26, "for this custom hath continued in the Church from the beginning, that the congregation have praised God with psalms singing altogether". But it belonged essentially to the office of Pastor to make prayer, and «the rest to pray with him in silence and to answer "Amen"» — I Cor. 4. 16. According to Fulke, the second duty of the pastor in worship was "the right administration of the Sacraments of God" — Matthew 28:19, Luke 22: 19:

> it is the duty of every pastor to administer the sacraments of

---

[19] THOMAS WATSON, *A Body Of Divinity*, p. 8.
[20] HORTON DAVIES, *The Worship of the English Puritans*, Oxford, 1948, pp. 13-24; 49.
[21] *Ibid.*, p. 50.
[22] in, ed. TRINTERUD, *op. cit.*

Christ, so this office apperteineth to none but to those which are ministers of the word [23].

However, such things as Confirmation and Churching of women, provided for in the *Book of Common Prayer*, were "mere devices of men and ought to have no place in the Church of Christ".

According to the Puritan, the basis for liturgical composition was quite straight forward:

$$\text{Scripture} \downarrow \text{Liturgy}$$

It was the monarch's duty to obey Scripture, and the resulting liturgy would bear little resemblance to the old Latin rites. Since the *Book of Common Prayer* had been compiled using other criteria, the Puritan believed it to be merely the remains of Roman Catholicism, containing many unscriptural elements. For example, there was no scriptural authority for such things as the ring in marriage, the sign of the cross in Baptism, or the wearing of any type of vestment [24]. Furthermore, it was too close in ethos to the Latin rites; according to Field and Wilcox, it was

> an unperfecte booke, culled & picked out of that popishe dunghil, the Masse booke full of all abhominations. For some, & many of the contents therin, be suche as are against the woord of God, and by his grace shall be proved unto you [25].

Popish remains included reading of services instead of preaching, observance of saints' days, kneeling at communion rather than sitting, the word "priest", private Baptism, questions to infants, god-parents' promises, the Gospel canticles, antiphonal singing of the psalms and the use of organs. Underlying these criticisms was the question of liturgical criteria: God's word, or the monarch's wishes:

> ·We must be in daunger of a premunire if we folowe not the lawes of the land, thoughe they be againste the Scriptures, and in daunger of a twelve monthes imprisonment, if we speake against the booke of common prayer, though it be againste the word of God [26].

---

[23] FULKE, *op. cit.*, in TRINTERUD, *op. cit.*, p. 266.
[24] *An Abridgment of that Booke which the Ministers of Lincoln Diocess delivered to his Maiestie upon the first of December last*, 1605; *The Millenary Petition*, 1603, in E. CARDWELL, *A History of Conferences and other Proceedings*, Oxford, 1841; *SPR*, 38, 57, 59, 72, 77, 78, 165.
[25] *An Admonition*, FRERE & DOUGLAS, *op. cit.*, p. 21; Cf. *SPR*, 50, "patched out of the Popes Portusses".
[26] T. CARTWRIGHT, *Second Admonition*, FRERE and DOUGLAS, *op. cit.*, pp. 93-4.

> Whereas once nothing but the Word of God had been taught, now there were

> Princes pleasures, mennes devices, popish ceremonies, and Antichristian rites in publique pulpits defended [27].

The Puritan endeavoured that Christ "might rule and raygne in his church by the scepter of his worde onely" [28].

The Puritans attempted to correct the defects of the *Book of Common Prayer* in two ways; either by private emendation of the Prayer Book, which Strype called "mangling the English book" [29], or by the adoption and promotion of a Reformed liturgy of a Calvinist type.

(a) *Mangling the English Book*

The precise forms of this liturgical anarchy are now lost to us; bearing in mind themany objections to the *Book of Common Prayer* we can for the most part only conjecture what some of these emendations may have been. Some information can, however, be collated from the charges brought against Puritans in the ecclesiastical courts. For example, in January 1584/5 Eusebius Paget, a particularly troublesome Puritan minister, admitted to the Court of High Commission that although he had sworn to use the enacted book, he had omitted certain parts:

> I have very willingly and with all humble obedience in the administration of the sacraments and other open prayers in the said parish use(d) rites, ceremonies and orders set forth in the said book, although I have not used all rites, ceremonies and orders ... as is (there) mentioned [30].

Paget pointed out that he had used no other order, but had left out certain parts:

1. Partly for that to my knowledge, there is not in the said church the said book.
2. Partly for that I am given to understand that you before whom I stand, and mine Ordinary, and the most part of the BBs and ministers do use greater liberty in omitting and altering the said rites, ceremonies and orders.
3. And especially for that I am not fully resolved in conscience that I may use divers of them.

---

[27] *An Admonition*, ibid., p. 12.
[28] *Ibid.*, p. 9.
[29] J. STRYPE, *Life of Parker*, 3 Vols., 1821, vol. 2, p. 65.
[30] *SPR*, 176. Ed. TRINTERUD, *op. cit.*, pp. 380-383; p. 380.

> 4. And for that when I took charge of that chruch, I was promised by mine Ordinary that I should not be urged to such ceremonies, which I am informed he might do by the law [31].

Here Paget appealed to the fact that many of the bishops had Puritan sympathies regarding the *Book of Common Prayer*.

Another minister who was suspended, one John Elliston, admitted that be had omitted the Epistle and Gospel "upon the saboth dayes" in the Ante-communion, and had refused communicants because they would not submit to being examined beforehand [32]. It was reputed that Richard Bowler, Rector of Leverington in the Isle of Ely, "addeth and diminisheth at his pleasure' in the use of the book [33]. Many prosecutions of Puritan clergy were for such offences as omitting the sign of the cross in Baptism and the refusal to use a surplice [34].

Besides these *ad hoc* Puritan alterations to rubrics and the omission of some texts, we must also consider a series of printed books, appearing from 1578 onwards, bound with the Genevan Bible, but differing in some details from the enacted *Book of Common Prayer*.

The precise nature and implications of these editions of the Prayer Book are by no means agreed upon by scholars. Proctor and Frere, in their *A New History of the Book of Common Prayer*, attributed these emasculated books to the Puritans [35]; Mr. J. F. Gerrard pointed out signs of hasty printing, and suggested that the variations in the text may be ascribed to the printers' vagaries [36]. And Dr. Collinson, noting the moderation of the alterations and the nature of the services which were omitted, described them as "successors to the mid-Tudor "primers", intended for domestic rather than congregational use" [37].

However, Mr. A.E. Peaston has argued strongly that these books are Puritan abridgements, representing a subtle attempt to alter the *Book of Common Prayer* by minor changes which might go undetected [38]. First, Peaston notes that the rubrics and services omitted were all ones to which the Puritans objected. Secondly, he points out that the books were bound with the Genevan Bible, being mainly the work of William Whittingham, a Marian

---

[31] *Ibid.*
[32] *SPR*, 177.
[33] Cited in, P. COLLINSON, *op. cit.*, p. 365.
[34] RONALD MARCHANT, *The Puritans and the Church Courts in the Diocese of York 1560-1642*, London, 1960. Passim.
[35] F. PROCTOR and W.H. FRERE, *A New History of the Book of Common Prayer*, London, 1901, p. 133-135.
[36] J.F. GERRARD, *Notable Editions of the Prayer Book*, Wigan, 1949, pp. 13-15.
[37] P. COLLINSON, *op. cit.*, p. 365.
[38] A.E. PEASTON, *The Prayer Book Tradition in the Free Churches*, London, 1964, pp. 16-32.

exile, husband of Calvin's sister, and ordained at Geneva. The Calvinist nature of the Genevan Bible was evident from its marginal notes, where episcopal hierarchy was condemned, and the equality of ministers was taught. Archbishop Parker refused to allow this version to be printed in England, and the bishops published their own version in 1568, the "Bishop's Bible". This latter was often bound with the 1559 *Book of Common Prayer*. However, Archbishop Grindal, noted for his Puritan sympathies, allowed the Genevan version to be printed *cum privilegio* by Christopher Barker. Later there appeared these adaptations of the Prayer Book; being bound with the Genevan Bible, it is logical to presume that both were for Puritan use [39].

Peaston's argument is supported by the evidence of Eusebius Paget; Paget pointed out that the Prayer Book in his Church, though printed "with privilege", was not the one authorised in 1559. He had not refused to use the enacted book; no one had offered it to him. It would appear that his book was one of the Puritan adaptations, and Paget could correctly claim that he had not deliberately omitted certain ceremonies or services, because they were not in his book to be omitted [40].

Ad hoc emendations to the Prayer Book, and printed adaptations, both had a precedent in *The Liturgy of Compromise*. This was the work of the Marian exiles at Frankfurt, who quickley set to work to bring the 1552 *Book of Common Prayer* into harmony with the Continental Reformed Rites [41].

(b) *The Use of Reformed Rites*

As well as "mangling the English Book", Strype informs us that some Puritans used a different liturgy in their meetings:

> And at these meetings, rejecting wholly the Book of Common Prayer, they used a Book of Prayers framed at Geneva for the congregation of English exiles lately sojourning there. Which book had been overseen and allowed by Calvin, and the rest of his Divines there, and indeed was for the most part taken out of the Genevan form [42].

The book in question was the *Genevan Service book*, 1556, compiled for use of a group of Marian exiles at Geneva. Its adoption by the Church of Sco-

---

[39] For the various editions, see *ibid.*, pp. 33-34.

[40] The prodution of Prayer Books with slight alterations or omissions, in the hope that the various modifications would gradually establish themselves, has a modern parallel in Anglo-Catholic editions of the Prayer Book, where parts of the Roman Rite have been interpolated.

[41] H.J. WOTHERSPOON and G.W. SPROTT, *The Liturgy of Compromise used in the English Congregation at Frankfort*, Edinburgh, 1905.

[42] J. STRYPE, *Life of Grindal*, Oxford, 1821, p. 169. Cf. 1572 Bill "Concerning Rites and Ceremonies", p. 149, in H.C. PORTER, *Puritanism in Tudor England*, London, 1970, pp. 148-150.

tland as the *Book of Common Order* in 1562 and 1564, and the not too infrequent exchange of clergy between Scotland and England, meant that despite the 1559 Act of Uniformity, this liturgy was far from forgotten. As early as 1567, it was in use by the Plumber's Hall congregation, and that which met in Goldsmith's House in 1568 [43]. In 1582 Cartwright was proposing to obtain Parliament's approval for a Prayer Book after the Genevan type, and in 1584 Dr. Peter Turner, a London Physician and the son of the Puritan naturalist, William Turner, attempted to present to Parliament a Bill to allow the use of an edition of the *Genevan Service Book* [44]. Again, in 1587, Peter Wentworth, Member of Parliament for Northampton, and Anthony Cope, Member of Parliament for Banbury, attempted to present a liturgy of the Genevan type [45]. Both these attempte were quashed by the intervention of the Queen. These two liturgies, both entitled *A Booke of the Forme of Common Prayers, administration of the Sacraments: &c. agreeable to Gods Worde, and the use of the reformed churches*, are both known after their respective printers, the Waldegrave book, 1584 and the Middleburg Book, 1586, by Richard Schilders of Middleburg, Zeeland. In 1583 Stephen Beamund, Rector of Easthorpe, was brought before the Assizes because he had neither worn the surplice, nor used the Prayer Book, but "had seditiously celebrated there other services" [46]. This may well have been the *Genevan Service Book*.

As well as the Genevan form, some Puritans had attempted in 1572 to authorise the liturgies of the French and Dutch "Stranger Churches" for use in the Church of England [47]. In 1564 Bishop Grindal of London had connived at the Calvinism of the English Merchant Adventurers, and advised their chaplain William Cole to water down the Prayer Book to fit the Protestant environment at Antwerp [48]. In later years several of the Puritan clergy who ministered in the Netherlands also adopted the Dutch liturgy.

The Separatists and Liturgy

The Puritans wanted a scriptural, Reformed liturgy; they objected to the *Book of Common Prayer* as enacted by Law, because it was to closely based upon the Roman rites, and because it was subject to the monarch's wishes.

---

[43] A. PEEL, *The First Conegational Churches*, p. 11.
[44] H. DAVIES, *op. cit.*, pp. 33-34, 123; COLLINSON, *op. cit.*, pp. 273-288.
[45] COLLINSON, ibid., pp. 303-316.
[46] F.G. EMMISON, *Elizabethan Life: Morals and the Church Courts*, Chelmsford (Essex County Council), 1973, p. 196.
[47] Text in, ed. H.C. PORTER, *op. cit.*
[48] KEITH L. SPRUNGER, *op. cit.*, p. 15.

Their objections were against a particular imposed liturgy, and not against a liturgy as such. So, for example, William Perkins defended the use of liturgical forms by appealing to the use of psalms in Scripture, and also by explaining that not everyone had the gift for extemporary prayer:

> It is alledged, that set formes of prayer doe limit and bind the holy Ghost.
> Ans. If we had a perfect measure of grace, it were somewhat, but the graces of God are weake and small in us. This is no binding of the Holy Ghost, but a helping of the Spirit, which is weake in us, by a crutch to leane upon: therefore a man may with good conscience, upon defect of memorie and utterance, &c. use a set forme of prayer [49].

The fact that Perkins felt it necessary to defend the use of liturgical forms indicates that in some quarters it was being questioned; some Puritans felt that prayer was a gift given to the minister, and that he should not be tied to a set form of prayer, enacted by Law. Field and Wilcox had appealed to the usage of the apostolic Church:

> Then ministers were not tyed to any forme of prayers invented by man, but as the spirit moved them, so they powred forth hartie supplications to the Lorde. Now they are bound of necessitie to a prescript order of service, and booke of common prayer in which a great number of things contrary to Gods word are contained, ... [50].

The belief that prayer was a gift of the Spirit, and that set forms quenched the Spirit, was one of the hall-marks of the Separatists. The Separatists such as Robert Browne and Henry Barrow may legitimately be regarded as the extreme left wing of English Puritanism. Although they attacked the Puritans for remaining within the Established Church, their views represented Puritan ideals taken to their logical conclusion. Scripture did not enjoin the use of the cross in Baptism; but neither did Scripture enjoin the use of a liturgy; for the Separatists, set forms of prayer had no scriptural authority.

The Separatist concept of worship was closely connected with their ecclesiology. The true Church was founded upon the Word of God, and established by him, and filled with his Spirit. Where a church was ordered according to God's Word, there true liturgy could be found. According to John Greenwood:

---

[49] WILLIAM PERKINS, "Cases of Conscience", Book 2, in *Works*, 3 Vols., London, 1628-31, Vol. 2, p. 67.
[50] FRERE & DOUGLAS, *op. cit.*, p. 11.

> The worde *leitourgia* signifieth *publicum munus, ergon laon*, the worck of, or for the people: that is the very execution of the ministeriall actions in the church, according to the worde of all the officers therof, that is the practise of those ministeriall duties prescribed by Christ, we may every where reade. ... Nowe, to make other leiturgia, in to lay an other foundation, and to make an other gospell, not that ther is an other gospell, but that ther are some willing to pervert the gospell of Christ [51].

Liturgy in the narrower sense of prayer was the gift of the Spirit; Greenwood cited John 4:23-24, "God is Spirit and must be worshipped in Spirit and truth" [52]. It was a sin to attempt to quench this gift by the use of set forms of prayer; true prayer must be of faith and knowledge, uttered with the heart, and lively voice to God [53]. Galatians 4:6 and Romans 8:26 were favourite proof texts [54]. In the apostolic Church, so Henry Barrow claimed,

> They alwaies used spiritual praiers according to their present wantes and occasions, and so taught all churches to pray, alwaies, with all maner of praier and supplication in the spirit, and therby to make knowen their wantes, and to shew their requestes in al thinges unto God their heavenly Father [55].

If prayer was essentially the gift of the Spirit, then written or "stinted" prayers represented a blasphemous attack on the Spirit; those who use written prayers

> ... take the office of the Holie Ghost awaie, quench the spirit of the ministrie, and of the whole church, stop and keepe out the graces of God, thrust their owne idle devises upon the whole church, yea, upon God himselfe, whether he wil or no [56].

This also applied to the Lord's Prayer; the Separatists believed that it provided the perfect pattern for prayer, but was not itself intended to be recited. Greenwood argued that the Hebrew *"Coh"* meant "Thus", or, "after this manner", and the Greek *"houtos"* introducing the Lord's Prayer had exactly

---

[51] JOHN GREENWOOD, *An Answere to George Gifford's Pretended Defence*, in, ed. LELAND H. CARLSON, *The Writings of John Greenwood 1587-1590*, London, 1962, pp. 73-74.
[52] CARLSON *ibid., Reasons against Read Prayers*, pp. 14-15.
[53] *Ibid.*
[54] *Ibid.* Cf. *A Fewe observations of Mr. Gifford's Last Cavlls about stinted read prayers and devised Leitourgies*, in, ed. CARLSON, *The Writings of John Greenwood and Henry Barrow 1591-1593*, London, 1970, p. 42 ff.
[55] *A Brief Discoverie of the False Church (1950)*, in, ed. CARLSON, *The Writings of Henry Barrow 1587-1590*, p. 366.
[56] BARROW, *A Plaine Refutation, The Writings of Henry Barrow 1590-1591*, ed. Carlson, London, 1966, p. 100.

the same meaning [57]. He also appealed to Calvin's comment upon Matthew 6:9, "It was not the intention of the Son of God (as we have already said), to prescribe the words which we must use, so as not to leave us at liberty to depart from the form which he has dictated" [58]. According to Barrow, the Lord's Prayer

> expresseth not our particular wantes, or estate of our heartes, neither do we understand those generall doctrines, by the bare saying or reading it over. This Scripture is not the grace of God's Spirit in us; it is not drawen out of the fountaine of our heartes. It is not our wordes to God, but his unto us, *etc.* It edifieth not the whole congregation so that they may al mind one thing, or say Amen. Therefore, and for all these reasons, it ought not and cannot be used of any Christian, either publiquely or privatly, as their praier [59]:

The Lord's Prayer was a perfect example because it was given by Jesus and was scriptural; but all other written prayer was the work of men, and as such was "carnal worship, a wearysomnes unto him, and lothsome in his sight" [60]. It was from this theology that the Separatists were able to reject the *Book of Common Prayer in toto*; true liturgy belonged to the true Church; the Church of England was not a true Church, and therefore could not possess true liturgy. The Separatists believed that their judgement was further confirmed by the fact that the *Book of Common Prayer* was a set liturgy, and by its Roman character; Cranmer and his fellow English reformers may have wished for reformation, but they were ignorant on the meaning of liturgy:

> Not withstanding, I saye this, their great sin of ignorance hath beene our great and deadlye plague, in that they translated out of the Latin portues of the pope in to Englishe, theyre deadlye collects and prayers, and soe made a booke of them. Not that they made the prayers and collects them selves, but antichrist, as I said, made them; and theise good men their ignorance was suche, that they translated those his prayers and collects into Englishe, and mended here and there places which were to to vitious, and put in some of their owne words in the romes of that vile stuffe: soe then you cannot well denye but theise prayers were first coyned in that Latin shopp of antichrist, and after were drawne out of the Latin shopp into Englishe by Cranmer, and patched up together by some of his owne coyning, and theirs with his; soe by this your common prayers are but patched prayers [61].

---

[57] *An Answere to George Gifford's Pretended Defence, op. cit.*, pp. 44-45.
[58] *A Fewe observations of Mr. Gifford's Last Cavills, op. cit.*, p. 50. *Ibid.*, p. 45.
[59] *A Brief Discoverie of the False Church, op. cit.*, p. 372.
[60] GREENWOOD, *An Answere to George Gifford's Pretended Defence, op. cit.*, p. 36.
[61] GREENWOOD, *Fragments of a Letter*, in, *The Writings of John Greenwood 1587-1590*, pp. 4-5.

But these arguments applied equally to the Genevan rite; whereas for the Puritans the problem was one of which liturgy, for the Separatists it was one of written liturgy versus inspiration of the Spirit.

Independent Puritans

The position of many of those who Champlin Burrage termed "Independent Puritans" seems to have been that of the Separatists, though with rather less vehement condemnation of the liturgies of other Churches. Dr. William Ames wrote of "Instituted Forms" of worship,

> No worship of this kind is lawfull, unlesse it hath God for the Author, and ordainer of it. *Deut*, 4.2. & 12.32. Keep you all things which I shall command you, Ad not to the word which I command you, neither take from it, every thing which I command you observe to doe: ad not to it, nor take from it every thing which I command you observe to doe: ad not to it, nor take from. 1 *Chron*. 16.13. Our Lord broke in upon us, because we did not seeke him aright [62].

Here Ames' statement suggests that some written forms might be lawful, since God might be the author. Elsewhere, however, he accepts the Separatist argument that the Lord's Prayer was "an example or patterne, according to which we are to direct our Prayers"; to keep to the text would mean "no proficiencie in the spirit and gift of praying" [63]. John Robinson also vigorously defended free prayer and praying "in the Spirit":

> The apostle Jude directeth us always to pray in the Holy Ghost, Jude xx: and Paul teacheth, that we cannot pray as we ought, but as the Spriit helpeth us, and begetteth in us sighs unutterable, Rom. viii. 26; by the work of which Spirit if our prayers be not conceived first in our hearts before they be brought forth in our lips, they are an unnatural, bastardly, and profane birth [64].

Therefore,

> We cannot but mislike that custom in use, by which the pastor is wont to repeat and read out of a prayer-book certain forms, for his and the churches' prayers, ... [65].

---

[62] W. AMES, "Of Instituted Worship", in *The Marrow of Sacred Divinity*, London, 1642, p. 271.

[63] W. AMES, *Conscience with the Power and Cases Thereof. Divided into 5 Books*, London, 1643, Book 4, p. 41.

[64] J. ROBINSON, *A Justification of Separation from the Church of England*, 1610, in, ed. R. ASHTON, *The Works of John Robinson*, 3 Vols, London, 1851, Vol. 2, p. 451.

[65] J. ROBINSON, "Of Written Liturgies", in *A Just and Necessary Apology*, 1625, in *Works*, Vol. 3, p. 19.

Robinson attacked the *Book of Common Prayer*, the papists' St. Peter's Liturgy, and that of St. James; he too maintained that the Lord's Prayer was but an example, and not a form of prayer to be imposed upon the Church [66]. Prayers could indeed be written down and read with profit, but in private meditation, not public worship [67].

The argument for free prayer was put forcefully by John Cotton, the leader of the New England Independents. Like the Separatists and Robinson, Cotton insisted that prayer should be "with the Spirit":

> *Now hee hath commanded us to pray in the spirit.* Ep. 6:18, which implies not onely with such affections as his spirit kindleth and stirreth up, but also with such matter and words as his spirit helpeth us unto: For his spirit is said to helpe us what to pray, which else we should not know, *Rom.* 8:26 [68].

According to Cotton,

> From the patterne of all the Churches, both in the old and new Testament, God never gave leave to any ordinary Officers of his Church, neither did any of them take leave to impose any formes of Liturgie upon any Church [69].

Another point against the use of a set form

> is taken from the meaning of the second Commandment, which wee conceive prohibiteth such prescript Liturgies [70].

Cotton maintained that it was unlawful to bring books other than the Bible into public worship and for the magistrate, or our ancestors, to prescribe a set form of prayer; also for prayers composed by others to be used as ordinary prayer, or for one Church to receive such set forms from another and use them as their own [71]. However, he allowed that set forms were justifiable in some circumstances; a man might lawfully compile a book of prayers, and give holy directions and rules for prayer to another, and set down some forms of prayer as examples. He also conceded that a man might be affected with some petitions in a prayer devised by others and may insert them in his own prayer [72]. Set forms were not therefore ruled out *a priori*.

---

[66] *Ibid.*, p. 22.
[67] *Ibid.*, pp. 26-27.
[68] J. COTTON, *A Modest and Cleare Answer to Mr. Balls Discourse of Set formes of Prayer*, London, 1642, p. 14.
[69] J. COTTON, *The Way of the Churches of Christ in New-England*, London, 1645, p. 70.
[70] *Ibid.*, p. 71. Cf. THOMAS SHEPHARD, *A Treatise of Liturgies, Power of the Keyes, And of matter of the Visible Church*, London, 1653.
[71] *A Modest and Cleare Answer*, pp. 4-5.
[72] *Ibid.*

In their *Apologeticall Narration*, the "Dissenting Brethren" described their forms of service in Holland. Wishing to repudiate the charge of Brownism, and to affirm their agreement with the Reformed Churches, they insisted:

> Our *publique worship* was made up of no other parts than the worship of all other reformed Churches doth consist of [73].

And later they asserted:

> Againe, concerning the great ordinance of *Publique Prayer* and the *Lyturgie* of the Church, whereas there is this great controversie upon it about the lawfulnesse of set formes prescribed; we practiced (without condemning others) what all sides doe allow, and themselves doe practice also, that the publique Prayers in our Assemblies should be framed by the meditations and study of our own Ministers, out of their own gifts (the fruits of Christ's Ascension), as well as their Sermons use to be [74].

Thus although they did not use set forms, they insisted that the forms which they did use were in general agreement with the liturgies of the Reformed Churches.

Laudianism

At various times the Puritans attempted to effect changes in the English Liturgy, through Parliament, by tracts, and by appealing direct to King James at the Hampton Court conference. Despite their efforts, the 1559 *Book of Common Prayer* remained intact. But the Puritan wing of the Church of England and the Separatists were not alone in desiring change in the public worship of the English Church; another group of divines, known — albeit inaccurately — as the "Laudian" school, also wanted change, but of rather a different nature. Wheres the Puritans appealed to the Word of God alone, the Laudians appealed to the usage of the Church in the first four or five centuries, and to the use of the Greek Church [75]. At first their liturgical ideas found expression only in outward adorning and ceremonial; chapels and churches were furnished with sumptuousness, with the communion table co-

---

[73] T. GOODWIN et al, *An Apologeticall Narration*, p. 8.
[74] *Ibid.*, p. 12.
[75] So for example, JEREMY TAYLOR'S *A Collection of Offices*, 1658?, drew upon material from the Greek Offices. See, G.W.O. ADDLESHAW, *The High Church Tradition*, 1941; G.J. CUMING, *A History of Anglican Liturgy*, 1969, pp. 140-146.

vered with a rich "carpet" or frontal, with two tapers, a silver bason, and a Bible and Prayer Book with fine bindings; the woodwork was richly carved; the minister often wore a cope as well as the detested surplice, and certain ceremonies were elaborated; for example, infants were not only signed with the cross in Baptism, but were then carried to the altar. These practices the Laudians sought to justify by appealing to the early Church, the Prayer Book of 1549, or to the Elizabethan injunctions on ceremonial.

Little was done with regard to actual revision of the text of the *Book of Common prayer*. The nearest approach to this was John Cosin's *Collections of Private Devotions* for the ladies of the Court, in which Matins and Evensong were supplemented with some material from the old Roman Catholic monastic offices (Breviary), and some prayers from the Prayer Book of 1549. This collection brought forth a bitter attack from the Puritan lawyer, William Prynne [76].

Cosin's use of the 1549 *Book of Common Prayer* epitomises the liturgical aspirations of the Laudians; from a survey of the Classical liturgies and the Roman rite, they concluded that the 1549 book was closer to the usage of the early church than subsequent enacted books [77]. They sought to rearrange the enacted Prayer Book to conform to that of 1549; thus with regard to the Eucharistic Prayer in the communion service, Cosin informs us that Bishop Overall used the "Prayer of Oblation" immediately after the "Prayer of Consecration", attempting to restore an anamnesis to the Prayer Book Eucharistic Prayer [78].

It was the policy of Archbishop Laud to preserve the unity of the Church of England by strict uniformity and by rigid enforcement of the law. He attacked slackness and disorder of every kind, ranging from cock-fighting in Churches and churchyards to Puritan disregard of rubrics in divine service. To enforce uniformity and obedience, he made wide use of the Court of High Commission, and it was here that the Puritan pamphleteers such as Prynne, Burton and Bastwick were tried for writing scurrilous attacks upon the bishops, and were sentenced to have their ears cut off. As John Watson wryly observed:

> If a man declines to use a liturgy and you crop his ears and split his

---

[76] W. PRYNNE, *A Briefe Survey and Censure of Mr. Cozens His Couzening Devotions*, London, 1628.

[77] In 1563 the Spanish Jesuit, FRANCISCUS TURRIANUS, had published a text of *Apostolic Constitutions*; his belief that it was taken down by St. Clement and was the Apostolic Liturgy was accepted by many. F.E. BRIGHTMAN, *Liturgies Eastern and Western*, p. xviii. For its subsequent influence and the flowering of the Laudian school, see W. JARDINE GRISBROOKE, *Anglican Liturgies of the Seventeenth and Eighteenth Centuries*, AC, London, 1958.

[78] J. COSIN, *Notes on the Book of Common Prayer*, in *Works*, LACT, 5 Vols, Oxford 1843-55, Vol. 5.

nose to encourage him, human nature is so constituted that he is apt to grow more obstinate, and to conceive a quite unreasonable prejudice against the book [79].

In the long run, Laud's policy resulted in the abolition of the Church of England as an episcopal Church during the Commonwealth, and the Prayer Book was replaced by the *Westminster Directory* [80]. Up until the 1640's, however, various Puritan ministers made their way to Holland to minister to English congregations without the necessity of using the Prayer Book.

Is summary, therefore, the Puritans desired a reformed *Book of Common Prayer*, or the adoption of a Reformed rite. The Separatists, believing that prayer was a gift of the Spirit, objected to any set forms of prayer at all. Many "Independent Puritans" adopted a middle position, not objecting to others using set forms, but themselves using extemporary prayer.

---

[79] JOHN WATSON, *The Cure of Souls*, New York, 1896, p. 254.
[80] For the subsequent development, see BRYAN D. SPINKS, *Freedom or Order? The Eucharistic Liturgy in English Congregationalism 1645-1980*, Pittsburgh, 1984.

CHAPTER 2

THE OFFICIAL EUCHARISTIC LITURGY: THE DERIVATION OF THE COMMUNION SERVICE OF THE BOOK OF COMMON PRAYER 1559 AND 1604

The Eucharistic liturgy which was enforced by the Act of Uniformity in 1559 was little changed from that found in the *Book of Common Prayer* of 1552, being Archbishop Cranmer's latest reform of the medieval Latin mass. In order to understand its structure, it will be useful to trace briefly its development from the Latin Mass itself.

The evidence for the early development of the Roman rite is fragmentary; the witness of Justin Martyr, c.150 A.D., and the evidence of the *Apostolic Tradition* attributed to Hippolytus, c.210 A.D., may be supplemented by the casual references to parallel rites from Cyprian and Ambrose [1]. As with other Classical rites, it consisted of two parts, the *missa catechumenorum*, or Synaxis, consisting of Scripture readings, a homily and intercessions [2], derived from the Synagogue liturgy, forming a Liturgy of the Word; and the *missa fidelium*, or Eucharist proper, concerned with the preparation, thanksgiving, and consuming of the elements of bread and wine, derived from the Lord's actions at the Last Supper. Like other rites, some parts became abbreviated, others became expanded.

Its use as a uniform rite in Western Europe seems to have begun in the eighth century when Charlemagne obtained a copy of the Roman sacramentary form Pope Hadrian. The sacramentary was incomplete, and it was the task of Alcuin of York to complete the rite with various pieces from the other Western rites, the Mozarabic and Gallican. His enlarged text eventually displaced older local uses, including that of Rome itself. It was this text, with

---

[1] JUSTIN MARTYR, *Apology* 65 and 67; *Dialogue with Trypho*, 41 and 70; *The Apostolic Tradition*, ed. G. Dix, London, 1937; AMBROSE, *De Sacramentis* IV; CYPRIAN, *Epistle* 63; J.A. JUNGMANN, *The Mass of the Roman Rite*, 2 Vols., New York, 1951-55; see also other possible non-Roman fragments in ed. R.C.D. JASPER and G.J. CUMING, *Prayers of the Eucharist: Early and Reformed*, London, 1975, pp. 101-103.
[2] G. DIX, *The Shape of the Liturgy*, London, 1945, p. 36 ff.; W. JARDINE GRISBROOKE, "Intercession at the Eucharist. 1. The Intercession at the Synaxis", in *SL*, 4 (1965), pp. 129-155. But for the view that the intercessions belong to the *missa fidelium*, see G.G. WILLIS, *Essays in Early Roman Liturgy*, AC, London, 1964, p. 3.

minor regional differences, which became universal in the medieval West. In England the dominant version of this text was that of Sarum.

Underneath the Latin Mass there was still to be discerned the chief constituent parts of the Eucharist as described by Justin Martyr — Word and Sacrament. But, as Dr. G. J. Cuming has said, "the bare bones have been clothed with a good deal of flesh" [3].

The Liturgy of the Word was prefaced with preparatory prayers said in the sacristy, consisting of *Veni Creator Spiritus*, the Collect for Purity, Psalm 43, the Lord's Prayer, *Ave Maria*, and, during the Introit or *officium*, the *Confiteor* and absolution. These preparatory prayers seem to have been Gallican in origin.

The Introit, originally a whole psalm, had been reduced to a verse. A ninefold *Kyrie Eleison* followed, being the remnant of a litany which had replaced the solemn prayers of intercession [4]. The *Gloria in excelsis*, originally a hymn sung at matins, and introduced into the Eucharist on festivals, now followed always except in Lent. Then came the collect(s) of the day, following the liturgical calendar.

The lections followed, reduced to an Epistle and Gospel, and separated by the Gradual chant and prayers. These were followed by the Nicene Creed, originally introduced in the West in Spain and France to counter heresy, and only coming into use in the Eucharist at Rome in 1014. A sermon could follow, but was rare; preaching was often without a liturgical setting.

The Eucharist proper began with the Offertory of bread and wine, accompanied by a chant, and the elements prepared with a series of collect, or offertory prayers, known as the "Litle Canon". These prayers, mostly Gallican and Mozarabic in origin, anticipated the Eucharistic Prayer, anaphora, or Canon [5]. The Congregation was exhorted:

> *Orate, fratres et sores: ut meum ac vestrum sacrificium acceptabile fiat apud Deum patrum omnipotentem.*

After the washing of the celebrant's hands *(Lavabo)* and the secret, or *Oratio super Oblata*, the celebrant started the Eucharistic Prayer with the *Sursum corda*, preface and, according to the season or day, a proper preface, leading into the *Sanctus* and *Benedictus*. The remainder of the Canon was printed in paragraphs, marked with initial letters, and divided by rubrics. The paragraphs *Communicantes, Hanc igitur, Supplices te, Memento etiam* and *Nobis*

---

[3] G.J. CUMING, *op. cit.*, p. 15.
[4] G.G. WILLIS, *op. cit.*, p. 48.
[5] *Ibid.*, pp. 107-110.

quoque had a conclusion *Per (eundem) Christum Dominum nostrum*, and to this was added Amen in every case except the last [6].

Although the salutations, preface and *Sanctus* formed part of the Classical Anaphora, the medieval missal regarded them merely as a preliminary, and the Canon itself started with *Te igitur*. *Te igitur* made little sense, for there was nothing for the *igitur* to refer back to. Professor Ratcliff and Dr. Willis have suggested that this originally referred back to a Thanksgiving through Christ [7]. The *Memento Domine* and the *Memento etiam* were perhaps once recited by the deacon, and only in his absence by the celebrant, and thereby became part of the Canon [8]. The *Hanc igitur* commended the offerers to God, and the *Quam oblationem* asked God to bless and accept the oblation of bread and wine, that it might be the body and blood of Christ. This led into the Words of Institution, *Qui pridie*, much of which is derived from the Old Latin version of Matthew 26:26-28 [9], and the anamnesis, *Unde et memores*, offering the consecrated elements to God. The prayer *Supra quae* asked God to accept the new covenant as he did the offerings of Abel and Abraham under the old covenant, and the *Supplices te* asked that the oblation might be carried to the heavenly altar, and also for benefits for the communicants. These were followed by the remembrance of the departed, *Memento etiam*, and of the saints, *Nobis quoque*. Finally came the Doxology and Amen.

The prayers of the Canon were followed by the Lord's Prayer, the fraction with *Agnus Dei* and the *Pax*. Usually only the celebrant communicated. During the communion chant, the vessels were cleansed, the actions accompanied by collects. The rite concluded with the post-communion prayer, the dismissal and blessing, and the "Last Gospel", John 1:1-14.

Parts of the Latin Mass were of great antiquity, much of the Canon being quoted by St. Ambrose. According to Professor E.C. Ratcliff, the sacrificial language of the Canon goes back to the doctrine taught by Irenaeus [10]. However, the medieval Church used the language of the Canon to teach the doctrines of Transubstantiation, and of the Sacrifice of the Mass of living and dead. Understandably, the Mass became the target of the Reformers' attacks.

---

[6] G.G. WILLIS, *op. cit.*, p. 121 ff.
[7] E.C. RATCILIFF, "Christian Worship and Liturgy", in K.E. KIRK, *The Study of Theology*, London, 1939, p. 433; G.G. WILLIS, *op. cit.*, p. 124.
[8] E.C. RATCLIFF, *ibid.*, p. 441; G.G. WILLIS, *op. cit*, p. 38. But see, RALPH A. KEIFER, "The Unity of the Roman Canon: An Examination of its unique Structure" in *SL*, 11 (1976) pp. 39-58.
[9] E.C. RATCLIFF, "The Institution Narrative of the Roman Canon Missae; Its beginnings and early background", in *Studia Patristica*, II, pp. 64-82, *Texte und Untersuchungen*, 64 Berlin, 1957.
[10] E.C. RATCLIFF, "Christian Worship and Liturgy", p. 443.

If it could be used to support Transubstantiation and a doctrine of Sacrifice for living and dead, it was a liturgical tradition which must be destroyed.

The first official change in the Latin Mass in England was in 1548 with *The Order of the Communion* [11]. The *Order* was a communion devotion in English, designed to be inserted into the Latin Mass after the priest's communion, providing communion in two kinds for the laity. Prefaced by an exhortation giving notice of the communion and urging worthy reception, the *Order* consisted of an exhortation with warning against unworthy communion, an exhortation to confession, confession said by one of the congregation or by a minister, an absolution, comfortable words of Scripture, a prayer of approach, "We do not presume", and formulae for administration:

> The bodye of oure Lorde Jesus Christ,
> which was geven for the, preserve thy
> body unto everlastyng life.
>
> The blud of oure Lorde Jesus Christ,
> which was shed for the, preserve thy soule
> unto everlastyng life.

The *Order* also provided a blessing.

Parts of the confession and some of the Scripture sentences had been borrowed from the Lutheran Consultation of Archbishop Hermann of Cologne, an English version of which had appeared in 1547 [12]. The term "spiritual" eating and drinking, a key protestant term, appeared several times in the *Order*, and the protestant demand for communion in two kinds was conceded; but there was nothing in it which made it strongly protestant, and, even less, identifiable with a particular school of protestantism.

As a separate Order, the 1548 work was short lived. The accompanying Proclamation referred to "further godly orders", and most of the material of the 1548 Order was incorporated into the communion service of the next "godly order", the 1549 *Book of Common Prayer*.

The 1549 Eucharistic liturgy [13], entitled "The Supper of the Lorde and the Holy Communion, commonly called the Masse", represented a conservative, though subtle, vernacular revision of the Latin Mass. The liturgical calendar was greatly pruned of saint's days, but the traditional Sunday sequence was maintained, and the Eucharist was to be celebrated every Sunday, and on week days. The structure of the Mass remained largely unchanged. It was still Word and Sacrament, with many of the traditional parts of the Mass.

---

[11] Text, ed. H.A. WILSON.
[12] WILSON, pp. 47-52.
[13] Detailed analysis, F.E. BRIGHTMAN, *The English Rite*, vol. 1, pp. xcviii-cxii.

It was still celebrated with vestments and with some of the old ceremonial. But there had been some abbreviation, and some careful rephrasing of the old words.

All that remained of the preparation was the Lord's Prayer and the Collect for Purity, now said by the priest at the altar. A full psalm was appointed for the Introit, followed by the *Kyries* and *Gloria in excelsis* in English. Collects for the King preceded the collects of the day. The Epistle and Gospel were retained, though the old Gradual chant was removed, possibly because in the Sarum rite, the Offertory of bread and wine began here. The Creed remained, and a sermon was to follow. The Liturgy of the Word ended with an exhortation to worthy communion.

The second part of the service, the Eucharist proper, began with the Offertory, but it was an offertory of alms, not of bread and wine; the bread and wine were merely prepared. The "Little Canon" disappeared, being replaced by Scripture sentences relating to alms.

The Eucharistic Prayer commenced with the traditional Western salutations, preface, proper preface, *Sanctus*, and *Benedictus*. The remainder of the Canon had been rewritten in three sections. In the first, corresponding to the *Te igitur, Memento Domine, Communicantes* and *Hanc igitur*, the offering of "these gifts", the bread and wine, and the prayer for the Pope and the King, were replaced by offering of prayer for the Church and the world, and those in need. The second paragraph took the place of the *Quam oblationem* and *Qui pridie*. It emphasised the single and complete offering and sacrifice of Calvary, and spoke of the Eucharist as a memorial. It asked:

> and with thy holy spirite and worde, vouchsafe to blesse and sanctifie these thy gyftes, and creatures of bread and wyne, that they mai be unto us the bodye and bloude of thy moste derely beloved sonne Jesus Christe.

The Words of Institution followed. The final paragraph, replacing the corresponding prayers of the Latin Canon, contained a petition to God for the benefits of communion, and the self-oblation of the communicants, their prayers and supplications. There was no offering of the consecrated elements. F.E. Brightman summarised the new Canon thus:

> The Canon is an eloquent paraphrase and expansion of the Roman Canon (l) adjusting it clearly to the conception of the Eucharistic Sacrifice as threefold: viz (a) as a commemoration of our Lord's *historical* self-oblation in his Death upon the Cross; (b) as a sacrifice of praise and thanksgiving for the benefits of redemption so secured;

and (c) as the offering of the Church, of ourselves, our souls and bodies: concentrating all sacrificial language on these three moments [14].

Brightman could have added that it represented the replacing of any language supporting the medieval concept of Eucharistic sacrifice by a protestant conception of the Eucharist.

After the Canon came the Lord's Prayer, a communion sentence, the devotions from the 1548 *Order* with the *Agnus Dei*. The 1548 words of administration were used, though now each set of words was applied to both "bodye and soule". After a post-communion Scripture sentence the service concluded with a post-communion prayer and a blessing.

The rephrasing of the 1549 communion service could easily be mistaken for conservatism. Bishop Gardiner, appealing to the petition for the Spirit to bless and sanctify the elements, could pronounce it not distant from the catholic faith [15]. Many clergy continued to celebrate it as if it were merely the old Mass in English [16]. The Strasbourg reformer, Martin Bucer, then Regius Professor of Divinity at Cambridge, subjected the book to an analysis in his *Censura*, and listed several points in the communion service which needed further reform [17]. On account of its conservative nature, and of the "curiousity of ministers and mistakers", the book was replaced by another book in 1552.

It has been argued by Dr. C.W. Dugmore that although Cranmer was responsible for the book of 1549, that of 1552 must be attributed to the Anglo-Zurich party, led by Hooper; Cranmer, by that time having lost favour with Northumberland, was unable to prevent the new book replacing that of 1549 [18]. Certainly the 1552 book shows some influence of reformers of the more extreme wing, of Hooper and Knox, and of John à Lasco [19]. However, E.C. Ratcliff [20] and A.H. Couratin [21] have maintained that the "godly orders" promised in the Royal Proclamation of the 1548 *The Order of the Communion* imply a series of planned reforms, viz., 1549, 1552, and possibly the Prayer Book rumoured by the Frankfurt exiles. Couratin also noted that in his reply to Bishop Gardiner in 1550, Cranmer interpreted the text and ru-

---

[14] *Op. cit.*, Vol. 1, p. cvi.
[15] T. CRANMER, *On the Lord's Supper*, p. 92.
[16] *Original Letters*, Vol. 1, p. 72, Hooper to Bullinger.
[17] E.C. WHITAKER, *Martin Bucer and the Book of Common Prayer*, AC Gt. Wakering 1974, for text.
[18] C.W. DUGMORE, "The First Ten Years 1549-59", in, M. RAMSEY et al, *The English Prayer Book 1549-1662*.
[19] *Ibid.*, G.J. CUMING, *op. cit.*, p. 102; but Cf. BRIGHTMAN, *op. cit.*, Vol. 1, p. civi.
[20] E.C. RATCLIFF, "The Liturgical Work of Archbishop Cranmer", in *JEH*, 7, (1956), pp. 189-203.
[21] A.H. COURATIN, "The Holy Communion 1549" in *CQR*, 164 (1963), pp. 148-159; "The Service of Holy Communion 1552-1662", in *CQR*, 163, (1962), pp. 431-442.

brics of the 1549 book in accordance with the subsequent book of 1552, and once used language reminiscent of the second book; "it is", he suggests, "hard to resist the conclusion that the book of 1552 was already taking shape as early as 1550" [22]. The more recent review by C.O. Buchanan supports this suggestion [23].

Whatever the truth of the authorship question, it remains a fact that the protestant nature of the 1552 communion service was unmistakable. The service represented a drastic pruning and rearrangement of that of 1549. The rubrics were carefully framed to exlude the possibility of disguising the service as the Mass, and with the exception of the *Gloria in excelsis*, all singing disappeared from the service [24].

The service commenced with the Lord's Prayer and Collect for Purity, and these were followed by the Ten Commandments; the Introit psalm and *Kyries* were removed. The remainder of the Liturgy of the Word followed the 1549 sequence — collect for the King, of the day, the Epistle, Gospel, Creed and sermon, and Offertory sentences. These sentences were followed by a "Prayer for the Church Militant", being the first part of the 1549 Canon, thought with modification taking account of Bucer's *Censura*. This was followed by a series of exhortations, leading to an exhortation to confession (Ye that do truly and earnestly), confession (Almighty God, Father of our Lord Jesus Christ), absolution and comfortable words of Scripture, these being from the 1548 *Order of the Communion*. At this point came the *Sursum corda*, preface and *Sanctus*, with the prayer "We do not presume". Then came a prayer containing the Words of Institution, with emphasis on the one oblation of Calvary. The 1549 petition for the blessing and sanctification of the gifts by the Spirit and word was replaced by

> and grant that we, receiving these thy creatures of bread and wine ... may be partakers of his most blessed body and blood.

Communion followed, the words of administration carefully excluding any notion that the bread and wine were connected with the body and blood of Christ:

> Take and eat this, in remembraunce that Christ dyed for thee, and feede on him in thy hearte by faythe, with thankesgeuing.

---

[22] "The Holy Communion 1549", p. 151.
[23] C.O. BUCHANAN, *What did Cranmer Think he was Doing?*, Grove Liturgical Study 7, Bramcote 1976, 1982.
[24] Detailed analysis F.E. BRIGHTMAN, *op. cit.*, clxi-clxii.

> Drinke this in remembraunce that Christ's bloude was shed for thee, and be thankefull.

After the Lord's Prayer came a thanksgiving, the *Gloria in excelsis* in a new position, and finally a bessing.

A rubric inserted at the last moment, the "Black Rubric", explained that although communion was to be received kneeling, this was not to be taken as reverence for the bread and wine.

The 1552 communion service was carefully constructed so as to exclude any notion of the Sacrifice of the Mass, and any notion of presence in the elements. The precise identity of the eucharistic doctrine in the service is disputed. Y. Brilioth [25] and G. B. Timms [26] have argued that Cranmer's own doctrine approximated to Calvinism; on the other hand, Dom Gregory Dix [27] and C. C. Richardson [28] have made out a plausible case that Cranmer was a Zwinglian, and that this is the doctrine enshrined in the 1552 service. C. W. Dugmore, while denying that it represents Cranmer's doctrine, in attributing it to the Anglo-Zurich party, implies that the doctrine enshrined in it is of the Zurich type [29]. According to the study by Peter Brooks, Cranmer's doctrine was of the Swiss type, but his ideas were not of one school to the exclusion of others [30].

It was the 1552 communion service which was re-enacted in 1559. But three significant alterations were made to the rite [31]: the old Eucharistic vestments and ornaments in use in the second year of Edward's reign (1548/9) were, in theory, re-introduced [32]; the 1549 words of administration were combined with those of 1552, suggesting that the bread and wine did have some connection with the body and blood of Christ; and the "Black Rubric" which had explained the practice of kneeling for reception was removed.

In 1604 James I issued a revised text of the *Book of Common Prayer*, but the communion service was unaltered [33]. Yet, as far as the Puritans and Separatists were concerned, its pedigree was still clearly discernable; it had a great deal of its structure and contents in common with its parent, the Latin Mass.

---

[25] Y. Brilioth, *Eucharistic Faith and Practice Evangelical and Catholic*, ET. A.G. Hebert, London, 1930.
[26] G.B. Timms, "Dixit Cranmer", in *CQR* 143 (1946-7), pp. 217-34; 144 (1947), pp. 33-51.
[27] G. Dix, *The Shape of the Liturgy*; "Dixit Cranmer et non Timuit", in *CQR* 45 (1947-8), pp. 145-76; 146 (1948), pp. 44-60.
[28] C.C. Richardson, *Zwingli and Cranmer on the Eucharist*, Illinois, 1949.
[29] C.W. Dugmore, *op. cit.*
[30] P.N. Brooks, *Thomas Cranmer's Doctrine of the Eucharist*, London, 1964.
[31] Brightman, *op. cit.*, pp. clxix-clxx.
[32] In practice only the surplice and cope were worn.
[33] Brightman, *op. cit.*, pp. clxxx-clxxxi.

CHAPTER 3

EARLY PURITAN EUCHARISTIC LITURGIES

The existence of unofficial liturgical revision was already hinted at in the Royal Proclamation which prefaced the 1548 *The Order of the Communion*; addressed to "all and singular of our loving subjects", it announced the intention of introducing communion in two kinds,

> least every man phantasying and devisyng a sondry way by hym selfe in the use of this moste blissed Sacrament of unitie, there might thereby arise any unsemely and ungodly diversitie [1].

Perhaps some ministers were already "phantasying and devisyng" their own liturgical novelties, for the Proclamation was careful to warn against those who,

> roune afore, and so by their rashenes, become the greatest hynderers of suche thynges, as they more arrogantly then godly, wolde seme (by their awne private authoritie) moste hotly to set forwarde [2].

Thus independent liturgical revision was contrasted unfavourably with official liturgical revision. Nevertheless, a promise was given that true reformation would be brought to effect, in due time.

We know, however, that further advances were made without official authority; the Grey Friar's Chronicle records that at Easter 1548 St. Paul's cathedral and some London parishes used English forms of service, and at the obit of Henry VII at Westminster, Mass was said in English and the *Canon missae* was omitted [3].

Reforms of a more radical nature may well have been encouraged by the arrival of continental divines such as Peter Martyr Vermigli, 1548, and Mar-

---

[1] Text in ed. WILSON, *op. cit.*
[2] *Ibid.*
[3] *Ibid.*, p. xix; C. WRIOTHESLEY, *A Chronicle of England*, II, Camden Society, New Series 20, London, 1877, p. 2. According to PETER LE HURAY, the Chapel Royal and some London Churches were experimenting with prototypes of the new English services. *Music and the Reformation in England 1549-1660*, London, 1967, pp. 9-10.

tin Bucer, 1549, and, complete with their own congregations and liturgies, Valerand Poullain and John à Lasco.

The growth of liturgical independency of a Puritan ethos is evidenced by four liturgies: William Huycke's translation of Calvin's liturgy in 1550, John Knox's liturgy for Berwick on Tweed, 1550, the *Liturgy of Compromise*, 1554, and the *Genevan Service Book*, 1556.

1. *William Huycke's Translation of Calvin's "La Forme", 1550.*

In 1550 there appeared a book of prayers entitled:

> Geneva: The Forme of common praiers used in the churches of Geneva: The mynystracion of the sacramentes, of Baptisme and the Lordes supper: The vysitacion of the sycke: And the Cathechisme of Geneva: made by master John Calvyne.
>
> In the ende are certaine other Godly prayers privately to be used: translated out of frenche into Englyshe. By William Huycke.

It was printed in London by Edward Whitchurche, "the VII daye of June 1550", and "cum privilegio". We are, then, dealing essentially with John Calvin's Genevan liturgy of 1542 and 1547 [4].

The question arises as to the purpose of the publication of this translation. Little is known of Huycke; an introduction to the reader by a certain Thomas Broke explained:

> There is also contayned in thys boke, ye common prayers, used in the congregacion of Geneva, the maner of the mynystracion of the Sacramentes there, ... All these were by master Wylliam Huicke, a man of Godlye learninge, and right honest conversacion, translated out of frenche whyle he was at Geneva, where he heared, and sawe, the same putte in use.

Perhaps this was the same William Huycke who graduated at Oxford, B.A. 19th February, 1532/3 and M.A. 18th June, 1537 [5]. No indication was given by Broke as to the date or length of time that Huycke was in Geneva, and he may well have been in exile there in the reign of Henry VIII.

Much more, on the other hand, is known of the printer, Edward Whitchurche, and his connection with the book may well be significant.

---

[4] Text in *Corpus Reformatorum*, Calvini opera VI; English translation in Bard Thompson, *Liturgies of the Western Church*.
[5] JOSEPH FOSTER, *Alumni oxonienses*, 1500-1714, Oxford, 1891, Vol. 1, p. 780.

Whitchurche [6] had well-known advanced protestant sympathies. In 1537 he had joined with Richard Grafton in arranging for the distribution of printed copies of the Bible in English; in 1543 he had been imprisoned for displays of protestant zeal; and later he was to be excepted from the pardon in the proclamation of 1554, and was to marry Cranmer's widow. From 1544 Whitchurche received jointly an exclusive patent for printing church service books, and later printed some editions of the enacted *Book of Common Prayer*. Thus, bearing the name of Whitchurche, Huycke's work might have commended itself to some as being an official translation having some degree of authority for use in England. If Huycke's work was merely to bring Calvin's liturgy to the attention of English scholars, we should have expected a Latin edition, as in the case of the liturgies of Poullain and à Lasco, and as in the case of the Latin edition of the 1548 *The Order of the Communion* and the 1549 *Book of Common Prayer* for continental scholars. The fact that this work was in English, and that the style of translation lent itself for public use, suggest that it was intended for a wider audience than scholars, and it may have been as an alternative, albeit an "independent" one, to the enacted liturgy.

Calvin's Genevan liturgy of 1542 and 1547 was itself an abbreviated edition of his Strasbourg liturgy of 1540 and 1545 [7]. Several sources underlie the latter:

(a) The ideal reformed Eucharistic liturgy was outlined by Calvin in his *Institutes of the Christian Religion*. The ceremonies of the Mass having been abandoned, the Evangelical Supper takes its place (we have divided it into the constituent parts).

> The commencement should be with public prayer; next, a sermon should be delivered:
> then the minister, having placed bread and wine on the table, should read the institution of the Supper.
>
> He should next explain the primises which are therin given; and, at the same time, keep back from communion all those who are devarred by the prohibition of the Lord.
>
> He should afterwards pray that the Lord, with the kindness with which he has bestowed this sacred food upon us, would also form and instruct us to receive it with faith and gratitude; and, as we are of ourselves unworthy, would make us worthy of the feast by his mercy.

---

[6] *DNB.*
[7] There is no extant copy of the 1540 edition. It is known by a reprint in 1542 by Pierre Brully. W.D. MAXWELL, *The Liturgical Portions of the Genevan Service Book*, Edinburg, 1931, p. 21.

> Here, either a psalm should be sung, or something read, while the faithful, in order, communicate at the sacred feast, the minister breaking the bread, and giving it to the people.
>
> The supper being ended, an exhortation should be given to sincere faith, to charity, and lives becoming Christians.
>
> Lastly, thanks should be offered, and the praises of God should be sung.
>
> This being done, the Church should be dismissed in peace [8].

This outline occurs quite naturally in Calvin's systematic treatment of the Lord's Supper. It appeared in the first edition of the *Institutes*, 1536, and we may presume that it represents his own reflections on the nature of the Lord's Supper in the biblical accounts, together with his knowledge of Reformed worship, in particular that of the city of Basle where he had settled for a short time in 1535 [9].

As early as 1502 Basle had been provided with a vernacular preaching service by John Ulrich Surgant in his *Manuale Curatorum*. Surgant had compiled this service from the medieval vernacular service called "pronus" or "pronaus", being derived possibly from *praeconium* (public speaking), or from πρόναος (nave). This vernacular service seems to have developed in the eighth and ninth centuries, and came after the reading of the Gospel in the Mass [10]. It usually included biddings, the Lord's Prayer, the *Ave Maria*, the Creed, Decalogue, a confession and absolution. Surgant used this as the basis for a separate preaching service before Mass, consisting of:

> Announcement of Text.
> Lord's Prayer.
> Ave Maria.
> Sermon.
> Bidding Prayers concluding with remembrance of the departed.
> Lord's Prayer.
> Ave Maria.
> Apostles' Creed.
> Decalogue.
> General Confession.
> Absolution.

---

[8] *Institutes*, 4-17-43.
[9] For this period see, T.H.L. PARKER, *John Calvin: A Biography*, London, 1975, p. 32 ff. Also at Basle were Capito, Sebastian Munster, Bullinger and Farel.
[10] V. THALHOFER, "Vom Pronaus, speciell von den an die Pfarrpredigt sich anschliessenden Gebeten und Verkundigungen", in *Theol. praktisch Quartalschrift* 38 (1885), pp. 25-42; F.E. BRIGHTMAN, *The English Rite*, vol. 2, pp. 1039-1043.

Conclusion: "Pray God for me as I will for you in the Office of the Holy Mass" [11].

Basle had been won for the Reformation by the efforts of Oecolampadius, and both he and his close friend Zwingli at Zurich, used a reformed version of Surgant's service as their main Sunday service in place of the Mass.

Although he did stress the concept of mystery, Oecolampadius was very close to Zwingli in his doctrine of the Eucharist, denying both the concept of sacrifice, and the presence of Christ in the eating and drinking at the Supper. The Supper they regarded as a visible exhortation to faith in the benefits of the Passion of Christ. The Eucharist was therefore primarily a declaration of faith and an exhortation to belief. Oecolampadius had prepared a Eucharistic liturgy for Basle as early as 1525, entitled *Form und gstalt Wie das Herren Nachtmal*, and consisting of the following:

> Sermon.
> Admonition.
> Preparation of elements.
> Confession.
> Psalm 130:1-8.
> Absolution.
> Isaiah 53:1-7. Contemplation.
> Matthew 27:35-50.
> Exhortation.
> Lord's Prayer.
> Brief exhortation.
> Administration. "The undoubted faith, which you have in the death of Christ, lead you into eternal life". "The faith, which you have in the spilt blood of Jesus Christ, lead you into eternal life".
> Commendation to love, and peace [12].

(b) While making for Strasbourg in July 1536, Calvin passed through Geneva, and the reformer Guillaume Farel, now a minister there, pressed Calvin to abandon his academic career and to assist with the reformation of Geneva. In use was Farel's own liturgical compilation, *La Manière et fasson*, prepared for Neuchâtel in 1533. Farel had compiled this order after his own experience of the worship of Basle, Bern and Strasbourg. The preaching service followed the Pronaus-type service, with biddings, Lord's Prayer, reading and exposition, exhortation, Decalogue, Confession, Apostles' Creed, intercessions and dismissal in peace. The Eucharistic liturgy also has many points of contact with that of Oecolampadius:

---

[11] Text in, F. SCHMIDT-CLAUSING, *Zwingli als Liturgiker*, Gottingen 1952, pp. 88-112. Surgant's *Manuale* was a guide, and was not suggesting a fixed liturgical text.
[12] ET in BARD THOMPSON, *op. cit.*, pp. 211-215.

Exhortation.
Institution.
Self-Examination.
Excommunication.
Confession.
Creed.
Assurance of Pardon.
Words of Institution.
Exhortation to true communion.
Communion.
Post-communion Bidding Prayer.
Peace and Blessing [13].

We may assume that this formed the basis of the Genevan services until Calvin's Genevan liturgy of 1542. Commenting on Farel's rite, W. D. Maxwell said:

> This was an utterly barren rite, a result of Zwinglian influence and the extreme views of Farel. It had no influence whatever upon any succeeding rite, except that Calvin borrowed from it considerably for his marriage service [14].

In fact, as we shall later see, Calvin used part of Farel's Eucharistic liturgy in his own Strasbourg rite, and his amended Genevan rite was influenced by the meagre provisions of Farel's liturgy.

(c) The major source of Calvin's Strasbourg liturgy was the Strasbourg German liturgy. Calvin himself explained:

> Quant aux prières des dimanche, je prins la form de Strasbourg et en empruntay la plus grande partie [15].

The Strasbourg liturgy to which Calvin referred was Martin Bucer's *Psalter mit aller Kirchenubing* of 1539 [16].

Farel and Calvin had been expelled from Geneva in 1538, and Bucer invited Calvin to take charge of the French congregation at Strasbourg [17]. The German magistrates had consented to allow the French congregation to hold their own preaching services, but for the Eucharist they had had to join with the Germans. On Calvin's arrival permission was given for them to celebrate the Eucharist once a month, and for this purpose Calvin had drawn up a

---

[13] *La Maniere et fasson*, ed. J.G. BAUM, Strasbourg, 1859; ET in BARD THOMPSON, *op. cit.*, pp. 216-224. Cf. E. JACOBS, *Die Sakramentslehre Wilhelm Farels*, Zürich 1978.
[14] W.D. MAXWELL, *An Outline of Christian Worship*, Oxford, 1936, p. 112, note I.
[15] *Corpus Reformatorum*, Calvini opera, IX, p. 894.
[16] ET in BARD THOMPSON, *op. cit.*, pp. 167-179.
[17] T.H.L. PARKER, *op. cit.*, p. 62 ff.

complete liturgy for all services, basing the Morning service and the Eucharist on the existing Strasbourg rite.

Bucer's *Psalter mit aller Kirchenubing* was the most recent of a whole series of editions of a reformed liturgy, extending over a period of fifteen years, and unlike those of Oecolampadius and Farel, deriving directly from the Roman Mass. Each successive revision had to a greater or lesser degree diverged from the parent rite in structure and content.

The first reforms of a liturgical nature in Strasbourg were those of Diobald Schwarz's vernacular mass, *Die Teutsche Messe* of February 1524. Four particular points of revision are worthy of notice.

(1) The long prepartion which had come to preface the Mass before the Introit was replaced by a shorter *Confiteor* serving as a general confession of sin, and followed by an absolution into which Schwarz interpolated 1 Timothy 1:15. The *Breviarium Argentinense* seems to have been the source of this *Confiteor* [18].

(2) The Offertory exhortation, *Orate Fratres*, was rewritten to incorporate the self-oblation of Roman 12:1: *"Lieben bruder und Schwester, bitten Gott den Vatter durch unsern herren Jesum Christum, das er mache unsern Leib zu ein lebendigen, heiligen, wohlgefelligen Opfer, das do ist der vernunftig Gottesdienst, der Gott gefelt. Das bestehe uns allen, Amen".*

(3) The invocation to the saints and the virgin Mary was omitted.

(4) The *Canon missae* was freely paraphrased, and prayer for te civil powers was introduced into it.

The structure of the Mass remained, as did most of the prayers themselves; but although the reforms were modest, Hastings Eells is correct when he says that "liturgically speaking, Strasbourg had crossed the Rubicon" [19]. In passing, it should be noted that in (1) and (2), Schwarz had paid particular attention to items which were late additions to the Western Eucharistic liturgy.

Schwarz's Reformed Mass was followed by four printed editions in the same year between Easter and September, and a fifth followed shortly after [20]. In these early editions features were already to be found which would become the hallmarks of Bucer's revisions: the Apostles' Creed might be substituted for the Nicene; the exhortation, *Orate Fratres*, increased in length; proper prefaces for the calendar were pruned; the *Canon missae* was further modified; and the Aaronic blessing was introduced.

After 1525 a whole series of revised liturgies began to appear in rapid succession, being the work of Bucer. Using the *Teutsche Messe* as a basis,

---

[18] G.J. VAN DE POLL, *Martin Bucer's Liturgical Ideas*, Assen, 1954, p. 10.
[19] HASTINGS EELLS, *Martin Bucer*, New Haven, 1931, p. 43.
[20] W.D. MAXWELL, *The Liturgical Portions of the Genevan Service Book*, p. 26.

each one of Bucer's revisions differed in some detail from its predecessor [21].

In these revisions the liturgical calendar with the traditional Sunday sequence was gradually abandoned; the Lord's Day and festivals of Christmas, Easter and Pentecost alone remained, resulting in the disappearance of the seasonal propers. Furthermore, the Cathedral excepted, the Eucharist was celebrated only monthly. On three Sundays out of four, the Synaxis or Liturgy of the Word alone was celebrated; Word and Sacrament were separated.

When the revisions themselves are examined, various modifications are found to have taken place. The opening confession was lengthened, and alternatives were provided; the Introit was replaced by a metrical psalm, and the *Kyrie eleison* and *Gloria in excelsis* became optional and fell into disuse. The collect for the day was replaced by a prayer for illumination to hear God's Word; the Epistle disappeared, and the Gospel was read chapter by chapter. The sermon might be followed by an exhortation, and the Apostles' Creed could be replaced by a psalm or hymn.

In the Eucharist proper, we find that in the 1539 rite, the *Canon missae* had been completely metamorphosed. The traditional salutations had disappeared. Three alternative prayers were provided, all having a similar content — prayer for the civil authorities, for the congregation, and, when applicable, for true communion, concluding with the Lord's Prayer. The Words of Institution had been detached from the prayer and were read immediately before the administration, presumably as a warrant, though G. J. Van De Poll has suggested thatit was in order to bring the words into closer association with the fraction and distribution [22]. A psalm was sung during the administration, and was followed by one of three thanksgivings which replaced the old postcommunion prayers.

At this point the question must be raised as to whether or not the *Psalter mit aller Kirchenubing* was influenced at all by the *Pronaus*. F. E. Brightman suggested that the substance of the Strasbourg Sunday Morning Service, and also that of Geneva, was morely a perpetuation of the *Pronaus* [23]. G. J. Van De Poll has implied that the Long Prayer was less a reform of the *Canon missae* than the substitution of the intercessions from Surgant's *Manuale* [24]. Against this must be set the textual evidence amassed by L. Büchsenschütz [25] and W. D. Maxwell [26] which demonstrates overwhelmingly that the liturgy of Strasbourg was derived directly from the Roman Mass.

---

[21] *Ibid.*, pp. 27-32.
[22] G.J. VAN DE POLL, *op. cit.*, p. 42.
[23] BRIGHTMAN, *op. cit.*, p. 1039.
[24] VAN DE POLL, *op. cit.*, p. 37.
[25] L. BÜCHSENSCHÜTZ, *Histoire des Liturgies en Langue Allemande dans l'Eglise de Strasbourg au XVIe siècle*, Cahors, 1900.
[26] W.D. MAXWELL, *op. cit.*, p. 66 ff.

However, it should be admitted that Brightman had compiled some interesting parallels which cannot be ignored. The evidence suggests that the vernacular *Pronaus*, simply by being in the vernacular, commended itself to the reformers, and perhaps influenced Bucer in the manner in which he revised the Mass; possibly Bucer's Antecommunion is the Mass judged by and reformed from the standpoint of the acceptable features of the *Pronaus*.

THE DERIVATION OF BUCER'S PSALTER MIT ALLER KIRCHENUBING.
1539

The Mass	Reforms, 1524-38	Bucer 1539
Preparation: Psalm Our help is in the name of the Lord. Who made heaven and earth.	→	Scripture sentences
confiteor.	→	Confession, choice of three. Scripture sentences of Remission.
Absolution	→	Absolution
Versicles and responses		
Introit	→	Psalm or hymn
Kyries	→	Sometimes, Kyries, and
Gloria	→	Gloria
Salutation and collect	→	Collect for illumination
Epistle		
Gradual	→	Psalm
(Priest's Prayer)		
Gospel	→	Gospel
(Sermon)	→	Sermon, with communion exhortation
Creed (Nicene)	→	Creed (Apostles) or psalm or hymn
Offertory Offertory Prayers Lavabo Pray brethren that my sacrifice and yours may be accepted by God the	→	Preparation of elements

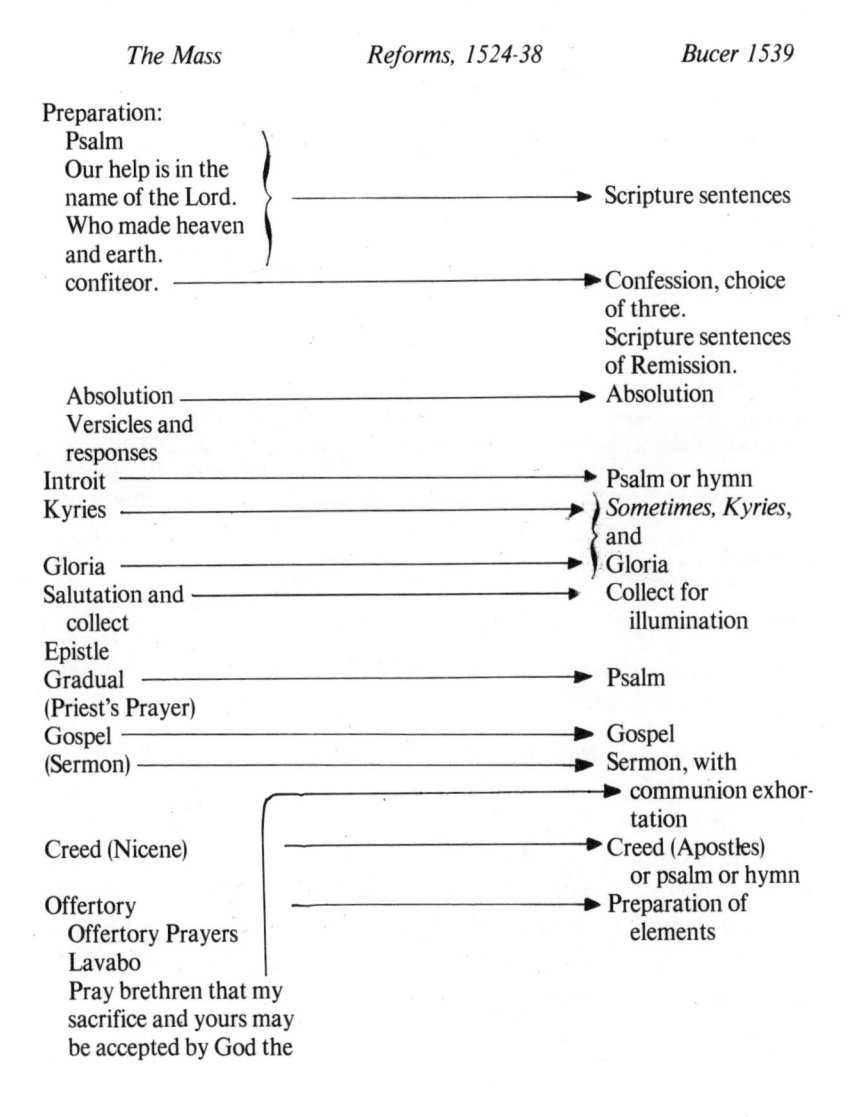

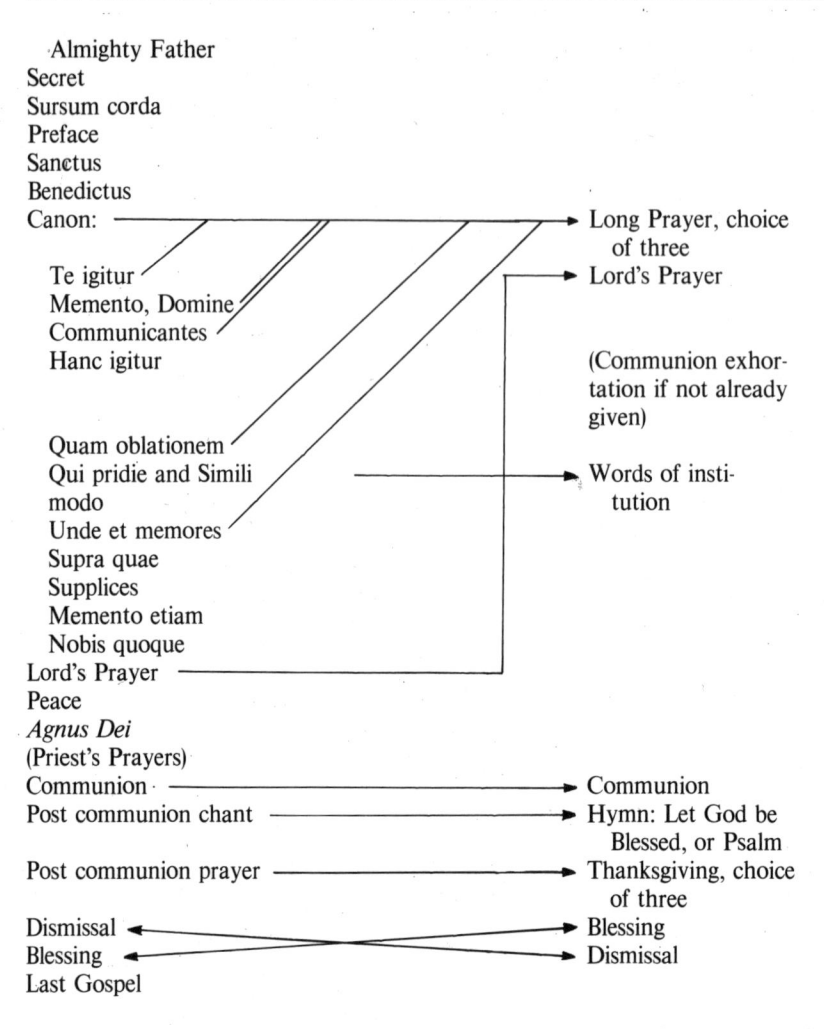

Almighty Father	
Secret	
Sursum corda	
Preface	
Sanctus	
Benedictus	
Canon:	Long Prayer, choice of three
Te igitur	Lord's Prayer
Memento, Domine	
Communicantes	
Hanc igitur	(Communion exhortation if not already given)
Quam oblationem	
Qui pridie and Simili modo	Words of institution
Unde et memores	
Supra quae	
Supplices	
Memento etiam	
Nobis quoque	
Lord's Prayer	
Peace	
Agnus Dei	
(Priest's Prayers)	
Communion	Communion
Post communion chant	Hymn: Let God be Blessed, or Psalm
Post communion prayer	Thanksgiving, choice of three
Dismissal	Blessing
Blessing	Dismissal
Last Gospel	

When there was no communion, after the Long Prayer Bucer's liturgy ended with a psalm, the blessing and dismissal.

    With certain alterations derived from the Neuchâtel rite of Farel, Calvin's Strasbourg liturgy was that of the *Psalter mit aller Kirchenubing*, entitled *La Manyere de faire prieres*, the most notable differences were that no alternative prayers were provided, and the Decalogue was sung after the absolution. This latter practice had been recommended by Bucer in *Grund und Ursach*, but although he had used the Decalogue as the basis of a confession, he himself never used it in this form [27]. Possibly Calvin took up Bucer's suggestion, or it may have been suggested to him from Farel's rite.

[27] VAN DE POLL, *op. cit.*, p. 75.

In 1541 Calvin returned to Geneva. Farel's liturgy was probably still in use, and the Genevan magistrates were reluctant to make changes. The 1542 Genevan rite, entitled *La Forme des Prieres*, represents a modified version of his Strasbourg liturgy, taking into account the bleak rite of Farel. However, Hughes Oliphant Old is surely correct when he says of Calvin's liturgy:

> Like all liturgies, it has passed through many hands: Surgant, Zwingli, Marot, Luther, Oecolampadius, Schwarz, Farel, Geiler, Blarer, Capito, and Zwick. Like all true liturgies it has passed through just as many cities: Bern, Memmingen, Aigle, Neuchâtel, Ulm. Augusburg, Paris and Strasbourg. In each hand and in each city it has picked up a bit more polish and has joined itself a bit more closely to history. It is in a very real sense the liturgy not of Calvin, not of Geneva, but the liturgy of the Reformed Church [28].

It was this liturgy which Huycke and Whitchurche presented to the English Churches.

At Strasbourg Calvin had celebrated the Eucharist once a month; thus on three Sundays out of four, the Liturgy of the Word was separated from the Eucharist. At Geneva, despite his protests [29], the Eucharist was celebrated only quarterly. This division was further emphasised by the physical separation of the two services in the printed books by the baptismal rite.

The Forme of Common Prayers (Sunday Morning Service)

Huycke (Geneva)	Calvin's Strasbourg Rite
Scripture sentence: our ayde and Succour is in the name and power of God, which made bothe heaven and earth. So be it.	Scripture sentence (*idem*)
Bidding to confession	Bidding to confession
Confession	Confession
	Scripture sentence of remission.
	Absolution.
	1st Table of Decalogue sung in metre
	Prayer for instruction in the law
Psalm in plainsong	2nd Table of Decalogue
Prayer for illumination	Prayer for illumination
Lection	Lection
Sermon	Sermon
Long Prayer, for civil powers, pastors and	Long Prayer (*idem*, but no special communion paragraph)

---

[28] H.O. OLD, *The Patristic Roots of Reformed Worship*, Zurich, 1975, p. 96.
[29] *Corpus Reformatorum*. Calvini Opera, IV. 1051-1052.

congregation, and for all people, and long paraphrase of Lord's Prayer. A Special paragraph to be added on communion Sundays.	
Open Confession of the Christian faith, (Apostles's Creed said by minister)	Apostles' Creed sung in metre,
Psalm	Psalm
Aaronic blessing	Aaronic blessing

In the Scripture sentence, or "call to worship", and the bidding and confession, Huycke followed Calvin closely, though with the liberty of a translator. Calvin had followed Bucer, using the second alternative confession given in *Psalter mit aller Kirchenubing*; this appears to have been Bucer's own composition [30].

The Strasbourg service followed Bucer in having Scripture sentences of remission and an absolution, and then Calvin's own addition, the singing of the Decalogue. At Geneva he was unable to use an absolution [31], and dropped the singing of the Decalogue. Since the liturgical calendar was abandoned, the old collect for the day disappeared, its place being taken by a prayer for illumination. This led up to the lection, and the sermon.

The Long Prayer which followed the sermon had been adapted from Bucer's third alternative "Canon" of 1539. When the Eucharist was celebrated at Geneva, a special "Eucharistic" section was added to the Long Prayer. In Calvin's Strasbourg Liturgy, this section had formed a separate prayer coming after the Creed and the preparation of the elements; at Geneva it ceased to be a separate "Eucharistic" prayer.

The substance of this Eucharistic prayer has been recently analysed by Jean Cadier, who has stressed that throughout it is concerned to express the double grace of Justification and Sanctification, by participation in the whole Christ [32]. Huycke's rendering of the prayer is as follows:

> And accordyng as oure Lord Jesu thought it not sufficient only to offer up once his blessed body and bloud on the crosse to acquite us of all our sinnes: but doth vouchsafe also spirituallye, to deale and dystribute the selfe same unto us, for a sustenaunce to nouryshe us unto everlastynge lyfe: Even so maye it please thee to endue us with

---

[30] VAN DE POLL, *op. cit.*, p. 34.
[31] *Corpus Reformatorum*, Calvini Opera, X, p. 213.
[32] JEAN CARDIER, "La Priere Eucharistique De Calvin", in *Eucharisties d'Orient et d'Occident,* Lex Orandi 46, Paris, 1970, pp. 171-180.

thy specyall grace, that with moste upryghte synglenesse of heart, and earneste ferventenesse of affeccyons, wee maye moste thankefullye receyue at hys hande so hygh a benefite, and so worthy (that is to say), that we may with a constante and assured faythe, receave bothe hys bodye and bloude, yea, verelye CHRIST hymselfe wholye, even as he, beeynge both verye GOD and manne, is moste woorthelye named to bee the holye breade of heaven, to quicken and refreshe oure soules: to the ende that from hencefoorthe wee maye cease to lyve in our selves, and after the course or inclinacion of our owne most corrupt and defyled nature: and that wee may lyve in hym, whiles we have hym also lyvyng in us, to conducte and guyde us unto the holy, most blessed and everlastynge lyfe. Graunte us also that in receyving the same, we become in verye deede partakers of the newe and everlastyng testament (that is to say) of the covenaunt of grace and mercy, being most certayn and assured, that thy good pleasure is to be oureverlastyng mercifull FATHER, whyles thou layest not to our charge oure manifolde offences, and providest for us, as for thy dearely beloved chyldren and heyres, all thynges needefull as well for the body as for ye soule: so that we may without ceassing render laudes and thankes unto thee, evermore extollyng, and magnifyinge thy holye name both by worde and deede. And fynallye, geve us grace so to celebrate thys day the holy remembrauce of thy blessed and dearelye beloved sonne, yea in suche sorte to use and practyse oure selves therein, and so to shewe foorthe and declare the woorthy benefites of hys precious death: that we receiving thereby farther strengthe and more ample increase in faythe and all good thynges, maye with the lustier courage, and the more confidence prayse the our FATHER, rejoysyng and glorifying onely in thy name.

Participation in the whole Christ, Cadier points out, leads to thanksgiving:

> Par la participation à la personne du Christ et à l'alliance de grâce, nous sommes replacés par la Cène devant les merveilles de l'amour divin et conduits à la reconnaissance, à la louange, à l'action de grâces, à l'eucharistie au sens littéral du terme [33].

It is interesting to compare one particular petition with the *Quam oblationem* of the *Canon missae*.

Quam oblationem	*Calvin*
Which oblation do thou, O God, we beseech thee, vouchsafe in all things to make blessed, approved, ratified, reasonable, and acceptable: that unto us it may be become the Body and Blood of thy most dearly beloved Son, our Lord Jesus Christ.	Even so may it please thee ... that we may with a constante and assured faythe, receave bothe hys bodye and bloude, yea, verelye CHRIST hymselfe wholye, ...

[33] *Ibid.*, p. 179.

In Calvin's petition, as well as there being no concept of oblation regarding the elements, faith is made and explicit precondition for a true communion.

It was the practice at Geneva to follow the Long Prayer with the Apostles' Creed, recited by the minister, leading into the Eucharistic liturgy proper. When there was no communion — on most Sundays in the year — the service concluded with a psalm and the Aaronic blessing.

The maner of celebrating the Supper of the Lord.

Huycke: Geneva.	Calvin's Strasbourg rite.
(preparation of the bread and wine during the Creed)	(preparation of the bread and wine during the Creed)
	Eucharistic Prayer.
	Lord's Prayer.
Exhortation, with Words of Institution and excommunication.	Exhortation, with Words of Institution and excommunication.
Breaking of bread and delivery.	Breaking of bread and delivery.
	Words of administration.
Psalm or Scripture reading.	Psalm 138.
Thanksgiving (from *The Forme*).	Thanksgiving.
	Nunc Dimittis.
Aaronic blessing (from *The Forme*).	Aaronic blessing.

The Eucharist was to follow immediately after the sermon and Long Prayer, and in this respect Word and Sacrament were regarded as a unity; indeed, the Eucharistic liturgy required the rubrics and prayers of the Morning service to make any sense.

There was no rubric for the preparation of the bread and wine, but W. D. Maxwell observed that at Strasbourg the practice was to prepare them after the Creed, whereas Calvin seems to have prepared them during the Creed [34]. The omission of any rubric may have been deliberate in order to eradicate any possible idea of offering of the elements: the preparation was purely utilitarian.

In his Strasbourg rite, Calvin had commenced with a Eucharistic Prayer and the Lord's Prayer; in the Genevan rite, he began with an exhortation, starting with the Words of Institution from 1 Cor. 11:23 ff, the scriptural warrant for what was about to take place.

In the Classical Anaphoras, the Words of Institution formed part of the prayer, addressed to God. In the Oriental liturgies the narrative was considerably embellished in the interests of symmetry. As has been noted above, the

---

[34] W.D. MAXWELL, *The Liturgical Portions*, pp. 132-3.

narrative in the *Canon missae* was probably based upon the Old Latin version of Matthew 26 and 1 Cor. 11, though it too had been embellished [35]. However, as far as the reformers were concerned, since the narrative in the Mass did not accord with the Vulgate or Greek versions of Scripture, it was to be rejected and replaced with one of the accounts from the received texts [36]. Bucer moved the words from the Eucharistic Prayer and read them immediately before the communion; they were preceded by an extemporary exhortation if one had not been given earlier.

When Calvin's rite is compared with Bucer's rite, it appears at first sight that Calvin had taken over Bucer's arrangement, and had interpolated a lengthy exhortation with excommunication between the Institution and the communion.

Bucer	Calvin Strasbourg	Calvin Geneva
Long Prayer	Eucharistic Prayer	
Lord's Prayer	Lord's Prayer	
(Short exhortation)		
Institution	Institution with exhortation	Institution with exhortation
Communion	Communion	Communion

However, in Calvin's liturgy the Words of Institution are not separate from the exhortation, but form part of it. Our attention is turned, therefore, to the exhortation as a whole.

The exhortation has no textual parallel in the 1539 *Psalter mit aller Kirchenubing*, and this led W. D. Maxwell to the conclusion that "Calvin's is a product of his own pen"; "Calvin (is) the ultimate source" [37]. His conclusion has been endorsed by G. J. Van De Poll [38] and Stephen Mayor [39].

It is true that already in the outline of the Lord's Supper given in the *Institutes*, Calvin had in mind an exhortation at this point, and furthermore, several parallels in language may be found in his treatment of the supper in the *Institutes* [40]. However, although Calvin admitted that for his Sunday Morning service he had used a large part of the Strasbourg rite, the same dependence is not necessarily implied as regards the Eucharist. We have already observed that Calvin had experienced the Reformed worship of Basle, and

---

[35] See above, Chapter 2.
[36] For example, Luther's criticism in "The Abomination of the Secret Canon", 1525; B.D. SPINKS, "Luther and the Canon of the Mass", in *LR* 3 (1973), pp. 34-46.
[37] W.D. MAXWELL, *The Liturgical Portions*, pp. 130-131.
[38] G.J. VAN DE POLL, *op. cit.*, p. 114.
[39] STEPHEN MAYOR, *The Lord's Supper in Early English Dissent*, London, 1972, p. 7.
[40] e.g. *Institutes* 4-17-42. "Let us remember that this sacred feast is medicene to the sick, comfort to the sinner and bounty to the poor".

had in all probability used Farel's *La Maniere et fasson*. It seems that Dr. Bard Thompson is alone in recognising that in his exhortation, Calvin has used Farel's "Reformed Sursum corda", but even he has not recognised the full extent of the dependence [41]. A comparison of Farel's Supper rite with Calvin's exhortation reveals both a parallel of ideas and of language, though not in the same sequence [42].

Calvin	*Farel*

1. *Words of Institution.*

Bucer's narrative had no introduction, and could be from the Gospels or 1 Cor. 11. Both Calvin and Farel exhort the congregation to hear the Words from 1 Cor. 11.

Escoutons comme Jesus Christ nous a institué sa saincte Cene, selon que saincte Paul le recite en l'unziesme chapitre de la premiere aux Corinthiens.	Escoutez comme nostre seigneur Jesuchrist a institute sa saincte cene en la premiere des Corinthiens, en lunziesme chapitre.

2. *Excommunication.*

Parquoy, suyvant ceste reigle, au Nom et en l'aucthorité de nostre Seigneur Jesus Christ: je excommunie tous idolatres, blssphemateurs, contempteurs de Dieu, heretiques et toutes gens qui font sectes à part pour rompre l'unité de l'Eglise, tous periures, tous ceux qui sont rebelles à peres et à meres, et à leurs superieurs, tous seditieux, mutins, bateurs, noiseux, adulteres, paillars, larrons, ravisseurs, avaricieulx, yvrognes, gourmans et tous ceulx qui meinent vie scandaleuse et dissolue: leur denonceant qu'ilz ayent à s'abstenier de ceste saincte Table de paour de polluer et contaminer les viandes sacrées, que nostre Seigneur Jesus Christ ne donne sinon à ses domestique et fidelles.	Aultrement tous ceulx qui nont vraye foy, ne presument point de venir a la saincte table faisant semblant et faulsement tesmoingnans estre du corps de Jesuchrist, duquel ilz ne sont pas, comme tous idolatres, adorans et seruans aultre que le seul Dieu, tous parjureurs, gens oysifz qui ne seruent et ne proffitent a rien, combien quilz le puissent faire, tous ceulz qui sont desobeissans a pere et mere, et a ceulx que Dieu a constitute sur nous en bien, sans contreuenir au commandement de Dieu. Tous batteurs, noyseux qui injustement battent et frappent leur prochain et les ont en hayne. Tous paillardz, yurognes, viuans dissoluement en boyre et manger. Tous larrons qui font tort et injure au prochain, tous faulx tesmoingz, et imposeurs de crimes, et tous ceulx qui viuent meschamment et contre les sainctz commandemens de Dieu, qui ne veulent suyure la saincte loy de Dieu et viure selon sa parolle, en suyant le sainct evangile, com-

---

[41] BARD THOMPSON, *op. cit.*, p. 193.
[42] 'TEXTS: *Corpus Reformatorum*, Calvini Opera VI; *La Maniere et fasson*, ed. J.G. Baum, Strasbourg, 1859. The English, using the translations of Bard Thompson, *op. cit.*, is given in an Appendix.

	me vrays enfans de Dieu ne presument point venir a ceste saincte table, en laquelle doibuent venir seulement ceulx qui sont veritablement du corps de christ, vnis et enracinez en luy par vraye et vifue foy, laquelle soit ouurante par charite.

3. *Self-Examination.*

Pourtant, selon l'exhortation de sainct Paul, qu'un chascun espreuve et examine sa conscience, pour scavour s'il a vraye repentance de ses faultes, ... Sur tout, s'il a sa fiance en la mesericorde de Dieu, ...	Vng chascun regarde et espreuue soymesmes, ... sil croyt parfaictement ... que Dieu nous est propice, et que son ire est appaisee par le benoist sauueur Jesus ...

4. *Confession.*

Et combien que nous sentions en nous beaucoup de fragilité et misere, comme de n'avoir point la Foy parfaicte: mais estre enclins à incredulité et defiance, comme de ne estre point entierement si adonnez à servir à Dieu, et d'un tel zele que nous devrions, mais avoir à batailler journellement contre les consupiscences de nostre chair:	Mais pour tant que cependant que nous conuersons en ce monde, enuironnez de ce corps de mort et de peche, nous sommes tous pouures pecheurs, et ne puuons dire que soyens sans peche, ...

5. *"Reformed Sursum Corda".*

Pour ce faire eslevons noz espritz et noz coeurs en hault, ou est Jesus Christ en la gloire de son Pere, et dont nous l'attendons en nostre redemption. Et ne nous amusons point a ces elemens terriens et corruptibles, que nous voyens à l'oeil, et touchons à la main pour le chercher là, comme s'il estoit encloz au pain ou au vin.	Pourtant leuez voz cueurs en hault, cherchans les choses celestielles, es cieulx, ou Jesuchrist est assis en la dextre du pere, sans vous arrester aux choses visibles qui se corrompent par lusaige.

The section on excommunication seems to have been derived from Oecolampadius's rite for Basle [43].

The clear verbal parallels between Calvin and Farel in 1, 2 an 5, suggest that although this is no slavish copy, nevertheless Calvin was drawing directly upon his knowledge of Farel's Supper rite. As with Farel's rite, the exhor-

---

[43] Text in BARD THOMPSON, *op. cit.*, p. 212.

tation was immediately followed by the administration. Against W. D. Maxwell, we may conclude that it was Farel, and not Calvin, who was the ultimate source of the exhortation.

Related to this is the question of the purpose and rationale of this exhortation, described by the Swedish scholar, Yngve Brilioth, as "a controversial digression", and "a liturgical monstrosity" [44].

The New Testament accounts of the Institution of the Eucharist are quite clear that before Jesus broke the bread and distributed it, and before he offered the wine to the disciples, he "gave thanks"; he did not read an exhortation. Why, then, should Calvin, whose authority was the Word of God, follow Farel in placing a long exhortation before the distribution? Prayer at this point was recommended in the outline given in the *Institutes*, but even in his Strasbourg rite, Calvin had the exhortation immediately before the administration; furthermore, the "Eucharistic Prayer" is concerned for a true communion; it is hardly a "Eucharistia" [45].

Calvin carefully observed that Jesus gave thanks at the Supper:

> For at the commencement of the supper, I have no doubt, he prayed, as he was accustomed never to sit down at table without calling on God [46].

But the reformer does not appear to have been interested in the nature of Jewish blessings and thanksgivings; in fact, Calvin implied that the Passover prayers were quite irrelevant to the Christian church:

> I do not understand these words to mean that with the paschal supper was mixed this new and more excellent supper, but rather, that an end was then put to the former banquet [47].

Accorcing to Calvin, the thanksgiving at the Supper served a specific purpose:

> The *thanksgiving* was a sort of preparation and transition to consider the mystery. Thus when the supper was ended, they tasted the sacred *bread* and *wine*; because Christ had previously aroused them from their indifference, that they might be all alive to so lofty a mystery [48].

---

[44] YNGVE BRILIOTH, ET. A.G. HESBERT, *Eucharistic Faith and Practice Evangelical and Catholic*, London, 1930, p. 178.

[45] See above, p. 144. There is no textual authority for placing a "Consecration Prayer" (VAN DE POLL, *op. cit.*, p. 119) or an "Eucharistic Prayer" (HORTON DAVIES, *The Worship of the English Puritans*, p. 264) after the exhortation in the Genevan rite.

[46] *Commentary on a harmony of the Evangelists*, ET W. PRINGLE, 3 Vols., Edinburgh, 1846, vol. 3. p. 203.

[47] *Ibid.*, on Matthew 26:26, pp. 203-4.

[48] *Ibid.*, p. 204.

Again, commenting upon 1 Cor. 11:24:

> This *giving of thanks*, however, has a reference to something higher, for Christ *gives thanks* to the Father for his mercy towards the human race, and the inestimable benefit of redemption; and he invites us, by his example, to raise up our minds as often as we approach the sacred table, to an acknowledgment of the boundless love of God towards us, and to have our minds kindled up to true gratitude [49].

In these two passages there is a strong hint that Calvin regarded the thanksgiving as being addressed, not to God, but to the disciples to draw their attention to "so lofty a mystery". It would appear to Calvin to have an exhortatory nature about it.

Calvin also interpreted the ancient "sursum corda" as being exhortatory in nature; in his *Short Treatise on the Holy Supper of our Lord and only Saviour Jesus Christ*, 1541, he wrote:

> Moreoever, the practice always observed in the ancient Church was that, before celebrating the Supper, the people were solemnly exhorted to lift their hearts on high, to show that we must not stop at the visible sign, to adore Jesus Christ rightly [50].

Likewise in the *Institutes*:

> That the pious soul may duly apprehend Christ in the sacrament, it must rise to heaven. ... And for no other reason was it formerly the custom, previous to consecration, to call aloud upon the people to raise their hearts, *sursum corda* [51].

There is some evidence, therefore, for suggesting that Calvin regarded the "thanksgiving" as a device for underlining the gravity of the sacrament, addressed to the hearts and minds of the congregation. If it was exhortatory in nature, then it is the equivalent of an exhortation; Calvin's exhortation served precisely the same purpose as he believed Christ's thanksgiving had served — as a "preparation and transtion to consider the mystery".

If this a correct understanding of Calvin, then the exhortation makes some sense. First, the Words of Institution (the Pauline version, "I received of the Lord", in which Calvin noted — no doubt with the *Canon missae* in mind — "received" implied that the words had not been tampered with) [52], were

---

[49] *Commentary on the Epistles of Paul the Apostle to the Corinthians*, ET J. PRINGLE, 2 vols., Edinburgh 1848, vol. 1, p. 374, on 1 Cor. 11: 23 ff.
[50] ET in *Calvin Theological Treatises*, ed. J.K.S. REID, *Library of Christian Classics*, Vol. 22, London, 1954, pp. 140-166, p. 159.
[51] *Institutes*, 4-17-36.
[52] *Commentary on the Epistles of Paul the Apostle to the Corinthians*, Vol. 1, p. 373.

read to impress the congregation with the gravity of the sacrament. Since they were the Word of God to men, they were not addressed in prayer to the Father; and to direct words of proclamation to the elements was, in Calvin's thinking, preaching to bread and wine. In several passages, Calvin makes it clear that the Words of Institution are addressed to men:

> This error (that the intention of the priest is required for consecration) has originated from not observing that those promises by which consecration is effected are intended, not for the elements themselves, but for those who receive them. Christ does not address the bread and tell it to become his body, but bids his disciples eat, and promises them the communion of his body and blood [53].

> We must hold that bread is not consecrated by whispering and breathing, but by the clear doctrine of faith. And certainly it is a piece of magic and sorcery, when the consecration is addressed to a dead element; for the bread is not made for itself but for us, a symbol of the body of Christ. In short, consecration is nothing else than a solemn testimony, by which the Lord appoints to us for a spiritual use an earthly and corruptible sign. This cannot take place unless his command and promise are distinctly heard with the purpose of edifying the faithful [54].

The solemn excommunication was a necessary part of understanding the gravity of the sacrament, as was self-examination and confession [55]. Kilian McDonnell has admirably summarised Calvin's teaching on this point.

> The sacrilege of the unworthy who approach the communion table is that they receive the sign of faith without faith, their unworthiness consisting essentially in the fact "that they do not believe that the body is their life" (Ins. 4.17.40). Because the unworthy man is a man without faith and without love he does not, cannot receive the body of Christ which is offered to him. Because the efficacy of the sacrament comes from the power of the Holy Spirit and because this power is manifested in the comunicant through faith and love, which are works of the Holy Spirit, there cannot be any eating of the body on the part of the unworthy. Because the unworthy man is a man without faith and without love, he does not, cannot receive the body of Christ which is offered to him. What is objectively offered to him cannot be received, not because he lacks moral righteousness, but because he is devoid of an objective religious gift and disposition: faith and love, which are acts of the Holy Spirit [56].

[53] *Institutes*, 4-17-39, cf. 4-17-15.
[54] *Corpus Reformatorum*, 45, p. 706, commenting on Matt. 26.26; Quoted by K. McDonnell, *John Calvin, the Church, and the Eucharist*, Princeton, 1967, P. 236.
[55] *Institutes*, 4-17-40, 42.
[56] K. McDonnell, *op. cit.*, pp. 274-275.

The duty of a man to prove himself according to the norms of faith does not dispense him from proving himself in relation to a moral concern, in relation to moral striving.

Finally, the worshipper was exhorted to lift his mind to heaven to receive Christ spiritually, Calvin here using Farel's refurbishing of the *sursum corda*. This latter element was the complete opposite of the "Epiklesis" of the Classical Anaphoras; wheras the "Epiklesis" called down the Holy Spirit (or Logos) upon the bread and wine, here the worshipper was exhorted to rise to heaven where the heavenly Christ was seated [57]. It might be termed an "anaklesis".

If we have interpreted Calvin correctly on this point, then on his premises, this was not a digression, but an accurate apprehension of the purpose of Christ's thanksgiving. However, as well as being a rather artificial interpretation of "thanksgiving", it also represented a complete turning inside out of the Classical Eucharistic prayer.

The administration followed immediately after the exhortation, the minister being directed to break the bread and give the cup to the people. No words of administration were provided, though in his Strasbourg rite Calvin had the following:

> Take, eat, the body of Jesus which has been delivered unto death for you.
> This is the cup of the new testament in the blood of Jesus which has been shed for you.

Calvin did not accept Zwingli's interpretation of the Eucharistic presence. For him it was more than mere remembrance; through faith and the Holy Spirit the communicant received what Christ had promised to give, namely the substance of his body and blood.

During the communion some psalms were to be sung, or one of the ministers was to read an appropriate passage of Scripture. The service concluded with a thanksgiving, being the second of four found in Bucer's 1539 rite, and the Aaronic blessing, both these texts being contained in *The Forme of Common Prayers*.

At the end of the service there was an *apologia* for the replacement of the mass by this rite.

Since Calvin's rite was derived mainly from Bucer, it was therefore a direct descendent form the Western rite. However, although of the same parentage, it differed considerably from the Eucharist of the *Book of Common*

---

[57] *Institutes*, 4-17-18.

Prayer. There was no liturgical calendar, and therefore no variable collects and no selected Epistles and Gospels; gone also were the *Kyries, Gloria in excelsis, Sursum corda*, preface and *Sanctus*. Word and Sacrament were separated.

The usage of Strasbourg, with ideas from Oecolampadius and Farel, all refracted through the mind of John Calvin, now appeared alongeide the official English revisions.

2. *John Knox's Liturgy for Berwick on Tweed, 1550.*

John Knox (c.1514-1572) is usually considered as the father of the Reformation in Scotland, and through the *Book of Common Order,* did much to shape the forms of Scottish worship. But as Peter Lorimer pointed out, "It is not usually remembered that a large portion of the best and most energetic part of his life was spent in England, and among Englishmen out of England. ... for ten of the best years of his life and work he was chiefly in contact with English, not with Scottish, minds" [58].

After studying philosophy at Glasgow, and probably at St. Andrew's, Knox took Orders in the Church [59]. During the mid 1540's he was influenced by the preaching of Thomas Guillaume and George Wishart, and Wishart's martyrdom in 1546 seems to have been a turning point in his life. In 1547 he became preacher at St. Andrew's, and after the fall of the city to the besieging Catholic forces, was imprisoned as a slave on a French galley. Through the intercession of Edward VI, Knox was released in 1549, and was appointed chaplain to Edward, and it would seem that he was partly responsible for the "Black Rubric" in the 1552 communion rite.

After the accesion of Mary, Knox fled to Geneva. For a short time he was minister to the English exiles at Frankfurt, but after disputes over liturgy, be returned to Geneva where a group of English Calvinists followed him. His tract *The First Blast of the Trumpet against the Monstrous Regiment of Women,* 1558, asserting that government by a woman is contrary to the law of nature and to Divine ordinance, offended Elizabeth I, and Knox was prevented from returning to the English church; he thus returned to his native Scotland.

During his ministry at Berwick, he drew up a liturgy for use in that city. Like his fellow reformers, Knox had little idea of the origin and development

---

[58] P. LORIMER, *John Knox and the Church of England*, London, 1875, p. 1.
[59] *The Works of John Knox*, ed. D. Laing, 6 Vols., Edinburgh, 1864, (cited as *Knox's Works*) Vol. 1, Life; P. LORIMER, *op. cit.*

of the Eucharistic liturgy; it was the Mass which formed practically his whole liturgical knowledge. His views on the Mass are preserved in a statement given before Bishop Cuthbert Tunstall of Durham and the council of the North in April 1550, entitled *A Vindication of the Doctrine that the Sacrifice of the Mass is Idolatry* [60].

Knox had learnt from Wishart that "in the worship of God, and especially in the administration of the sacraments, the rule prescribed in Holy Scripture is to be observed without addition or diminution, and that the church has no right to devise religious ceremonies and impose signification upon them" [61]. As with the Calvinist School, Knox therefore made the Word of God alone the criterion for liturgy:

> ... all whilk is addit to the religioun of God, without his awn express Word, is Idolotrie [62].

Thus,

> All wirschipping, honoring, or service inventit by the braine of man in the religioun of God, without his own express commandment, is Idolotrie: The Masse is inventit be the braine of man, without any commandement of God: Thairfoir it is Idolatrie [63].

As with Calvin, Knox found particular significance in Paul's words in 1 Cor. 11:23 ff, "I have received of the Lord...":

> Paule wryting of the Lordis Supper, sayith, *Ego accepi a Domino quod et tradidi vobis*, "I have ressavit and learnit of the Lord that whilk I have taught you". And consider yf one ceremony he addeth or permitteth to be usit other than Chryst did use him self; but commandeth thame to use with reverence the Lordis institutioun untill his returnyng to judgement [64].

Knox could not believe that the Mass was of any great antiquity in terms of the Apostles or the Apostolic Fathers:

> It will not satisfie the hairtis of all godlie to say, St James and St Petir celebrated the first Masse in Jerusalem or Antiochia ... But I sall prove that Pope Sixtus was the first that did institut the aulteris. Felix, the first of that name, did consecrat thame and the tempillis boith. Bonifacius commandit the aulteris to be coverit with cleane

---

[60] *Knox's Works*, Vol. 3, pp. 33-70.
[61] *Ibid.*, Vol. 1, p. 192.
[62] *Ibid.*, Vol. 3, p. 42.
[63] *Ibid.*, p. 34.
[64] *Ibid.*, p. 42.

> clothis. Gregorius Magnus commandit the candellis to be lychtit at the Evangile; and did institute certane clothis. Pontianus commandit *confiteor* to be said. ... [65].

The reading of an Epistle and Gospel was merely a cloak for idolatry [66]. But it is the *Canon missae* which Knox found particularly offensive. To begin with, it is late in composition:

> Who is the author of the Canon, can thai precislie tell? Be weill avysit befoir ye answer, lest by neglecting your self ye be proved lyaris. ... Yf the Canon discendit frome the Apostillis to the Popes, bold and maleparte impietie it had bene to haif addit any thing thairto; for a Canon is a full and sufficient reule, whilk in all partes and poyntis is perfyte. But I will prove dyverse Popes to haif addit thair portionis to this halie Canon [67].

He attributed additions to Sergius, Leo, and two Alexanders. For the saints mentioned in the *Communicantes* and *Nobis quoque*, Knox applied the simple logic that since many of the saints named in these prayers lived after the time of the Apostles, they could hardly have been used by the Apostles themselves.

> For who useit to mak mentioun of a man in his prayeris befoir he be borne [68]?

Regarding the words of Institution, Knox denied that they were "words of consecration", because Christ never called them by that name. But in any case, the words in the Canon were not the words of Christ; *ex hoc omnes* was said of the cup, but the Canon applies it to the bread also, and of course, the laity are denied the cup; and *enim* is an addition

> Is not this thair awn inventioun, and addit of thair awn braine [69]?

The Canon had omitted the words "given for you or broken for you"

> Theis last wordis, whairin standis our haill comfort [70].

Knox, like all the reformers, also objected to the sacrificial language of the Canon, which even references to Melchizedek or Malachi could not

---

[65] *Ibid.*, p. 48.
[66] *Ibid.*, p. 51.
[67] *Ibid.*, p. 49.
[68] *Ibid.*, p. 49.
[69] *Ibid.*, p. 50.:
[70] *Ibid.*, p. 51.

justify [71]. Like Luther, Knox insisted that the Eucharist was a gift to men, not a sacrifice to God [72].

From this summary, it is quite evident that Knox had little time for the Mass. He could hardly, then, have been particularly impressed with the Eucharistic liturgy in the 1549 *Book of Common Prayer* which he found in use in England. It may be this that accounts for the origin of his own "independent" Eucharistic liturgy which he prepared for Berwick on Tweed in 1550, though Lorimer suggested that the border counties of England were exempted from the obligation of conformity [73]. Whether Lorimer is correct or not, Knox's liturgy had no other authority than his own.

The text which we have is of a fragmentary nature, there being no rubrics to indicate at what point the administration came, or how. We do know that, contrary to the Prayer Book rite, it was administered sitting at the table [74]. The fragment gives the following order [75]:

> Sermons of the benefits of God, John 13-16.
> "In the name of the Father, and of the Son and of the Holy Ghost".
> Prayer — praise for creation, and redemption; petition for faith and thanksgiving.
> 1 Cor. 11:20-31.
> (Declaration of the Apostle's mind upon the same place)
> Excommunication.
> Confession.
> Scriptural assurance of forgiveness.
> Prayer for the Congregation.
> A Prayer for the Queen's majesty.

The "Prayer for the Queen's majesty" suggests that the copy which has come down to us dates from the reign of Mary, or possibly, Elizabeth [76]. Peter Lorimer suggested that Knox's *A Summary according to the Holy Scriptures of the Sacrament of the Lord's Supper* may have been used for the "Declaration of the Apostle's mind" [77].

This Order seems to have been entirely Knox's own work, for until this time, he had had little contact with continental Reformed worship. However, the sequence Institution — excommunication — confession is not too dissimilar from that of Calvin, Farel, and the rite of Basle.

---

[71] *Ibid.*, pp. 60-61.
[72] *Ibid.*, p. 65. Cf. BRYAN D. SPINKS, "Luther and the Canon of the Mass".
[73] P. LORIMER, *op. cit.*, pp. 29, 160.
[74] *Ibid.*, p. 31; Letter to the Congregation at Berwick, pp. 251-265.
[75] Lorimer, pp. 290-292.
[76] *Ibid.*, p. 292.
[77] *Ibid.*, p. 292.

3. *The Liturgy of Compromise, 1555.*

With the death of Edward VI, the plans of the English reformers came to an abrupt end; Edwardian legislation was repealed, and Queen Mary retraced the steps that led to Rome. The 1552 *Book of Common Prayer* was replaced by the old Latin service books; its Eucharistic liturgy was replaced by the Mass. However, the 1552 book did not entirely disappear. It remained in use in some churches in Scotland; and, as G. J. Cuming has said, "on the continent its history was more eventful" [78]. Indeed, it was to the Continent that a group of English Calvinists fled:

> and, in the year of our Lord 1554, and the 27th of June, came EDMUND SUTTON, WILLIAM WILLIAMS, WILLIAM WHITTINGHAM, and THOMAS WOOD, with their companies, to the City of Frankfort in Germany [79];

This company at Frankfurt had in its possession some copies of Huycke's work [80]. The ensuing liturgical struggle is recorded for us in *A Brieff Discours off the Troubles begonne at Frankford in Germany Anno Domini 1554*. Traditionally attributed to William Whittingham [81], *A Brief Discourse* represented the beginning of the conflict between those who remained content with the provisions of the *Book of Common Prayer*, and those who wished for further reform along the lines of the Genevan liturgy. Professor Edward Arber, who edited *A Brief Discourse*, stated that "it records the very beginning of the Rift between the English Conformists and Nonconformists; or, to put it in other words, the Origin of English Puritanism" [82].

Whittingham and his fellow exiles had come to Frankfurt-on-the-Main after hearing that the magistrates there had granted the use of their Church of the White Ladies to Valerand Poullain and his congregation of French exiles. Seeking a similar privilege, the English were granted the use of the French church on alternate days.

> But it was with this commandment, That the English should not dissent from the Frenchmen in Doctrine and Ceremonies [83].

---

[78] G.J. Cuming, *A History of Anglican Liturgy*, p. 117.
[79] *A Brieff Discours off the Troubles begonne at Frankford in Germany Anno Domini 1554, abowte the Booke off Common Prayer and Ceremonies*, ed. E. Arber, 1908, p. 23. Cited as *A Brief Discourse*.
[80] *Ibid.*, p. 42.
[81] For a discussion on Authorship, see P. Collinson, "The Authorship of A Brieff Discours off the Trouble Begonne at Frankford", in *JEH*, 9 (1958), pp. 188-208.
[82] *Op. cit.*, p. xii. For the view that A Brief Discourse is a projection back into the reign of Mary of the controversies of the late 1560's and 1570's, M.A. Simpson, *John Knox and the Troubles Begun at Frankfurt*, West Linton, Tweeddale, 1975.
[83] *Ibid.*, p. 24.

Having organised themselves into a church with officers, the exiles then faced the problem of what Order of Service they should use.

At length, the English Order (1552) was persued; and this, by common consent, was concluded:

> That the answering aloud after the Minister should not be used: the Litany, Surplice, and many other things also omitted: for that, in those Reformed Churches, such things would seem more than strange. It was farther agreed upon, that the Minister, in place of the English Confession, should use another, both of more effect, and also framed according to the state and time. And the same ended; the people to sing a Psalm in metre in a plain tune; as was, and is accustomed in the French, Dutch, Italian, Spanish, and Scottish, Churches. That done, the Minister to pray for the assistence of GOD's HOLY SPIRIT and so to proceed to the Sermon.
>
> After the Sermon, a General Prayer for all Estates, and for our country of England, was also devised: at the end of which Prayer, was joined the Lord's Prayer, and a rehearsal of the Articles of our Belief. Which ended, the people to sing another Psalm as afore. Then the Minister pronouncing his blessing, "The peace of GOD", etc., or some other of like effect; the people to depart.
>
> And as touching the Ministration of the Sacraments: sundry things were also, by common consent, omitted, as superstitious and superfluous [84].

The significance of this order has been aptly put by W. D. Maxwell:

> In structure and content this first order of service is distinctly Calvinistic, and while its connexion with the BCP is extremely slight ... what connexion there exists is with Ante-Communion and not with Matins [85].

It was in fact a similar type of order to Calvin's *Form of Prayers*.

After organising themselves, this Frankfurt congregation sent out a general letter to other English exiles, inviting them to come to Frankfurt, in the meantime appointing John Knox and Thomas Lever as ministers. Knox, having fled from England, was at this time in exile at Geneva, and Lever was at Zurich.

However, some of the exiles at Zurich and Strasbourg, on being invited to join the English Church at Frankfurt, were prepared to come only if the 1552 *Book of Common Prayer* was used in full. Thus, from those at Zurich:

---

[84] *Ibid.*, pp. 24-25.
[85] W.D. MAXWELL, *The Liturgical Portions of the Genevan Service Book*, p. 4.

> If, upon the receipt hereof, ye shall (without cloak or forged pretence; but only to seek CHRIST) advertise us, by your Letters, that our being there is so needful as ye have already signified, and that we may all together serve and praise GOD as freely and as uprightly (whereof private Letters received lately from Frankfort make us much to doubt) as the Order last taken in the Church of England permitteth and prescribeth — for we are fully determined to admit and use no other — ... [86].

This in turn led to disputes among the Frankfurt congregation as to which order they would ultimately use.

> At length, it was agreed that the Order of Geneva which then was already printed in English, and some copies there among them, should take place, as an Order most godly, and farthest of from superstition [87].
>
> But Master KNOX, being spoken unto, as well to put that Order in practice as to minister the Communion, refused to do either the one or the other; ... Neither yet would he minister the Communion by the Book of England; for that there were things in it placed, as he said, "only by warrant of Man's authority, and no ground in GOD's Word for the same; and had also a long time very superstitiously in the Mass been wickedly abused [88].

In fact, according to Knox, there were in the English book "things superstitious, impure, unclean, and unperfect" [89]. Thus the disputation was prolonged. Eventually it was decided that:

> Master KNOX, Master WHITTINGHAM, Master GILBY, Master FOX, and Master T. COLE, should draw forth some Order meet for their state and time.
>
> Which thing was by them accomplished, and offered to the Congregation; being the same Order of Geneva, which is now in print.
>
> This Order was very well liked by many; but such as were bent to the Book of England could not abide it. ...
>
> In the end, another way was taken by the Congregation; which was that Master KNOX and Master WHITTINGHAM, Master PARRY and Master LEVER, should devise some Order, if it might be, to end all strife and contention [90].

---

[86] *A Brief Discourse*, p. 33.
[87] *Ibid.*, p. 42.
[88] *Ibid.*
[89] "A Narrative of the Proceedings of the English Congregation at Frankfort in March, 1555" in *Knox's Works*, Vol. IV., p. 43.
[90] *A Brief Discourse*, p. 52.

Finally we are informed:

> Whereupon, after some conference, an Order was agreed upon: some part taken forth of the English Book; and other things put to, as the state of that Church required. ... Yea, the holy Communion was, upon this happy agreement, also ministered. And this friendship continued till the 13th of March following [91].

It was this Order that the Scottish liturgiologist, G. W. Sprott, so fittingly named *The Liturgy of Compromise* [92]. We are concerned here with the Eucharistic liturgy of this order.

From *A Brief Discourse* it is possible to glean some information as to the reason for the rejection of the 1552 *Book of Common Prayer*. It has already been noted that Huycke's version of the Genevan order was in their possession, "an Order most godly, and farthest off from superstition", and presumably they preferred this latter [93].

Although the "Genevan" party at Frankfurt did not outrightly reject the *Book of Common Prayer*, nevertheless, they could not use it in full. To the English exiles at Zurich they explained:

> As touching the effect of the Book, we desire the execution thereof as much as you, so far as GOD's Word doth commend it: but as for the unprofitable Ceremonies, as well by his consent as by ours, are not to be used [94].

They believed that but for King Edward's untimely death, further reforms would have been carried out:

> And if GOD had not, in these wicked days, otherwise determined, they would hereafter have changed more: yea, and in our case, we doubt not bt that they would have done the like [95].

From the Frankfurt exiles came the rumour of the existence of a third Prayer book, a 'hundred times more perfect' than that of 1552 [96].

The particular objections to the communion service of the Prayer Book were partly revealed in a summary, or plat, which the exiles sent to Calvin for his opinion:

---

[91] *Ibid.*, p. 53.
[92] Ed. H.J. Wotherspoon and G.W. Sprott, bound with the 1552 BCP, 1905. For the view that this liturgy really belongs to the late 1560's, SIMPSON, *op. cit.*, p. 8.
[93] *A Brief Discourse*, p. 42.
[94] *Ibid.*, p. 37.
[95] *Ibid.*
[96] *Ibid.*, p. 75.

Now the manner of the Supper is thus. The number of Three, at the least, is counted a fit number to communicate: and yet it is permitted, the pestilence or some other common sickness being among the people, the Minister alone may communicate with the sick man in his house.

First, therefore, the Minister must be prepared after this manner, in a white linen garment, as in saying the other Service he is appointed; and must stand at the North side of the Table.

Then it had the Lord's Prayer, after the custom. Then he reciteth the Collect; and after follow in order The Ten Commandments: but so notwithstanding that every one of the people may answer "Lord, have mercy upon us; and incline our hearts to keep this law"!

After the rehearsal of the Commandments; the Collect of the Day, as it is called, and another for the King, are had. By and by the Epistle and Gospel followeth: to wit, such as the Calendar appointeth for that day.

And there in this place, there is a note, that every Holy Day hath his Collect, Epistle, and Gospel; which fill seventy-three great leaves of the Book, when the rest scarce fifty. For all Holy Days are now in like use, as were among the Papists; only very few excepted.

Then he goeth forth to the Creed; and after that, to the Sermon, if there be any.

Afterwards, the Parish Priest biddeth the Holy Days and Fasts on their Eves; if there by any that week. And here the Book warneth, That none defraud the Parish Priest of his due or right; specially on those Feast Days that are dedicated to offerings.

Then followeth, A Prayer for the state of the Church Militant; and that without a long heap and mixture of matters: until they come, after a certain Confession of Sins, to

"Lift up your hearts"!

The people answering, "We give thanks to the Lord,

"Let us give thanke to our Lord GOD"!

The answer, "It is very meet, right, and our bounded duty", etc.: and so the Preface, according to the Feast, is added.

Afterwards, he saith, "Therefore with Angels and Archangels"; and so ended with Holy, Holy, Holy, Lord GOD"; till he come to, "Hosanna in the highest"!

Now the Priest boweth his knee; acknowledging our unworthiness in the name of all that shall receive: and, setting out GOD's mercy, he beseecheth GOD that our body be made clean by his body, and that our souls may be washed through His blood.

And then he again standeth up, and taketh in hand afresh another

Prayer appointed for this purpose; in which are contained the Words of the Institution.

All which being done, he first communicateth: then by and by, he saith to another kneeling, "Take and eat this, in remembrance that CHRIST died for thee: and feed on him in thy heart by faith with thanksgiving".

Now, about the end, the Lord's Prayer is again used, the Minister saying it aloud, and all the people following.

To conclude. They have a giving of thanks in the end; with "Glory to GOD in the highest!", as it was used among the Papists.

If it happen that there be no Sermon; only a few things are omitted: but all other things are done in order as aforesaid [97].

The summary betrays a dislike of collects, Epistles and Gospels, together with the liturgical calendar; the reference to the *Gloria in excelsis* "as it was used among the Papists" suggests that any remnant of the Mass was suspect.

The Eucharistic rite in the *Liturgy of Compromise* had the following order:

> Collect for Purity.
> Ten Commandments.
> A Prayer for the time, and the whole State of Christ's Church.
> Nicene Creed.
> Exhortation "We come together at this time dearly beloved".
> (Sometimes the Exhortation "Dearly beloved forasmuch as")
> Exhortation "Dearly beloved in the Lord ye that mind".
> Exhortation to Confession, "Ye that do truly".
> Confession "Almighty God the Father of our Lord Jesus Christ".
> Absolution "Almighty God, our heavenly Father".
> Comfortable Words.
> Communion Devotion "We do not presume" (Humble Access).

The remainder of the order follows the 1552 order.

In this compromise rite, we find that the word "priest" has been replaced by "Minister", and everything having any connection with the liturgical calendar had been removed. The collect, Epistle and Gospel were replaced by "A Prayer for the Time, and the whole state of Christ's Church"; and after the comfortable words, the *Sursum corda*, preface, proper preface and *Sanctus* disappeared, probably because of their connection with the liturgical calendar, but possibly simply because they were used in the Mass [98]. The *Glo-*

---

[97] *Ibid.*, pp. 46-47.
[98] A.E. PEASTON, *The Prayer Book Tradition in the Free Churches*, 1964, p. 14, suggested that the placing of the "Prayer of Humble Access" after the comfortable words anticipated theri

ria in excelsis seems to have been retained.

The alterations to the text of the 1552 rite were slight; nevertheless they represent an "independent", Puritan adaptation of the *Book of Common Prayer*.

4. *The Genevan Service Book, 1556.*

At one particular stage of the liturgical disputes among the English exiles at Frankfurt we learn that a decision was taken to the effect that:

> Master KNOX, Master WHITTINGHAM, Master GILBY, Master FOX and Master T. COLE, should draw forth some Order meet for their state and time.
>
> Which thing was by them accomplished, and offered to the Congregation; being the same Order of Geneva, which is now in print [99].

The liturgy here referred to, known as the *"Genevan Service Book"* [100], was drawn up for the use of the congregation and to replace all previous orders, viz. 1552, the exiles own amended service, and Huycke's translation of Calvin. However, it was too far removed from the Prayer Book for some of the congregation, and therefore the *Liturgy of Compromise* came into being. With the arrival of Dr. Cox with a large number of pro-Prayer Book exiles, the *Liturgy of Compromise* was ousted by the 1552 rite, and Knox was expelled, taking refuge in Geneva. Some of the Calvinist exiles joined him in Geneva, and there founded and English Church with Knox as their minister, later succeeded by William Whittingham. For their worship, they revised the book referred to above; with a new preface it appeared in 1556 printed by John Crespin.

The book itself is often referred to as "John Knox's Genevan Service Book". However, it should be noted that Knox was only one of five compilers. Lorimer commented upon Knox's involvement:

---

position in the Deposited Book of 1928. *Pace* Mr. Peaston, this seems to illustrate one of the dangers of comparative liturgy. On the one hand, in the *Liturgy of Compromise*, a Puritan work, the sequence was the result of the abolition of the *Sursum corda - Sanctus*. On the other hand, in the Deposited Book, the result of years of Tractarian demand for enrichment, the sequence was the result of a deliberate repositioning of the "Prayer of Humble Access". The resulting sequence, as Mr. Peaston observed, is the same; the motive for alteration was rather different! Any "anticipation" of 1928 on the part of the authors of the *Liturgy of Compromise* was purely by accident.

[99] *A Brief Discourse*, p. 52.
[100] The full title is: *The Forme of Prayers and Ministrations of the Sacraments, & c., used in the English Congregation at Geneva, and approved by the famous and godly learned man, John Calvyn.*

> In its published form it was substantially, probably all but verbally, the same (except the Preface) which had been prepared at Frankfurt; and in determining the substance and arrangement of that draft, it cannot be doubted that his influence was paramount, ... The style, however, we do not claim to be his; it is much smoother and fluenter than his English style ever became, and was, in all probability, from the accomplished pen of Whittingham, to whom the Preface is usually ascribed [101].

Lorimer's suggestion that Whittingham may have been responsible for the final text which appeared in 1556 is certainly feasible; Whittingham, later Dean of Durham, translated the New Testament into English at Geneva, and had prepared some psalms in metre. His literary skills may well have been brought to bear upon the 1556 *Genevan Service Book*.

The text of the *Genevan Service Book* has been edited by W. D. Maxwell, and it is this edition which we have used here [102].

The *Genevan Service Book*, at least with regard to the Morning service and the Eucharistic rite, was basically that of Calvin, "with certain rearrangements and additions peculiar to itself" [103]. As in Calvin's liturgy, the Sunday Morning service and the Eucharistic liturgy belonged together, but were separated physically in the liturgical book by the rite of Baptism, and by the fact that communion was celebrated only once a month — a more frequent celebration of the rite than Calvin was able to establish.

The sunday Morning Service.

> A Confession of our synnes, framed to our tyme, out of the 9. chap. of Daniel.
> or, An other Confession, for all states and tymes.
> Psalm.
> Prayer for illumination.
> (Lection and)
> Sermon.
> A Prayer for the whole estate of Christes Churche.
> Lord's Prayer.
> Creed.
> Psalm.
> Aaronic Blessing and the Grace.

The structure of the Morning service is almost identical with Calvin's *La Forme*, and we know that the compilers had before them Huycke's translation of Calvin.

---

[101] LORIMER, *op. cit.*, p. 212.
[102] W.D. MAXWELL, *The Liturgical Portions of the Genevan Service Book*.
[103] *Ibid.*, p. 51. Cf. also, G.J. CUMING, "John Knox and the Book of Common Prayer: a short note", in *LR* 10 (1980), pp. 80-81.

The first confession was an innovation; being based upon Daniel 9, it may possibly have originated in the first order of service drawn up by the exiles on their arrival at Frankfurt, which contained a confession "in place of the English Confession ... both of more effect, and also framed according to the state and time" [104]. W. D. Maxwell drew attention to the fact that John à Lasco's *Forma ac ratio*, published at Frankfurt in 1555, although itself not containing such a confession, does allude to a confession as in Daniel 9, and may have suggested the idea to the compilers [105]. The second confession was based on Huycke and Calvin, though the latter part was an independent addition by the compilers, serving the purpose of an absolution [106].

The "Prayer for the whole estate of Christes Churche" after the sermon was in place of Calvin's Long Prayer. It was followed immediately by the Lord's Prayer and the Creed, and it too might have belonged to the original service compiled by the exiles:

> After the Sermon, a General Prayer for all Estates, and for our country of England, was also devised: at the end of which Prayer was joined the Lord's Prayer, and a rehearsal of the Articles of our Belief [107].

Perhaps this was the same prayer of the *Liturgy of Compromise* which was entitled "A Prayer for the time, and the whole state of Christ's Church".

The overall nature of this service has been admirably described by Horton Davies:

> This form of service is Calvinistic in three main characteristics. It is Biblical, didactic and congregational. Its Biblical basis is seen in the opening Confession of Sins, based largely on the 9th chapter of the Book of Daniel; in the use of metrical psalms; and in the preference for Biblical Blessings as compared with the Anglican Blessing ... It is didactic in that the climax of the service is approached by a prayer for Illumination, and reached in the reading and exposition of the Word of God; whilst the Apostles' Creed immediately precedes the closing acts of worship. Its congregational character is shown by the singing of two metrical psalms and by the particular intercessions for the members of the mystical Body of Christ in the Intercessory Prayer, as also in the personal and intimate petition with which this prayer opens. The clearest indication of Calvinism is, of course, the extreme statement of the doctrine of original sin so dominant in the Confession with which the service begins [108].

---

[104] *A Brief Discourse*, pp. 24-25.
[105] MAXWELL, *op. cit.*, p. 943.
[106] *Ibid.*, pp. 95, 97.
[107] *A Brief Discourse*, p. 25.
[108] HORTON DAVIES, *The Worship of the English Puritans*, p. 119.

As in the case of the Morning service, the 1556 Eucharistic rite was closely modelled upon that of Calvin's Genevan rite; as with Calvin, it presupposed that the rite was to be added to the Morning service, not substituted for it. However, although Calvin's rite had suggested the structure and much of the content of this rite, there were distinct differences.

> *The Maner of the Lordes Supper.*
> (after the Creed and psalm).
> Institution Narrative.
> Exhortation with excommunication.
> Eucharistic Prayer.
> Fraction and delivery; reading of Scripture during delivery.
> Thanksgiving.
> Psalm 103 or a similar psalm.
> Blessing (from the Morning service).
> To the Reader (note).

The Institution Narrative was now quite distinct from the exhortation, and as the note "To the Reader" confirms, was read as a warrant for the rite. Its separation from the exhortation was made distinct by a rubric:

> This done, the minister proceadith to the exhortation.

The exhortation itself was taken in part from the third exhortation of the 1552 communion rite, and the remainder from Calvin. After the exhortation, a rubric directed the minister to come down from the pulpit, go to the table, and sitting at the table, take the bread and wine and give thanks; the communicants were also to sit at the table. Thus, the Institution Narrative was not read in association with the elements, and could not be regarded as a "consecration"; it was addressed to the Church as the Divine command for the rite to take place. Knox's practice of sitting for communion introduced at Berwick was continued here.

There followed a Eucharistic Prayer, a feature which was an innovation to Calvin's rite. It would appear that the compilers, while recognising that an exhortation was desirable, felt that it could not be a substitute for a "Eucharistia" to God before the delivery. In obedience to the scriptural accounts, the compilers restored the sequence of taking, thanksgiving, and delivery.

With the Eucharistic Prayers of the Classical rites in mind, W. D. Maxwell has drawn attention to the similar themes found in this prayer: adoration, thanksgiving for creation and redemption, commemoration of the incarnation, death, resurrection, and the Last Supper, with an ascription of praise; and the Roman Catholic liturgical scholar, Louis Bouyer, has also remarked that there "seems to be a direct echo of those of Christian antiquity" in this prayer [109]. Despite these observations, the likelihood of there being any conscious echo is highly remote.

The prayer does appear to have been the work of the compilers themselves, but W. D. Maxwell is incorrect in his assertion that it is not derived from any known source [110]. The first part of the Prayer was based upon the first prayer of Knox's Berwick liturgy:

Berwick	1556
Omnypotent and everlasting God, whome all creatures do know and confesse thee to be Governor and Lorde, but we thy creatures, created to thyne own image and symilitude, ought at all tymes to feare, adore, love and prayse thye godlye Majestie - fyrst for owr creation, but principally for own redemption when we were dead and lost by sin.	O Father of mercye and God of all consolation, seinge all creatures do confesse thee, as governor, and lorde, it becommeth us the workmanship of thyne own handes, at all tymes to reverence and magnifie thy godli maistie, first that thou haste created us to thyne own Image and similitude: but chieflye that thou haste delivered us from everlasting death and damnation into the which Satan drewe mankinde by the meane of synne:

After the Eucharistic Prayer, the minister was directed to break the bread and give it to the people who distributed it and the cup among themselves "accordinge to our saviour Christes comandement"; this may refer to the use of scriptural words of delivery, for no words were provided.

The thanksgiving which came after the communion was that of Calvin's rite, and the service concluded with a blessing as contained in the Morning service.

The note "To the Reader" served as an *apologia* for the rite, possibly inspired by that in Calvin's liturgy. The reader is informed that in this liturgy the error of the papists is rejected, and a return to the primitive form of celebration has been made. The Institution Narrative is read, not to consecrate the elements, but as a warrant. It is a rite which is in accordance with the Word of God:

> so that without his Woorde, and warrante, there is nothyng in this holy action attempted.

---

[109] W.D. MAXWELL, *op. cit.*, p. 134; LOUIS BOUYER, *Eucharist. Theology and Spirituality of the Eucharistic Prayer*, Ed. C.U. QUINN, Notre Dame Indiama, 1968, p. 422. When Stephen Mayor, *The Lord's Supper in Early English Dissent*, 1972, p. 9, asserts that there is an "Epiklesis" in the prayer, he has misread both the text and Maxwell's comments.

[110] W.D. MAXWELL, *op. cit.*, p. 134.

It would seem, however, that the rite was not inspired solely by the Word of God, but was greatly indebted to Calvin's *La Forme*, possibly the first liturgy compiled by the Frankfurt congregation, the 1552 *Book of Common Prayer*, and in at least one place, Knox's Berwick liturgy. The resulting order, in its structure and content, is without doubt, Genevan.

From the above consideration of these four Eucharistic liturgies, we may make the following observations:

(1) These English Eucharistic liturgies had only the authority of the translator (Huycke), author (Knox), or compilers (*Liturgy of Compromise* and the *Genevan Service Book*). They may be divided into two types of liturgy:

> (a) The Genevan (Huycke, Knox and the *Genevan Service Book*).
> (b) The *Book of Common prayer*, sultably adapted (*Liturgy of Compromise*).

(2) The authors or compilers of these liturgies believed that they were restoring the Eucharist to its apostolic and early Christian form, simply by their appeal to Scripture. Calvin could claim:

> Ainsi donques tout l'ordre et la rayson d'administrer la Cene nous est notoyre par l'institution d'icelle, aussi avec l'administration de L'eglise ancienne des Apostres, des Martirs et des saintz Peres [111].

Similarly, the *Genevan Service Book* appealed to Christ's institution and St. Paul's rule. Hughes Oliphant Old has argued strongly — sometimes rather labouring his case — that the structure of the continental Reformed rites was based on the Reformed understanding of the writtings of the Fathers, particularly Chrysostom, Cyprian and Augustine [112].

However, for the modern scholar, these claims by the Reformers seem rather weak. There is no evidence to suggest that the compilers were at all interested in any examination of liturgy wich can remotely be described as historic or academic. Insofar as they made no attempt to reintroduce a meal into the Lord's Supper, their appeal to Scripture was selective. A study of these texts reveals the very opposite of their compilers' intentions. Through Bucer, and the influence of Oecolampadius's and Farel's use of *Pronaus*, many elements of these rites represent merely a "protestantisation" of medieval elements. Gregory Dix has commented upon the Reformed rites:

> Their compilers were far more concerned to follow what they regarded as "scriptural warrant" than anything within the liturgical tradi-

---

[111] *Corpus Reformatorum*, Calvini Opera VI, pp. 195-6.
[112] H.O. OLD, *op. cit.*, pp. 338-9.

tion against which they were in revolt. But the Reformers themselves thought largely in terms of the Western tradition within which they had been trained. In consequence their rites all reveal under technical analysis not "primitive" characteristics at all, nor anything akin to the special Eastern tradition, but a marked dependence on the basic Western liturgical tradition at a particular stage late in its development [113].

So for example in Calvin via Bucer we see the development of the *Confiteor* and the use of exhortatory material developed from the *Orate fratres*.

(3) These liturgies were already shorn of many of the traditional features of the Eucharistic liturgy — *Gloria in excelsis*, salutations, *Sanctus*, *Benedictus* and *Agnus Dei*. With the rejection of the liturgical calendar there also disappeared collects, and selected Epistles and Gospels. The element of thanksgiving tended to be shifted away from the setting apart of the bread and wine to after the act of communion [114].

(4) With regard to Calvin's rite and the *Genevan Service Book*, these two liturgies were derived from the Mass; the Morning service was not from the Divine Office, but from the Synaxis, and the influence of the *Pronaus*. However, the Calvinist tradition failed to restore weekly communion to the Church. Whereas the Mass was celebrated frequently, but communion by the laity was infrequent, the Reformed liturgies simply accepted infrequent communion and accordingly had infrequent celebration of the Eucharist. The result with regard to the liturgical texts was the separation of Word and Sacrament. They were indeed intended to be joined in one rite, but it would be a temptation to regard them as two quite separate services.

(5) The confession which rehearsed original sin, the fall, and redemption, and the exhortation before communion, emphasise the didactic element which was introduced into the Reformed liturgy. As Stephen Mayor has observed, there is a total subordination of act to word — human word.

> The protest against a degree of ceremonial which concealed rather than revealed the nature of the rite was no doubt justified, but in the Puritan versions of the Supper the acts which are an essential part of it disappear equally effectively behind a barrage of preaching and verbose praying. It is difficult not to feel that there was here a superstition of the voice [115].

---

[113] G. Dix, *The Shape of the Liturgy*, p. 10.
[114] A.C. Honders, "Remarks on the Postcommunion in some Reformed Liturgies", in Ed. Bryan D. Spinks, *The Sacrifice of Praise*, Bibliotheca "Ephemerides Liturgicae" Subsidia 19, Roma 1981, pp. 142-157.
[115] S. Mayor, *op. cit.*, pp. 27-28.

What is more, this wordiness belonged to the minister; the congregation had little to say other than an occasional "Amen".

(6) Calvin's rite, Knox's Berwick liturgy and the *Genevan Service Book* represent Reformed liturgies of a quite different ethos from that of the *Book of Common Prayer*. Calvin may have derived his rite from the same source as Cranmer, but the results were quite different. The Puritan tradition belived that the Reformed tradition had liturgies which were in accordance with Scripture, whereas the Church of England had not. Thus they appealed against the *Book of Common Prayer* to God's Word, and the example of the "best Reformed Churches".

APPENDIX

A Comparison between the Exhortations of Calvin and Farel; translation from Bard Thompson, *Liturgies of the Western Church*, pp. 205-207; 219-223.

CALVIN

Let us hear how Jesus Christ instituted His holy Supper for us, as St. Paul relates it in the eleventh chapter of First Corinthians:

Therefore, following that precept, in the name and by the authority of our Lord Jesus Christ, I excommunicate all idolaters blasphemers and despisers of God, all heretics and those who create private sects in order to break the unity of the Church, all perjurers, all who rebel against father or mother or superior, all who promote sedition or mutiny; brutal and disorderly persons, adulterers, lewd and lustful men, thieves, ravishers, greedy and grasping people, drunkards, gluttons, and all those who lead a scandalous and dissolute life. I warn them to abstain from this Holy Table, lest they defile and contaminate the holy food which our Lord Jesus Christ gives to none except they belong to His household of faith.

Moreover, in accordance with the exhortation of St. Paul, let every man examine and prove his own conscience to see whether he truly repents of his faults ... Above all let him see whether he has his trust in the mercy of God.

FAREL

Hear how our Lord Jesus Christ has instituted His Holy Supper, as it is written in I Corinthians, the eleventh chapter:

On the other hand, all those who do not have true faith must not presume at all to come to the Holy Table, pretending and falsely testifying to be members of the body of Jesus Christ to which they do not belong. Such are: all idolaters who worship and serve other than the one God; all prejurers; the slothful who serve no purpose and are of no account, though they could be; all who are disobedient to their father and mother and to those whom God has purposely appointed to rule over us without contravening His authority; all ruffians, quarrelsome persons who unjustly beat and smite their neighbours, whom they hate; all lechers; the intemperate who live dissolutely in their eating and drinking; all thieves who work damage and injury upon their neighbours; all false witnesses and perpetrators of crimes; and all those who live wickedly and contrary to the holy commandments of God, who do not intend to obey His holy law nor live according to His Word by following the holy Go-

And yet, we may be conscious of much frailty and misery in ourselves, such that we do not have perfect faith, but are inclined toward defiance and unbelief, of that we do not devote ourselves, wholly to the service of God and with such zeal as we ought, but have to fight daily against the lusts of our flesh.

To do so, let us lift our spirits and hearts on high where Jesus Christ is in the glory of His Father, whence we expect Him at our redemption. Let us not be fascinated by these earthly and corruptible elements which we see with our eyes and touch with our hands, seeking Him as though He were enclosed in the bread or wine.

spel, like true children of God. Let them not presume to approach this Holy Table, to which only those are to come who really belong to the body of Christ, united and rooted in Him by true and living faith which works through love. (For it shall be to their judgment and condemnation if they come here; and they shall be rejected as traitors and the successors of Judas).

Let everyone take heed of himself and inquire ... whether he believes completely ... that God is gracious unto us, that his wrath is appeased by the blessed Saviour Jesus ...

Yet, while we abide in this world, surrounded by this body of death and sin, we are all poor sinners and cannot say that we are without sin.

Therefore, lift up your hearts on high, seeking the heavenly things in heaven, where Jesus Christ is seated at the right hand of the Father; and do not fix your eyes on the visible signs which are corrupted through usage.

Chapter 4

PURITANISM AND THE EUCHARISTIC LITURGY IN ENGLAND: THE SIXTEENTH AND EARLY SEVENTEENTH CENTURIES

In both its structure and content, the 1559 communion service of the Prayer Book, unaltered in 1604, was substantially that of 1552. The latter had sought to exclude any notion of the sacrifice of the Mass and of presence within the elements of bread and wine. Cranmer had regarded these two doctrines as being the roots of popery, which if removed, would effectively destroy it:

> But what availeth it to take away beads, pardons, pilgrimages, and such other like popery, so long as two chief roots remain unpulled up? Whereof, so long as they remain, will spring again all former impediments of the Lord's harvest, and corruption of his flock. The rest is but branches and leaves, the cutting away whereof is but like topping and lopping of a tree, or cutting down of weeds, leaving the body standing and the roots in the ground; but the very body of the tree, or rather the roots of the weeds, is the popish doctrine of transubstantiation, of the real presence of Christ's flesh and blood in the sacrament of the altar (as they call it), and of the sacrifice and oblation of Christ made by the priest, for the salvation of the quick and the dead [1].

Part of the effective removal of these two doctrines had been the last minute inclusion of the "Black" rubric concerning kneeling.

The Puritans, being firmly protestant, found no quarrel with these doctrinal changes in the Eucharistic liturgy [2]. However, the removal of the "Black" rubric in 1559 caused them some consternation. Query 61 of *A Survey of the Booke of Common Prayer*, 1606 [3] asked whether kneeling for communion was lawful according to the Word of God,

---

[1] T. Cranmer, *On the Lord's Supper*, p. 6.
[2] For a general survey of Puritan Eucharistic Theology, E. Brooks Holifield, *The Covenant Sealed: The Development of Puritan Sacramental Theology in Old and New England, 1570-1720*, New Haven and London, 1974.
[3] *A Survey of the Booke of Common Prayer, By way of 197, queres grounded upon 58, places*, London, 1606. Cited as *A Survey*.

> Seeing it is contrary to the example, not only of such reformed Churches, as condemne *consubstantiation* as well as *Transubstantiation* with whom there ought to be conformitie as well as amongst our seves, but also of Christ himselfe, and his Apostles who ministred and (of purpose) received sitting [4].

The author of *Reasons against kneeling at the receit of the Communion* maintained that

> Whatsoever is destitute either of commandement or example out of Gods word, is not to be done: The ground of this *maior* is the place of Deut. 12. ver. 32. *Therefore whatsoever I commaund you*, take heed *you doe it: thou shalt put nothing* thereto, *nor take ought therefrom.* And this place, Rom. 14. ver. 23. *Whatsoever is not of faith, the selfe same is sinne:* meaning by the terme faith, a certaine and an assured perswasion setled and builded uppon Gods worde, which alone is the obiect and ground of conscience [5].

He continued:

> But kneeling at the Communion is voide either of commandement or example out of the worde [6].

The writer appealed to Chrysostom, the Reformed Churches of France, Flanders, Hungary, Poland, Berne, Zurich, Savoy and Scotland, as well as to the authority of Bullinger and Beza to justify sitting for reception. Field and Wilcox had similarly complained:

> In this booke we are enjoined to receave the Communion kneeling, which beside that if hath in it a shew of papisterie doth not so wel expresse the misterie of this holy Supper [7].

These two writers had argued that sitting was the correct posture for reception because it signified rest and the perfect work of redemption. On the other hand, the Lincoln ministers who petitioned James I appealed to Dionysius of Alexandria to justify standing for reception [8].

However, had the "Black" rubric been restored, it is doubtful whether the Puritans would have been satisfied; it is apparent that the criticism was not primarily concerned with whether or not kneeling implied transubstantia-

---

[4] *Ibid.*, p. 73.
[5] in *PR*, pp. 410-411, p. 410.
[6] *Ibid.*
[7] *An Admonition to the Parliament*, 1572, ed. Frere and Douglas, *op. cit.*, p. 24.
[8] *An Abridgment of that Booke which the Ministers of Lincoln Diocess delivered to his Maiestie upon the first of December last*, London, 1605, p. 60.

tion, but rather with the question of whether or not it had scriptural authority. Whereas for Cranmer, it had been sufficient to remove two doctrines from the liturgy, for the Puritan every remaining item in the liturgy must have scriptural authority. The puritan Vicar of Wandsworth, John Edwine, therefore maintained:

> There are some thinges in the booke of common prayer that are against the worde of God, and therfore repugnant to the worde of God [9].

And similarly it was with the criterion of scriptural authority in mind that Anthony Gilby, once a Frankfurt exile, alleged that in the *Book of Common Prayer* the Holy Sacraments were "mixed with mens traditions" [10]. The judgment of the 1559 communion service by the criterion of scriptural authority had two implications for the Puritans. First, the English liturgy should be compared with those of the Reformed Churches which ordered things according to the Word of God. Thus one Puritan author demanded:

> Let the admynistration of the sacraments, joyned with the preaching of the worde, be simplie and syncerelye admynistred, accordinge to the rule thereof, our Liturgye being examyned according to that touchstone (i.e. Scripture) and the example of other apostolique and reformed Churches [11].

The Plumber's Hall congregation had declared:

> We wilbe tried by the *best reformed Churches* [12].

and the 1587 Bill for the further reformation of the Church of England alleged,

> Furthermore, the saied booke of Common praier and Ordination of ministers differeth from the simplicitie and sinceritie of Gods service and from the example of all reformed Churches, ... [13].

The second implication was that as far as the Puritans were concerned, a

---

[9] The true report of a conference had betweene the B. of Wintchester and John Edwine, Vicare and Minister of Wandworths in Surr. 30 Aprilis 1584, in *SPR*, (161).

[10] A. GILBIE, *A Viewe of Antichrist his lawes and ceremonies in our Church unreformed*, in *PR*, p. 62.

[11] Notes of the Corruptions of these our bookes to which the mynisters are urged to subscribe, as not repugnant to the word, *SPR*. (140).

[12] *The true report of our Examination*, 1567, in *PR*, p. 35.

[13] A Bill for the further reformation of the Church, offered with the booke in the Parliament. A. 1587. *SPR*, (231).

Eucharistic liturgy which had been reformed according to the Word of God would have little in common with the Roman Catholic Mass. The Latin Mass had been abrogated by Law, but Catholic priests from the English Seminary at Rheims said Mass in secret for the Recusants; the Puritans also complained that in some parishes within the Church of England Mass was still said [14], and in other places the 1559 communion service was disguised as a Mass [15].

The Puritans certainly had no love of the content of the Mass. The *Kyrie eleison* was to be rejected because Gregory acknowledged that he had himself introduced it, six hundred years after Christ, and for clerks only, not the people [16]. The *Benedictus* and *Hosannah* had been abused; there are in Scripture two comings of Christ, the Incarnation and the Second Coming; but in the Mass this anthem had been made to refer to a blasphemous third coming - transubstantiation [17]. The *Canon missae*, since it supported the sacrifice of the Mass for the living and the dead, and transubstantiation, could not be considered as a Eucharistic Prayer. Comparing it with the prayer of Christ in John 17, William Fulke stated:

> The Canon of the Masse, is too base to be matched with this divine praier of our Saviour Christ, which yet followed his Supper, and not went before it as the Popish Canon, beginneth before consecration [18].

Even the most scriptural parts of the Mass did not redeem it in the eyes of the Puritans; referring to the *Sanctus*, Thomas Cartwright pronounced:

> These words in your Masse and other mash of yours is like a gold ring in a swines snout. And it is one of her harlots trickes to overlay her writhen and wrinckled face with the faire colours of goodlie words, if happily hee may snare some fooles that know not her filthines [19].

A Reformed rite would be totally different from the Mass. Edward Dering, referring to "the forme of prayer, which the papistes used", pinted out

---

[14] *A Comfortable epistle written by Mai. D. W. Doctor of Divinitie*, 1570, PR, p. 9.
[15] A. GILBIE, *op. cit.*, p. 62.
[16] WILLIAM FULKE, *The Text of the New Testament of Jesus Christ translated out of the vulgar Latine by the Papistes of the traiterous Seminarie at Rheims... with a confutation*, London, 1589, p. 297, commenting on 1 Cor. 14.
[17] *Ibid.*, p. 42. commenting on Matthew 21:9.
[18] *Ibid.*, p. 169.
[19] THOMAS CARTWRIGHT, *A Confutation of the Rheimists traslation, glosses and Annotations on the New Testament*, Leiden, 1618, p. 717, on Rev. 4:8.

> at this day all reformed Churches in *Fraunce, Polonia, Helvetia, Scotlande*, and other places, have chaunged that forme of prayers [20].

But the pedigree of the 1559 communion service — as of many of the Prayer Book services — was clearly discernible:

> The fourme of it is more agreeable to the popishe churche then to the reformed Churches of the Gospell, bothe in the common course of the Service, as in the Scriptures sett downe here a peece and there a peece, and as in most of the prayers and Collects [21].

Cartwright was more explicit: the entire book was "culled out of the vile popish service booke, with some certaine rubrikes and gloses of their owne devise" [22].

Puritans differed in their individual assessments of the 1559 communion service; some simply objected to the wearing of the surplice and kneeling for reception, whilst others found a great many faults. But taken overall, there were few items in the service which escaped Puritan criticism. These criticisms will be considered in relation to the Antecommunion and Eucharist proper.

A. *The Antecommunion.*

1. The opening rubrics were objected to because the minister was called "priest", he was to stand at the North side of the table, and because the provisions for warning of and preparation for communion were too short [23].
2. In the Decalogue two criticisms could be made. The first related to the text:

> In the recitall of the first commandment, a part of the text is cut off "which brought them out of the land of Egypt out of the house of bondage" [24].

The second, by implication, was of the responses to the Decalogue, and indeed all use of salutations and responses:

---

[20] *Articles answered by Mai. Edm(w). Dering, anno 1573*, in *PR*, p. 73.
[21] A Note of certaine Speciall Corruptions in the Booke of common prayer, unto which the ministers are yet urged by the Byshopps to subscribe, as not repugnant to the Worde of God. *SPR*, (127).
[22] *Second Admonition*, Frere and Douglas, p. 93. cf. Field and Wilcox, *ibid.*, p. 21; The Generall Inconveniencies of the booke of common prayer. *SPR* (165).
[23] Exceptions to be taken against those articles proposed to be subscribed unto by the ministers and people. *SPR* (57).
[24] Faults of the booke gathered by Mr. L. *SPR* (77).

> Againe, where learned they to multiplie up many prayers of one effect, so many times Glorye be to the Father, so manye times the Lorde be with you, so many times let us pray. Whence learned they all those needelesse repetitions? ... Lorde have mercye upon us, Christe have mercy upon us, is it not Kyrie eleeson, Christe eleeson [25]?

3. The Puritans saw no reason why the minister should have to stand to read the collect [26]. But there were also serious theological objections to particular collects. Regarding the collect for Innocents Day, "Almightie God whose prayse this day the young Innocents, thy witnesses, have confessed & shewed forth, not in speaking but in dying", *A Survey* asked whether they were martyrs in the same sense as Stephen — were they killed for the Word of God and the testimonies they maintained [27]? In the same work, Query 43 asked concerning St. Michael's Day:

> Whither this be not a notable disparagement to our glorious Saviour that in our prayer to his heavenly Father, *who hath glorified his* Sonne, *and will glorifie him againe we should ioyne him in services with meere created Angels, or ministring spirits, and that without a convenient note of his proper difference* [28].

Cartwright had seized upon those of Christmas and Pentecost, and St. Bartholomew:

> upon the nativitie day I must say, that Christe vouchsafed this day to be borne, & when I read it another day, I must say, he vouchsafed this day to be borne, and the next day againe this day. Surely I lie, one of the dayes, and suche a prayer is at whitsontide appointed.

> wherin they pray that they may follow Bartholomews sermons, seeing there is never a sermon of his extant, and so we shall follow we wot not what [29]?

4. It might be reasonable to suppose that the lections, being the pure Word of God, would have escaped criticism. In fact, the "pistles and Gospells" were for the Puritans a major cause for complaint. Query 11 of *A Survey* raised objections to the introduction to the lections, "The Epistle or Gospel, is written in ...":

> As if they were the only Epistles and Gospels, or the most holy of all Epistles and Gospels [30].

---

[25] CARTWRIGHT, *Second Admonition*, Frere and Douglas, *op. cit.*, p. 114.
[26] Faults of the booke gathered by Mr. L.
[27] *A Survey*, p. 56.
[28] *A Survey*, p. 60.
[29] *Second Admonition*, Frere and Douglas, p. 116.
[30] *A Survey*, p. 36.

It was also noted with disapproval that many people still replied to the announcement of the Gospel with the response "Glorie to thee O Lord", even though the rubric authorising it had been removed from the Prayer Book after 1549. The ministers of the Lincoln diocese criticised them on the grounds that the order for appointing the lections was contrary to the Word of God, that chapters of the Bible were omitted, and that the pericopes for the Epistles and Gospels resulted in the Holy Scripture being "mangled into shreds and pecies" [31].

Query 10 of *A Survey* criticised the reading of the Epistle and Gospel on Sundays or weekdays when there was no communion service. It was argued that just as baptism, marriage and funeral offices were only said on their respective occasions, so too the collect, Epistle and Gospel, which belonged to the communion service, should be confined to when the Communion was celebrated [32].

5. Linked with the criticism of the collects, Epistles and Gospels was the objection to the liturgical calendar — the Sunday sequence, the seasons and saints' days. Query 14 of *A Survey* asked

Whither the catelogue of holy dayes be authenticall [33]

and Query 52

Whither men may, with warrant of the word, sanctifie any holy day to be observed [34],

since all holy days which God had prescribed of the Levites were abolished except the seventh day. Any other observance was tantamount to making the children of the marriage chamber fast when they had the bridegroom with them. One writer declared that to observe the fast of Lent and the keeping of saints days was unlawfull as well as superstitious [35]. Again, the observation of days and seasons was condemned by Paul (Galatians 4:10) [36]. Ambrose and Tertullian had taught that men were cast down to hell if they observed Jewish ceremonies; Solomon's policy of unfaithfulness led to his downfall, for the Word of God is clear, "Turne unto me with all your harte, saith the lorde, and put awaye thyn abominations" [37].

---

[31] *An abridgment of that Booke,...* p. 75.
[32] *A Survey*, pp. 33-34.
[33] *A Survey*, p. 59.
[34] *A Survey*, p. 66.
[35] Divers abuses to be reformed in the Church of England, *SPR* (166).
[36] Collections out of the communion book, *SPR*, (80).
[37] A Letter from Anthony Gilby to Thomas Cartwright. *SPR* (93).

6. The Creed was "as a peece of your masse"; there was nothing wrong with the Creed as such, but it should be taught and confessed in the sermon rather than merely recited [38]. (Yet the Reformed rites could also be indicted here.)
7. The provision for the reading of a homily instead of the preaching of a sermon was to be condemned [39].
8. The provision for the recitation of the Antecommunion without the Eucharist itself was the remains of the "Dry Mass" [40]. Field and Wilcox went so far as to question whether there was any scriptural authority for any Antecommunion before the actual communion:

> They shoulde first prove, that a reading service by the woorde of God going before, and with the administration of the sacraments, is according to the Woorde of God,... [41].

B. *The Eucharist Proper.*

It hac already been observed above that one of the major criticisms of the Eucharist of 1559 was the requirement of kneeling for reception. There were other criticisms.
1. The phrase in the Preface, "therefore with angels and Archangels" was questioned on the grounds

> Whether the Scripture do warrant that speech of any more than one, namely Jesus Crist [42].

The Proper prefaces could be criticised on the same grounds as some of the collects:

> In the proper prefaces (all which for the most part are taken out of the Mass booke). And namely in that appointed to be read on Whitsunday, and Six dayes after it, it is said that the Holy Ghost came downe that day from heaven, and so upon every of the Six dayes, which maketh the Minister to lye, as much at Whitsontide as at Christmas [43].

2. Query 63 of *A Survey* attacked the free rendering of the Words of Institution in the prayer later to be called the "Prayer of Consecration" [44]. Since

---

[38] *Certaine Articles... with an Answere to the same*, Frere and Douglas, p. 140.
[39] eg. Faults of the booke gathered by Mr. L. *SPR* (77).
[40] Exceptions to be taken against those articles, *SPR*, (57).
[41] *An Admonition to the Parliament*, Frere and Douglas, p. 21.
[42] Faults of the booke gathered by Mr. L.
[43] Exceptions to be taken against those articles, ...
[44] *A Survey*, p. 74.

Scripture faithfully records the words (apparently here overlooking the divergences of the New Testament) we should use them, and not make up our own. Furthermore, the joining of "unnecessary & dangerous Prayers" to them was not warrantable by the Word.

3. The words of delivery in the 1559 liturgy were a combination of those of 1549 and 1552. Some Puritans objected to both.

> Why content you not your selves with Christes words and the Apostles? Either folishe Paule and wise you, or folish you, and wise the Apostles [45].

Query 62 of *A Survey* complained that the delivery of Christ was in the plural, but that in the Prayer Book individual [46].

4. There was no need to include the *Gloria in excelsis* in the communion service:

> Not every thing that is good, is to be patched into the Communion, because that christians ought not to make quidlibet ex quolibet of a rede a rammes horne [47].

5. The reserving of blessings for Bishops, and the use of wafers were both contrary to the Word of God [48].

An overall assessment was given by Field and Wilcox, comparing the usage of the early church:

> They (the early church) had no introite, for Celestinus a pope broght it in, aboute the yeare 430. But we have borrowed a peece of one out of the masse booke. They read no fragments of the Epistle and Gospell: we use both. The Nicene crede was not read in their Communion: we have it in oures. Ther was then, accustomed to be an examination of the communicants, which now is neglected. Then they ministred the sacrament with common and usual bread: now with wafer cakes, brought in by Pope Alexander, being in forme, fashion and substance, lyke their god of the alter. They receaved it sitting: we kneelyng, accordyng to Honorius Decree. Then it was delivered generally, & in definitely, Take ye and eat ye: we particulerly and singulerly, Take thou, and eat thou. They used no other wordes but such as Chryste lefte: we borrowe from papistes, The body of our Lorde Jesus Chryst which was geven for thee, &c. They had no Glo-

---

[45] *Certaine articles*, Frere and Douglas, p. 141.
[46] *A Survey*, p. 73.
[47] *Ibid.*, p. 141.
[48] Articles sent to the Bishops and Cleargye in the convocation house... From the Marshalsye by John Nasshe the Lordes prisoner 1580 Januarye. *SPR* (99); Faults of the booke gathered by Mr. L. *SPR* (77); Exceptions to be taken against those articles ... *SPR* (57).

ria in excelsis in the ministerie of the Sacrament then, for it was put to afterward. We have now. They toke it with conscience. We with custume. They shut men by reason of their sinnes, from the Lords Supper. We thrust them in their sinne to the Lordes Supper. They ministred the Sacrament plainely. We pompously, with singing, pypyng, surplesse and cope wearyng. They simply as they receeved it from the Lorde. We, sinfullye, mixed with mannes inventions and devises [49].

The Puritan criticism of the 1559 Eucharistic liturgy appears to the modern liturgical scholar as nothing more than a tedious catena of complaints about rubrics and precise grammar. But the tedious catena betrays an underlying fundamental objection to the whole ethos of the liturgy; it was quite simply too much like the Mass.

In at least three particular ways the Puritans sought to overcome the problem of an unscriptural enacted Eucharistic liturgy: by adapting it; by attempting to legalise the use of the Reformed rites of the "Stranger" Churches; and by issuing revised editions of the *Genevan Service Book*.

1. *Adaptations of Prayer Book Communion Service.*

In a previous chapter we have already indicated that for the most part it is possible only to conjecture what individual Puritan ministers might have omitted or changed in the Prayer Book services. In addition to John Elliston who omitted the Epistle and Gospel, Josias Nichols of Kent omitted the collect and creed, and William Jenkynson of Croxton near Thetford omitted the commandments and replaced the Epistle and Gospel with a portion of Scripture, as in the *Genevan Service Book* [50].

Many Puritan clergy and laity were cited for receiving the sacrament standing [51]. On the other hand, Bishop Scambler of Peterborough was alleged to have sanctioned the practice of standing for communion at Northampton:

The maner of this communion is, beside the sermon, according to the order of the queen's Book; saving the people, being in their confession upon their knees, for the dispatch of many do orderly arise from their pews and so pass to the communion table, where they received the sacrament, and from thence in like order to their place,

---

[49] *An Admonition to the Parliament*, Frere and Douglas, pp. 13-14.
[50] P. COLLINSON, *The Elizabethan Puritan Movement*, p. 366. In the case of Nichols this seems to be in reference to Morning Prayer rather than the communion service.
[51] RONALD MARCHANT, *op. cit.*, passim.

> having all this time a minister in the pulpit, reading unto them comfortable scriptures of the passion or other like, pertaining to the matter in hand [52].

The reference to the reading of suitable passages of scripture during the administration may be compared with the *Genevan Service Book*:

> Duringe the which tyme (i.e. the administration), some place of the scriptures is read, which doth lyvely set forth the death of Christ, ... that our hartes and myndes also may be fully fixed in the contemplation of the lordes death, which is by this holy Sacrament representede.

The practice at Northampton would appear to be a Genevan feature interpolated into the Prayer Book service.

The method of administration of a certain Puritan Vicar of Ratesdale, "dealing the bread out of a basket, everyman putting in his hand and taking out a peece" [53], was judged to be irreverent and a breach of the rubrics.

A similar verdict was passed on Robert Johnson, preacher of Northampton, as regards the "consecration" of the elements. When the Communion wine had failed, Johnson had sent for some more and had simply administered it with the words of administration, without first repeating the prayer (Prayer of Consecration) containing the Words of Institution. Johnson argued that in the *Book of Common Prayer* there was no rubric which demanded its repetition in such circumstances, and "for that it being one entire action and one supper, the wordes of institution afore spoken were sufficient" [54]. Here Johnson was appealing to the conception of consecration found in Calvin's liturgy and the *Genevan Service Book*, and taught by such Puritan scholars as William Fulke and Thomas Cartwright [55], that the Words of Institution were a warrant making the use "lawfull unto us" [56], or in Johnson's words, "that holynes is in the use and end and not in the substance" [57]: The Commissioners, accepting St. Augustine's words *"Accedat verbum ad elementum et fit sacramentum"* to mean that the Words of Institution effected consecration or blessing of the elements, ruled against Johnson. Professor E. C. Ratcliff observed:

---

[52] P. COLLINSON, *op. cit.*, p. 369.
[53] The summe and substance of the conference... at Hampton Court Jan 14, 1603. Contracted by William Barlow, D.D. in Cardwell, *op. cit.*
[54] *The examination of Master Robert Johnson*, 1573, in *PR*, pp. 105-111, p. 106.
[55] WILLIAM FULKE, *The Text of the New Testament... with a confutation*, p. 54, commenting upon Matthew 26:26; THOMAS CARTWRIGHT, *A Confutation of the Rheimists translation*, p. 128.
[56] Cartwright, *ibid.*
[57] *The examination of Master Robert Johnson, PR,* p. 109.

> They were unmoved indeed by any arguments which Johnson adduced; and they declined his interpretation of a passage of Bullinger and of the Scottish and Genevan Liturgies [58].

The rubrics of the Prayer Book were not to be interpreted by the theology and rubrics of Geneva.

In the Puritan editions of the *Book of Common Prayer* which appeared from 1578 onwards, only minor alterations were to be found in the Eucharistic liturgy:

> 1. "Minister" was substituted for "Priest".
> 2. The introductory rubrics were omitted, including the direction for the minister to stand at the North Side of the Communion Table.
> 3. "Great number" was substituted for "good number" in the second rubric at the end of the service.

Although of an insignificant nature, all these points were ones to which Puritans objected; "priest" because of its Catholic associations, "North Side" as superstitious, and "great number" may have been to guard against private communion [59].

Both the *ad hoc* alterations, and the slight changes in the printed books give us adaptations of the Prayer Book Eucharist which stand in the tradition of the *Liturgy of Compromise*.

2. *The Stranger Churches: The Liturgies of Valerand Poullain, John à Lasco and Maarten Micron.*

In a report to the Privy Council of January 1634, Archbishop William Laud, a bitter opponent of all forms of Puritanism, stated:

> I conceive under favour that the Dutch Churches in Canterbury & Sandwich are great Nurseryes of Inconformity in those Partes. Your Majesty may be pleased to remember I have complained to your selfe and my Lords at the Counsell Board & humbly desired that they both of the French, Italian, & Dutch Congregations, which are borne Subjects, may not be suffered any longer to live in such Separation as they doe from both Church and State. And have accordingly ... commanded my Vicar Generall ... to beginn fairely to calle them to conforme with the English Church [60].

---

[58] E.C. Ratcliff, "The English Usage of Eucharistic Consecration, 1548-1662", I and II, in *Theology*, 60 (1957) pp. 229-236, 273-280, p. 278.
[59] A.E. Peaston, *The Prayer Book Tradition in the Free Churches*, pp. 31-32.
[60] Harleian MSS. 787, fol. 32, quoted in R.P. Stearns, *Congregationalism in the Dutch Netherlands*, pp. 61-62.

Laud's intention to bring the foreign protestant congregations, the so-called "Stranger" Churches, into conformity with the Established Church stemmed from that type of eccelsiastical nationalism admirably expressed by Fielding's Parson Thwackum, that religion, Christianity and Protestantism are synonymous with the Church of England. But Laud's remark also stemmed from his careful observations that while the Stranger Churches remained autonomous, they both spurred on and provided a court of appeal for the Puritan and Separatist movements.

The Stranger Churches had their origin with the congregations of continental Protestants who fled to England during the reign of Edward VI and after 1559 in order to escape Catholic persecution and civil strife on the Continent. Thus, in 1548 Jan Utenove was associated with a Walloon congregation at Canterbury [61], and in 1550 Valerand Poullain settled with his French congregation at Glastonbury.

The autonomy of these Stranger Churches can be traced to the charter granted by Edward VI in 1550 in which the medley of foreigners in London were placed under the supervision of the Polish reformer, John à Lasco.

John à Lasco, or Jan Laski, described by his contemporaries as a nobleman [62], had been carefully prepared for the Church under the guidance of his uncle, also Jan, who was Primate of Poland. During his education he had been acquainted with Erasmus and Oecolampadius at Basle, and later with Zwingli. He became Bishop of Vesprin, but by 1538 had adopted Protestantism and had married. Forced to flee Poland, he settled at Emden in 1542 and became Superintendent of the Church of East Friesland. The enforcement of the Augsburg Interim in 1548 again forced him to flee, and at the invitation of Edward VI and Cranmer, he eventually came to England. After his arrival Maarten Micron, a Dutch minister, wrote to Henry Bullinger, explaining that there were plans for establishing a German (Dutch) Church in England [63]. This plan was confirmed by the Royal Charter of 1550, appointing à Lasco Superintendent:

> We will that John à Lasco, a pole by race, a man very famous on account of the integrity and innocency of life and manners and singular learning, to be the first and present superintendent of the said church; and that Walter Leonus, Martin Flandrus, Francis Riverius and Richard Gallus be the four first and present ministers [64].

---

[61] C.H. SMYTH, *Cranmer & The Reformation under Edward VI*, Cambridge, 1926, p. 191.
[62] For a recent discussion of this and other biographical details, BASIL HALL, *John à Lasco 1499-1560. A Pole in Reformation England*, Dr. Williams's Trust, 1971.
[63] *Original Letters*, Vol. 2, p. 560. Micron to Bullinger, May 20, 1550.
[64] The Charter is given in Latin and English in, J. LINDEBOOM, *Austin Friars. History of the Dutch Reformed Church in London 1550-1950*, pp. 198-203.

The Dutch speaking congregation was given the Church of Austin Friars, and the French, St. Anthony's Hospital in Threadneedle Street. The "independent" nature of this Church was guaranteed in the Charter:

> We give also and grant to the said superintendent ministers and their successors faculty, authority and licence, after the death or voidance of the superintendent, from time to time to elect, nominate and depute another learned and grave person in his place; so nevertheless that the person so nominated and elected be presented and brought before us our heirs or successors, and by us, our heirs or successors instituted into the office of superintendent aforesaid.
>
> We order, and firmly enjoinng command as well the Mayor, Sheriffs and Alderman of our City of London, the Bishop of London and his successors, with all other our Archbishops, Bishops, Judges, Officers and Ministers whomsoever, that they permit the aforesaid superintendent and ministers and their successors freely and quietly to practise, enjoy, use and exercise their own rites, ceremonies and their own peculiar ecclesiastical discipline, notwithstanding that they do not conform with the rites and ceremonies used in our Kingdom, without impeachment, disburbance or vexation of them or any of them.

As in the case of the English Edwardian Church, the King's untimely death and the accession of his Cathilic sister Mary, brought to an abrupt and the peace of the Stranger Churches. Poullain and his Glastonbury congregation fled to Frankfurt; the Dutch Church fled to Denmark, from there to Emden, and arrived finally in Frankenthal in the Palatinate. However, sufficient numbers must have remained in England, for although neither Poullain, à Lasco or Micron were to return, in 1559 Jan Utenhove returned to London to take charge of the Dutch speaking congregation, and in 1560 Nicolas des Gallars, a pastor from Geneva, arrived to minister to the Walloon Church.

Utenhove presented the 1550 Charter to Elizabeth, but although the Stranger Churches were allowed to continue as before, the Queen never confirmed the Charter, and insisted that the Superintendent should be the Bishop of London. Despite suspicion from the English hierarchy, the Churches continued to use their own rites and ceremonies, though during Laud's ascendancy, many were pressurised into adopting the *Book of Common Prayer* [65].

Even a cursory survey of Puritan literature reveals that Laud's charge against the Stranger Churches of being "great nurseyres of Inconformity"

---

[65] D.N. GRIFFITHS, "The French Translations of the English Book of Common Prayer", in *Proceedings of the Huguenot Society of London*, Vol 22, (1972) pp. 90-114, pp. 94-95. The Dutch Church in London seems to have resisted the imposition.

was not without foundation. For instance, one Puritan critic attacking the practice of kneeling could appeal to

> all the churches of *France, Flanders, Hungarie, Polonia, Bernia, Zurick, Savoy, Scotland* ... besides the presidents and practise wee have heere at home before our owne eyes, in the French, Dutch, and Italian Churches at London, Norwicth, Sandwitch, and other places in this Realme [66].

Henry Jacob, in *A Third Humble Supplication* of 1605, requested a convenanted Church "As namely in the well ordered and peaceable Churches of the French and Dutch, which by your Maiesties gracious protection and allowaince doe liue within your Realme", and gave an assurance of keeping "brotherly communion" with the rest of the English Church "according as the French and Dutch churches do" [67]. Puritanism seems to have been particularly strong in those towns which had a Dutch or French Church. Their position from Laud's point of view has been put succinctly by Patrick Collinson:

> As members of organised Calvinist churches which were largely self-governing and free to elect their own officers and to exercise Reformed, congregational discipline, the foreign Protestants must have exercised a fascinating influence over their English brethren who longed for these rights but could not as yet enjoy them. ... they played the part of a Trojan horse, bringing Reformed worship and discipline fully armed into the midst of the Anglican camp [68].

The threat which the "Trojan horse" posed to the liturgy of the Established Church was only too well illustrated by the Bill presented to Parliament in May 1572, which would have empowered Bishops to licence their clergy to omit parts of the *Book of Common Prayer* in order to increase the time of preaching, and to use

> such forme of prayer and mynistracion of the woorde and sacraments, and other godlie exercises of religion as the righte godlie reformed Churches now do use in the ffrenche and Douche congregation, within the City of London or elsewheare in the Quenes maiesties dominions and is extant in printe, any act or acts, Iniunction, advertisement, or decree heretofore had or made to the contrarie notwithstandynge [69].

---

[66] *Reasons against kneeling at the recit of the Communion, PR*, p. 410. (Norwichth seems to be a misprint).

[67] BURRAGE, *The Early English Dissenters*, Vol. 2, pp. 161-165.

[68] P. COLLINSON, "The Elizabethan Puritans and the Foreign Reformed Churches in London" in *Proceedings of the Huguenot Society of London*, Vol. 20 (1958-64), pp. 528-555, pp. 529, 531.

[69] FRERE and DOUGLAS, *Puritan Manifestoes*, pp. 149-151, p. 151.

Any hopes the Puritans may have had concerning this Bill were dashed by the Queen's adamant refusal on this, or any other occasion, to grant them concessions. They were firmly ordered

> to kepe the order of common prayer, divine services and administration of the Sacramentes accordyng as in the sayde booke of divine service ther be set foorth, and none other contrary or repugnant, upon payne of her highnesse indignation and of other paynes in the sayde acte comprysed [70].

The "Trojan horse" was in quarantine, and would remain so.

Our concern here is to consider the liturgies which the Bill of 1572 sought to authorise for use in the Church of England.

Any consideration of the liturgies of the Stranger Churches must centre upon the liturgy of the Superintendent of the London Churches, à Lasco's *Forma ac ratio Ecclesiastici ministerii in peregrinorum potissimum vero Germanorum Ecclesia instituta Londini in Anglia*. However, a number of complex problems surround the *Forma ac Ratio* and the use of the Dutch and French Stranger Churches in 1572 [71].

1. The first known edition of the *Forma ac ratio* was published in Frankfurt in 1555, after à Lasco and a large number of the London Church had fled. A French edition, *Toute La forme & maniere du Ministere Ecclesiastique, en l'Eglise des estrangers, dressee a Londres on Angleterre, par le Prince tres fidele dudit pays, le Roy Edouard VI: de ce nom: L'an apres l'incarnation de Christ. 1550, avec le previlege de sa Majeste a la fin du livre*, appeared in 1556 printed by Giles Ctematius.

The historian of the Dutch Reformed liturgy, J. A. Mensinga, believed that during his years in London, à Lasco used only a handwritten copy of the forms which he later elaborated for publication. Professor Lindeboom, in his history of Austin Friars, tends towards this view:

> Less haste was made with the drafting of the church order and of a fixed liturgy, than had been applied to the compilation of the book of instruction ... There are indications of provisional rules relative to the liturgy having been drawn up, such as certain set prayers and a liturgy for the Communion Service [72].

However, this simple explanation is complicated by the fact that there exists

---

[70] *Ibid.*, p. 151.
[71] Too little is known of the Italian and Spanish congregations to consider them here. Already by 1571 the members of the Italian community asked the Dutch whether they might join in their communion service. J. LINDEBOOM, *op. cit.*, p. 98.
[72] *Ibid.*, pp. 18-19.

what appears to be a Dutch abridgement of the *Forma ac ratio* by Maarten Micron, entitled *Christian Ordinances of the Netherlands congregation of Christ which was established in London in 1550 by the Christian prince, King Edward VI; faithfully collected and published by M. Micron with the consent of the elders and deacons of the congregation of Christ in London; for the comfort and profit of all believers.* But this work appeared in 1554, a year before à Lasco's *Forma as ratio*.

The problem raised by Micron's work is complicated even further by statements of à Lasco and Micron themselves. In his dedication to Sigismund of Poland, à Lasco mentioned that Micron had translated his work into Dutch, and Micron acknowledged his debt to à Lasco. But Micron also mentioned that Jan Utenhove had translated the "present ordinances" into Dutch. Are we to infer from this that there was a liturgy connected with Utenhove — an elder associated with the Walloon Church at Canterbury and the Dutch Church at Austin Friars — which antedates both Micron and à Lasco, and what is the relationship between them all?

Utenhove did publish a Dutch catechism translated from à Lasco in 1551, and — for which his name is chiefly remembered — a Dutch version of the psalms which included the Decalogue, Lord's Prayer, Creed and a prayer before the sermon, all of which were important elements in the Dutch liturgy [73]. However, there is no actual liturgy of Utenhove.

In his introduction to Micron's work, Professor W. F. Dankbaar of Groningen University offered the following explanation [74].

The ordinances for the London Stranger Churches were drawn up by à Lasco in 1551, first of all being a rough scheme which was gradually developed. But à Lasco did not know much Dutch. The scheme had to be discussed by the community, and Utenhove undertook to translate à Lasco's work. This work was merely for the community to discuss amongst themselves. This scheme would correspond to the handwritten copy which Mensinga and Lindeboom mention. Later, after he had left London, à Lasco sought to defend the London Church by setting out its constitution in the *Forma ac ratio*. Here à Lasco elaborated and expandend his earlier rough scheme, the result being both a description of the practice in London between 1550 and 1553, and what he hoped that practice might eventually have been. At the same time, Micron was preparing a popular or practical version, using the original Latin drafts and Utenhove's translations. But Micron did not work indepen-

---

[73] *De Psalmen Davidis, in Nederlandischen sangs-ryme; door Ian Wtenhove van Ghendtt.* Copy of an edition of 1566 at Austin Friars.
[74] W.F. DANKBAAR, *Marten Micron, De Christlicke Ordinancen der Nederlantscher Ghemeinten te Londen (1554)*, Kerkhistorische Studien Deel VII. 's-Gravenhage, 1956.

dently of à Lasco; a letter of à Lasco to Bullinger of 7th June 1553 mentioned that he had been assisted by Micron. The two works were, then the result of co-operation between Micron and à Lasco, but the forms originate with à Lasco.

That there was an earlier form of the services of the *Forma ac ratio* is perhaps also suggested by the Italian congregation's *La forma delle publiche orationi, et della cōfessione, & assolutione, la qual si usa nella chiessa de forestieri che è nuouamente stata instituita in Londra (per gratia di Dio) con l'autorità & cōsentimento del Re*, translated by P. P. Vergerio, a copy of which is to be found in the British Museum. Consisting of eight leaves without pagination, it appears to be a slightly abbreviated version of the Morning service of the *Forma ac ratio*. However, if the British Museum's suggested dating of 1551 is correct, it antedates the work of both à Lasco and Micron, and would indicate that the services of the *Forma ac ratio* are revised and polished versions of services compiled for the "Strangers" in 1550.

Neither John à Lasco nor his *Forma ac ratio* were to return to the Dutch Church in London after 1559, but Micron's *Christian Ordinances* did. The liturgy is only slightly altered from à Lasco's, and the prayers, structure, and theology belong primarily to à Lasco.

2. After 1559 Micron's version of à Lasco's liturgy was in use in the London Dutch Church, together with the psalms of Utenhove. However, the Dutch Reformed Church in the Netherlands, which had its origin in the Palatinate, had another version of the psalms and another liturgy, being the work of Petrus Datheen, 1566. According to the archives of Austin Friars, the London congregation adopted Datheen's psalm on Easter Day 1571 [75]. The earliest copy of Datheen's psalms and liturgy in the library of Austin Friars is indeed dated 1571, being bound with the Bible; the next edition is dated 1582. Does this imply that on Easter Day 1571 Datheen's liturgy was also adopted, and that the Bill of 1572, as regards the Dutch church, referred to Datheen's liturgy and not that of à Lasco-Micron?

Even if Datheen's liturgy had been adopted in 1571, it would make little difference to our consideration of à Lasco-Micron. Datheen's liturgy will be considered later in a different context, but suffice it to say here that, for example, in the Morning service Datheen provided merely two prayers with a few rubrics; the à Lasco-Micron service is a lengthy one, and we would hardly expect this to have been replaced by a service of two prayers. Austin Frars

---

[75] *Kerkeraads-Protocollen Der Hollandische Gemeente te Londen 1569-71*, ed. A. Kuyper, Utrecht 1870, pp. 302, 311. The reason was that some members of the congregation were using Utenhove's version, and others Datheen's, resulting no doubt in a dreadful sound.

has an edition of Micron of 1554, possibly brought back to England in 1559, and another edition dated 1582, suggesting that Micron's order was used for some time after 1571 [76]. The prayers of Datheen may have been used, being inserted into Micron's order; Micron's liturgy was in no sense binding, and seems to have been to guide the minister, the people having their parts — psalms, creed and Lord's Prayer — in their psalm books. The *Christian Ordinances* was more of a directory than a *Book of Common Prayer*; this is also suggested by the alterations made by one minister, Godfried Van Wingen, who introduced some new prayers and changed others [77]. It appears that Micron's order was still used in the Netherlands after 1566 alongside that of Datheen [78].

3. Even more complex is the position of the liturgy in use in the French Stranger Churches.

Any consideration of the liturgy of the French Stranger Churches must begin with the *Liturgia Sacra* of Valerand Poullain [79]. A successor to Calvin and Brully in the ministry of the French congregation at Strasbourg, Poullain had taken over Calvin's Strasbourg liturgy, though making a number of modifications to phraseology and to the rubrics. It is therefore of the same pedigree as Calvin's rite [80].

In 1549 Poullain arrived in England with some of his congregation, and he eventually settled at Glastonbury, in charge of a small community of Walloons. In 1551 he published his Strasbourg liturgy in Latin under the title of *Liturgia Sacra*, dedicating the work to Edward VI. A second edition appeared in French in 1552, and Latin editions were published at Frankfurt in 1554 and 1555. We refer here to the critical edition prepared by A. C. Honders, giving a summary of Morning service and the Lord's Supper [81].

> *Morning service.*
>
> The first table of the Decalogue, sung. (Clement Marot's metrical version verses 1-5).
> "Our help is in the name of the Lord".

---

[76] The 1554 edition is printed by Collinus Volckwinner, *alius* Giles Ctematius, at Emden; the 1582 edition is confusing, the title page attributing it to Jaspar Troyens of Antwerp, the last page attributing it to Cornelius Jansz at Delft.

[77] DANKBAAR, *op. cit.*, pp. 23-24.

[78] *Ibid.*, p. 25.

[79] For a link between Poullain and Congregationalism, H.J. COWELL, "Valerand Poullain. A Precursor of Congregationalism?" in *CHST*, 12 (1933-36), pp. 112-119.

[80] Maxwell classed it as a fourth edition of Calvin's Strasbourg rite, *The Liturgical Portions of the Genevan Service Book*, p. 21.

[81] A.C. HONDERS, *Valerandus Pollanus Liturgia Sacra (1551-1555)*, Kerkhistorische Bijdragen 1, Leiden, 1970.

Exhortation to Confession.
Confession. (Calvin, from Bucer.)
Absolution, the pastor recites sentences of Scripture concerning the remission of sins, and pronounces the Absolution to those who believe and are penitent, in the name of the Father, Son and Holy Ghost.
The Second Table of the Decalogue, verses 6-8.
Prayer, that the commandments may be for our instruction, implanted in our hearts by the Holy Spirit and inscribed there, that we may serve and obey in all sanctity and Justice.
Last verse of Marot's metrical Decalogue [82].
Prayer of Illumination.
New Testament Lection.
Sermon.
Special Bidding Prayer for the sick or poor.
Offering.
Prayer for the Church. (Calvin, from Bucer.)
Apostle's Creed.
Psalm.
Aaronic Blessing.

The Order of the Supper (after the Apostle's Creed).

Eucharistic Prayer. (Calvin, Strasbourg).
Words of Institution.
Exhortation with excommunication. (Calvin)
Fraction and Delivery.
Words of Delivery: The Bread which we break is the communion of the Body of Christ. The Cup which we bless is the communion of the Blood of Christ.
Psalm during administration, at the minister's discretion.
Prayer of Thanksgiving. (Calvin)
Aaronic Blessing.

Since the text of the prayers is almost identical to that of Calvin's Strasbourg rite, there is little need for additional comment here.

The title of the edition of 1552 described this liturgy as *L'Ordre des prieres et ministere Ecclesiastique avec La forme de penitence pub. & certaines Prieres de l'Eglise de Londres*, and the Preface mentioned that for three years previously there had been a French speaking Church in London under the leadership of Richard Vauville, "homme vrayment entier et parfaict en la piete Chrestienne". However, there is no evidence to suggest that *Liturgia Sacra* was used in any other Church than Poullain's own congregation at Glastonbury [83]. Again in the 1552 Preface, Poullain explained that the Lon-

---

[82] See Honders' discussion, *ibid.*, p. 12. Also A.C. HONDERS, "Let us Confess our Sins...", *Concilium* 2:9 (1973) pp. 86-94, p. 89.

[83] My opinion is supported by Dr. A.C. HONDERS, in a letter dated 26th March, 1974. There is no evidence to support the claim of H. HAGEMAN, "The Liturgical Origins of the Reformed

don Churches, in order to provide stability and good order, had been placed under the charge of John à Lasco. We should expect that the foreign London congregations would have used the liturgy of their own Superintendent, the *Forma ac ratio*. Before 1550, or until the *Forma ac ratio* began to take shape, it may be the case that Vauville had used Calvin's Genevan rite. À Lasco himself recorded that as regards his own liturgy, he had in mind the examples of the Churches of Geneva and Strasbourg [84]. Poullain could provide the text of the latter; perhaps Vauville provided the text of the former. Once the *Forma ac ratio* had been drafted, we may presume that the London French Church adopted it.

However, which liturgy was in use in the French Churches in 1572? We have already drawn attention to the French edition of the *Forma ac ratio* of 1556; two copies of this edition are in the possession of Austin Friars, and a copy is also in the possession of the French Protestant Church in Soho Square, London, being the present-day successor to the original Threadneedle congregation. Although possession does not constitute proof of use, it might suggest rather more than academic interest. Nicolas des Gallars who became minister of the London congregation in 1560 came straight from Geneva, and presumably was familiar with Calvin's Genevan rite. Although he published no liturgy, des Gallars did publish the "Discipline" of the French congregation, and he seems to have based it upon the *Forma ac ratio*. A short section dealt with the celebration of the Eucharist: it was to be celebrated when the consistory ordained it, and when the congregation was so disposed, and when there were sufficient communicants present; the minister was to distribute the bread and wine for good order, and with reverence, and no one else was to assist with the chalice except the elders or deacons; the tables were to be near the pulpit so that the mysteries could be better and more easily expounded near the tables; children and strangers had to present themselves for instruction [85].

The use of the *Forma ac ratio* in the compilation of the "Discipline" might well suggest that à Lasco's liturgy provided a basic directory for the worship of the French Stranger Churches.

The tentative conclusion which we draw from the problems outlined above is that à Lasco's *Forma ac ratio*, either in the Dutch version of Micron, or in French and Italian translation, formed the basic directory of worship in the Stranger Churches.

Church", in ed. J.H. BRATT, *The Heritage of John Calvin*, Grand Rapids, Michigan, 1973, pp. 112, 116 that à Lasco's French speaking congregation used *Liturgia Sacra*.
 [84] Ed. A. KUYPER, *Joannis a Lasco Opera*, 2 Vols., Amsterdam, 1866, Vol. 2, p. 50.
 [85] NICOLAS DE GALLARS, *Polite et Discipline Ecclesiastique observee en l'Eglise Des Estrangiers François A Londres*, 1561.

As in the case of Calvin's rites, the Morning service and the Eucharist are separate orders, but they belong together. The Morning "form and order of ordinary services on Sundays and Festivals in the Churches of Foreigners in London" according to the *Forma ac ratio* was as follows [86]:

> Exhortation to Prayer.
> Prayer before the Sermon.
> Lord's Prayer.
> Psalm.
> Bible Lection.
> Sermon.
> Prayer after the Sermon, that the word may be inscribed in our hearts.
> Decalogue (Exodus 20).
> Admonition to confession.
> Confession.
> Absolution.
> Apostles' Creed.
> General Prayer for the Church and World.
> Lord's Prayer.
> Psalm.
> Commendation of the Poor and Aaronic Blessing.

The absolution included the binding of the sins of the unrepentant. The general prayer contained the following:

> a) That God who has delivered us from ignorance and from Roman Idolatry, might fortify us and arm us with the Holy Spirit.
> b) For the universal church; for true instruction, and deliverance from all false Pastors and teachers; for the edification of the Church.
> c) For the churches in England; for Edward VI.
> d) For the Royal family, Magistrates and the Parliament.
> e) For the whole Kingdom of England.
> f) For the City of London.
> g) For the Foreign Churches in England.
> h) For all Kings, rulers, magistrates, who are oppressed by antichristian tyranny.
> i) For all brothers who are dispersed and oppressed for their faith.
> j) For the members of the Church who are in sickness, affliction and poverty.
> k) Provision for free prayer — particular present needs.

The composition of this service is extremely interesting. It is clear that Poullain's *Liturgia Sacra*, or the use of Strasbourg, has had a marked influen-

---

[86] Latin text, ed. A. KUYPER, *Joannis a Lasco Opera*, Vol. 2. English text David G. Lane, Text B in this volume, pp. 157-175.

ce upon the structure of the *Forma ac ratio* here. Nevertheless, à Lasco did not simply adopt *Liturgia Sacra* which would have been the easiest course open to him. The reason — apart from the Polish reformer's own ability — may well be connected with the fact that à Lasco had learnt protestantism from Oecolampadius and Zwingli, and many of the Dutch speaking Walloons had been under the influence of Basle and Zurich rather than of Strasbourg and Geneva. In a dispute with the Anabaptist Menno, à Lasco had sided with Zwingli rather than Calvin, and he spoke of Zwingli and Bullinger as "our fathers". It is significant that the Church at Austin Friars practiced "Prophecyings" — the whole community had a chance to interpret Scripture — a practice which was imported from Zurich. Zurich seems to have been the source of much of à Lasco's theology, and of his liturgical thought; the Decalogue, Creed and Lord's Prayer feature prominently in the *Forma ac ratio*, these being prominent features also in the *Pronaus* - based liturgies of Zurich and Basle.

This "Zwinglian" influence is born out by the structure of à Lasco's Morning service. The exhortation to prayer, the prayer before the sermon with the Lord's Prayer recall Poullain's service, but there is a clear parallel here with the services of Zwingli and Farel which begin with a bidding prayer and Lord's Prayer before the sermon [87].

The Decalogue was of course also found in *Liturgia Sacra*, but there it came at the beginning with a confession before the sermon, and was to be sung. In *Forma ac ratio* it came after the sermon, was to be read by the minister, and led into the confessio, absolution, Creed and intercessions — precisely the same sequence as in Farel's *La Maniere et fasson*; the confession and absolution also came after the sermon in Zwingli and Oecolampadius. The sequence Creed, intercessions and Lord's Prayer, had a precedent in Oecolampadius, and the intercessions, although corresponding to the Long Prayer of Bucer/Calvin/Poullain, also recall the bidding prayers of Zwingli and Farel.

Finally, the blessing appears to be a combination of Oecolampadius's commendation of the poor with the Aaronic blessing as used by Bucer/Calvin/Poullain.

We have previously suggested that Bucer's Antecommunion was the Mass judged by and reformed from the standpoint of the acceptable features of the *Pronaus* [88]; perhaps this could be expressed in mathematical symbol as Mass/*Pronaus*. In the *Forma ac ratio*, à Lasco seems to have had in mind the Pronaus-based services of Basle and Zurich, to which he has added elements from Poullain's *Liturgia Sacra*, which via Calvin came from Bucer. We might

---

[87] For text of Zwingli, Farel and Oecolampadius, BARD THOMPSON, *op. cit.*
[88] Above, Chapter 3.

thus represent *Forma ac ratio* as (*Pronaus*-based service) + (Mass/*Pronaus*); the conclusion must be that *Pronaus* is a primary factor in this liturgy.

The order for the Lord's Supper followed the general prayer of the Morning service. It illustrates a blending of à Lasco's own ideas with the order in Poullain's *Liturgia Sacra*, although according to the study of Anneliese Sprengler-Ruppenthal, the 1535 Lutheran rite of East Friesland which was in use when à Lasco became Superintendent there, must also be taken into account [89].

> Public reminder of those who are excluded.
> Prayer (from the pulpit), that we may testify publicly the communion in the Body and Blood of Christ, and that we may be worthy.
> Words of Institution.
> Exhortation about worthiness, including the "Reformed *Sursum corda*".
> * 1 Cor. 5:7-8 (from the table).
> Fraction and delivery: The bread which we break is a sharing in the Body of Christ.
> Take, eat and remember, that the body of our Lord Jesus Christ was for us given up to death on the beam of the cross for the remission of all our sins.
> The cup of blessing which we bless is a sharing in the blood of Christ. Take, drink and remember that the blood of our Lord Jesus Christ was for us poured out on the beam of the cross for the remission of all our sins.
> During the administration one of the ministers may read John 6, or 13, 14 or 15.
> * Words of Assurance: Be sure and do not doubt, all of you who have participated in this Lord's Supper and meditated on his divine Mystery, that you have a sure and health-giving sharing with him in his body and blood to eternal life. Amen.
> * Exhortation on the fruits of communion.
> Thanksgiving.
> * Admonition.
> Psalm.
> Blessing.

À Lasco's order for the Eucharist is much closer to the corresponding rite in *Liturgia Sacra* than is his Morning service. If the structures of the two liturgies are compared, it will be seen that the basic outline of the *Forma ac ratio*

---

[89] ANNELIESE SPRENGLER-RUPPENTHAL, *Mysterium und Riterr nach der Londoner Kirchenordnung der Niederländer*, Köln, 1967. A Lasco's own statement that in the *Forma ac Ratio* he had in mind the liturgies of Geneva and Strasburg (*Opera*, Vol. 2., p. 50) would seem to suggest that the 1535 Lutheran rite was not a prime source for his liturgy. For the 1535 rite, E. SEHLING, *Die evangelischen Kirchenordnungen des XVI Jahrhunderts*, Niedersachsen: II.1. Tübingen, 1963, pp. 373-397; the Lord's Supper, pp. 376-380.

is that of Poullain to which has been added those items which we have marked by an asterisk. Sprengler-Ruppenthal draws attention to the exhortation about worthiness in the 1535 East Friesan rite, suggesting some influence [90]. However, as regards position, in the Lutheran rite the exhortation came before the Lord's Prayer and Words of Institution (being based upon Luther's *Deutsche Messe*, 1526), whereas à Lasco followed Calvin and Poullain in their sequence of Words of Institution followed by an exhortation. Since à Lasco's brief exhortation includes the "Reformed *Sursum corda*", it seems unnecessary to place too much weight on the 1535 rite and East Friesan usage.

Despite a similarity in structure to Poullain's rite there is an unmistakable difference in theological emphasis. Poullain's rite, being almost identical to Calvin's Strasbourg rite, implied that the bread and wine were not empty signs, but by eating and drinking the communicant received by faith and the Holy Spirit, the substance of the body and blood of Christ. Thus Poullain reproduces the words of Calvin's Eucharistic Prayer:

> *c'est qu'en certaine Foy, nous recevions son corps et son sang: voir luy entierement:*

This was also implied in the words of administration:

> The bread which we break is the communion of the body of Christ.
> The cup which we bless is the communion of the blood of Christ [91].

In Poullain's later Latin editions of 1554 and 1555, perhaps in turn influenced by à Lasco, the words were extended:

> 1554: *accipe, manduca, memor Christi corpus pro te fractum in remissionem peccatorum tuorum.*
> *accipe, bibe, memor Christum sanguinem suum pro te profudisse in remissionem peccatorum tuorum.*
> 1555: *Accipite Comedite, memores corpus Christi pro vobis esse fractum in remissionem peccatorum.*
> *qui pro vobis est fusus in remissionem peccatorum.*

All the words imply that there is some connection between the reception of the bread and wine and the body and blood of Christ.

We have already mentioned the Zurich influence upon à Lasco. Basil

---

[90] A. SPRENGLER-RUPPENTHAL, *op. cit.*, pp. 146-148.
[91] Panis quem frangimus, communicatio est corporis Christi.
Calix cui benedicimus, communicatio est sanguinis Christi.
Le pain que nous rompons est la communication du corps de Christ.
Le hanap au quel nous benissons, est la communication du corps de CHRIST.

Hall has drawn attention to the denial by à Lasco that he obtained his Eucharistic doctrine from either Karlstadt or Zwingli, though the Polish reformer cited in support of his own views Oecolampadius, Bullinger and Vadian, all of whom may be termed "Zwinglian" rather than Calvinist [92]. Although differing on some points from Zwingli, à Lasco's teaching on the Eucharist shows clear signs of this influence. In his *Epistola ad amicum quendam*, 1544, à Lasco wrote:

> And we call the symbols of the Supper «sphragidas» with Paul, i.e. seals of that very communion, which, while we receive them according to the Lord's institution, bring before our eyes in a mystery that same communion and renew it in our minds, and seal us wholly in certain and undoubted faith in it, by the operation of the holy Spirit, although we place in them no physical or real inclusion of the body and blood of Christ ... [93].

The main difference between à Lasco and Zwingli was on the interpretation of the Words of Institution; the words "Do this" à Lasco took to refer to the whole action of the Supper — breaking, partaking, drinking and giving thanks [94]. Nevertheless, C. H. Smyth's judgment that à Lasco may be reckoned as a Zwinglian from the year 1545 seems a fair one [95]. Certainly in the Eucharistic liturgy of the *Forma ac ratio*, a Zwinglian conception that the Supper was a fellowship meal by means of which the faithful were able to remember the benefits of the atonement, was prominent.

The opening prayer was hardly "Eucharistic" [96]; it asked that we may celebrate the memory of Christ's sacred body given up to death for us, and publicly witness to our sharing with him in the same body and blood. The Holy Spirit was requested to enable the worshipper to recognise the great kindness of Christ, the atonement.

The same emphasis was to be found in the detailed rubrics for the fraction and administration. The followship meal was emphasised by the communicants sitting at the table, in successive sittings. The words for the fraction were taken from Poullain, but the emphasis was changed. Poullain's use of the words were as words of administration. In the *Forma ac ratio* à Lasco gave the folowing:

> Fraction: *Panis quem frangimus communio est corporis Christi. Po-*

---

[92] Basil Hall, *op. cit.*, pp. 27-28; *Joannis à Lasco Opera*, Vol. 1, p. 564.
[93] *Joannis à Lasco Opera*, Vol. 1, pp. 465-479; cited in C.H. Smyth, op. cit., p. 185.
[94] *Joannis à Lasco Opera*, Vol. 1, p. 565; Vol. 2, pp. 143-4.
[95] C.H. Smyth, *op. cit.*, p. 188.
[96] Though in fairness it should be noted that à Lasco, as with Bucer/Calvin/Poullain, postponed "thanksgiving" until after reception.

culum laudis, quo laudes celebramus, communio est sanguinis Christi.
Administration: *Accipite, edite et memineritis, corpus Domini nostri Iesu Christi pro nobis in mortem traditum esse in crucis patibulo ad remissionem omnium peccatorum nostrorum.*
Accipite, bibite et memineritis sanguinem Domini nostri Iesu Christi pro nobis fusum esse in crucis patibulo ad remissionem omnium peccatorum nostrorum.

Sprengler-Ruppenthal suggests that the words of administration of the *Forma ac ratio* were in fact those that were in use at Emden during à Lasco's superintendency; he retained the formulae he knew, but used Poullain's words to a new purpose, before the administration as a fraction [97]. The ultimate source of à Lasco's Emden words of administration, she suggests, is Bucer's Strasbourg formula of 1525, noting that one finds traces of Bucer in the early reformation in East Friesland [98]. Noting also the similarity to the words of the 1552 *Book of Common Prayer* she suggests the following hypothetical scheme of derivation [99]:

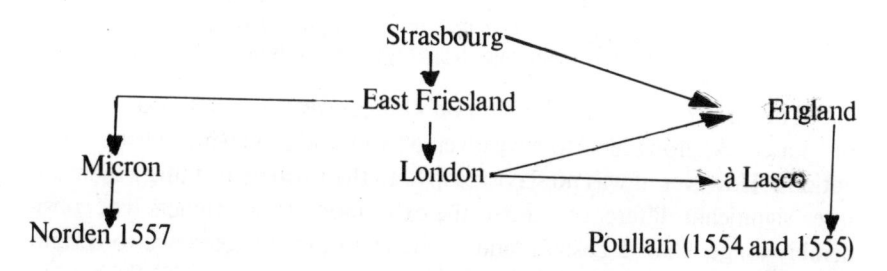

```
                    Strasbourg
                        ↓
         ┌─────── East Friesland ──────────┐
         ↓              ↓                   ↓
      Micron         London ←──────── à Lasco       England
         ↓                                           ↓
      Norden 1557                          Poullain (1554 and 1555)
```

However, whatever the ultimate source may have been — and Sprengler-Ruppenthal's suggestion is purely conjectural — the actual use of the words are of considerable significance. Sprengler-Ruppenthal notes that whereas in Poullain's version of 1 Cor. 10:16 the word *communicatio* is used — a favourite word of Calvin — à Lasco deliberately avoids this word in favour of *communio* [100]. It may be that whereas Poullain referred *communicatio* to a "communication" of the crucified and risen Lord's body and blood to the communicant through the reception of the bread and the wine, à Lasco took *corporis Christi* and *sanguinis Christi* to refer to the body of Christ, the Church, the bread and wine symbolising the *communio*, or fellowship of

---
[97] A. SPRENGLER-RUPPENTHAL, *op. cit.*, pp. 159-160.
[98] *Ibid.*, p. 161.
[99] *Ibid.*, pp. 162-165; we have simplified the diagram given on p. 165, omitting the later East Friesland and Dutch liturgies.
[100] *Ibid.*, pp. 160-161.

Christians at the Lord's table. In any case, they were carefully separated from the act of communion so as to give no suggestion that the bread and wine were in any sense the vehicles of Christ's body and blood. The words of administration resemble those found in the 1554 and 1555 editions of *Liturgia Sacra*, and it is not certain whether à Lasco influenced Poullain or *vica versa*. However, à Lasco kept the words quite separate from the words of 1 Cor. 10:16, and against Poullain, has the words "on the beam of the cross" (*in crucis patibulo*): the body of Christ would not be associated with the bread and wine, but rather the bread and wine were the means of remembering the death of Christ *on the cross*. They were a mental reminder of the atonement on Calvary.

The fellowship meal, though with an eschatological emphasis, was also to be found in the admonition after the communion:

> I hope too that in coming to this table you have all perceived with the eyes of your faith that blessed reclining at table in the kingdom of God with Abraham, Isaac and Jacob, and that in your trust in the righteousness, recompense and victory of Christ the Lord in the sharing of which we have now been pledged you are as sure of this as we have surely taken our places together at this table of the Lord.

The services in Micron's *Christian Ordinances* are very similar to those of à Lasco. Micron seems to have given a free translation with stylistic emendations. However, it was no slavish copy. In the Eucharistic liturgy there are three significant differences. First, the exhortation to worthiness was considerably longer than à Lasco's, and included an explicit reference to certain sins, reminiscent of Calvin's exhortation and excommunication. Second, in the words of administration Micron expanded them slightly, "Take, eat, remember *and believe* ...", though this made no difference to the Zwinglian theology. The other difference of significance was the thanksgiving prayer after the communion, which seems nearer to that of Calvin than of à Lasco. Sprengler-Ruppenthal suggests that à Lasco's thanksgiving reflects former East Friesan usage, and expresses the relationship thus [101]:

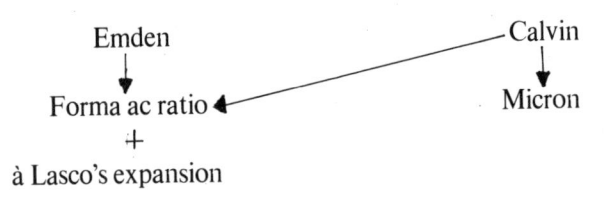

```
        Emden                              Calvin
          ↓                                  ↓
    Forma ac ratio ←                       Micron
          +
    à Lasco's expansion
```

---

[101] *Ibid.*, pp. 173-174.

Nevertheless, Micron's rite may be regarded simply as a version of à Lasco. The same applied also to the emendations made by Van Wingen [102].

Although we have considered in some detail the *Forma ac ratio*, it would be easy to over-estimate its importance and the extent of its influence on the English Puritans. it would be wrong, for example, to regard it as indicating a preference for a Zwinglian liturgy or theology [103]; furthermore, it has to be emphasised that the 1572 Bill came to nothing. Nevertheless, the significance of the appeal of the 1572 Bill is twofold. First, it illustrated that some Puritans were aware of the heritage of John à Lasco, and knew the liturgy of the Stranger Churches. But second, and of rather more significance perhaps, is the type of liturgy to which the Puritans were appealing; the liturgy of the Stranger Churches was in fact merely a directory of worship for the guidance of the minister. It provided a structure, but the minister was free to use his own prayers within the suggested structure.

3. Editions of the Genevan Service Book.

It is known that in 1567 the *Genevan Service Book* of 1556 was used by the congregation which met in the Plumber's Hall, London, and also by the Puritans who met in Goldsmith's House in 1568 [104]. Two attempts were made by the Puritans to authorise the use of revised editions of the *Genevan Service Book* of 1556. In 1584, Dr. Peter Turner attempted to present a Bill to Parliament which would allow its use, and a similar attempt was made in 1587 by Peter Wentworth and Anthony Cope [105]. As in the case of the Bill of 1572, the Queen's intervention meant that the Bills failed.

The two liturgies presented with the Bills of 1584 and 1587 were both entitled *A Booke of the Forme of Common Prayers, administration of the Sacraments: &c. agreeable to Gods Worde, and the use of the reformed churches*. They are known after their respective printers, the Waldegrave Book (1584), and the Middleburg Book (1586). The Waldegrave Book bears no date, but seems to have been printed by Robert Waldegrave, the printer of a great deal of Puritan literature, in 1584. Its authorship has been variously attributed to Cartwright, Dudley Fenner, Walter Travers, and Field and Wilcox. It is in fact merely a modified edition of the *Genevan Service Book*. The

---

[102] Van Wingen, for example, altered the wording of the administration. It made no difference to the structure of the litugy.

[103] E. BROOKS HOLIFIELD, *op. cit.*, p. 27ff. The English Puritans tended to see little difference between Zwingli and Calvin.

[104] *The true report of our Examination*, 1567, *PR*; A. PEEL, *The First Congregational Churches*, p. 11.

[105] Above, Chapter 2, p. 48.

same is true of the Middleburg Book, editions of which were printed in 1586, 1587 and 1602 by Richard Schilders of Middleburg, Zeeland. Schilders, it is worth noting for future reference, also printed the liturgy of the Dutch Reformed Church by Datheen.

A. The Waldegrave Book, 1584.

> *Morning Service.*
> (Reading Service).
> Our help be in the name of the Lord, who hath made both heaven and earth.
> Let us fall down before the majesty of Almighty God, humbly confessing our sins, and follow in your hearts the tenor of my Words.
> Confession.
> Psalm.
> Prayer extemporary for the assistance of God's Holy Spirit that the Word may be expounded faithfully.
> Lord's Prayer.
> Lection from Canonical Scripture.
> Sermon.
> A Prayer for the whole state of Christ's Church.
> (Two alternatives provided).
> Apostles' Creed.
> Decalogue.
> Lord's Prayer.
> Psalm.
> Aaronic blessing, or Grace.

The Morning service was prefaced by a rubric prescribing what has become known as the "Reader's Service". It provided for someone, appointed by the Eldership, to read chapters of canonical Scripture, singing psalms in between at discretion. W. D. Maxwell, noting that this became a feature of Scottish worship, has suggested that it was a Puritan form of Matins:

> All responses and versicles are omitted, the Psalms are sung in metre and the canticles dropped and the lectionary is discarded. But the New Testament and the Old Testament are read through consecutively, the Readings interspersed with Psalms. The Reader's Service looks very much indeed like a "purified" Matins [106].

The Call to worship, absent in the *Genevan Service Book*, was reintroduced from Calvin. The confession provided in Waldegrave was again Calvin's, the

---

[106] W.D. MAXWELL, *The Liturgical Portions*, p. 179.

1556 alternative based on Daniel 9 being omitted. The text of the confession differed in two places from that found in 1556:

> forasmuch as thou hast vouchsafed to offer pardon to all that repent, and seek it in the name of thy beloved Son Christ Jesus, and that by thy grace ...
>
> but also bring forth such fruits as may please thee, ...

The rubric after the confession was an expanded version of that of 1556, making more specific the content of the prayer of illumination, and including the Lord's Prayer. The "canonical Scripture" carefully excluded the Apocrypha.

The sermon was followed by "A Prayer for the whole State of Christ's Church", from the 1556 liturgy. The phrase "that Romyshe idoll, enemie to thy Christe" of the latter was rendered "the Antichrist of Rome", and the petition for the city of Geneva and its government was replaced by prayer for Queen Elizabeth and her government; "clamitie of bodie, or vexation of mynde" was rendered "grief of body, or unquietness of mind", and the portion of 1556 prayer for those in England under "Babylonicall bondage" was omitted, since no longer applicable. As an alternative, however, the Waldegrave Book gave Calvin's Long Prayer which was derived from Bucer's third Canon.

A significant variation was the provision for a third alternative Long Prayer after the Sermon, beginning "O God, almighty and heavenly Father, we acknowledge in our consciences", which also occurs in the Middleburg Book. In his edition of the Middleburg Morning service, Bard Thompson simply makes the following observation, referring to the original editors:

> They added still a third alternative version of the Great Prayer — a ponderous and penitential piece, with parts of Calvin's Great Prayer as an appendage [107].

In a note on the text Thompson commented:

> The editors of the Middleburg Liturgy likely supplied the third — a heavy, penitential piece, to which a substantial part of Calvin's prayer was to be appended [108].

But what was the source of this third alternative prayer? It was certainly not from the pen of the editors. It is in fact an English translation of the prayer after the sermon in the Dutch Reformed liturgy of Petrus Datheen. Many prominent Puritans, including Cartwright, spent some time in exile in the Ne-

---

[107] BARD THOMPSON, *op. cit.*, 315.
[108] *Ibid.*, pp. 340-341.

therlands, and were familiar with the Dutch liturgy. The inclusion of the Decalogue may have been suggested by the *Forma ac Ratio*.

> *The Manner of Administering the Lord's Supper.*
>
> Institution Narrative.
> Exhortation with excommunication.
> Eucharistic Prayer
> Fraction and delivery with words of Institution. Scripture reading during administration.
> Thanksgiving.
> Psalm 103, or a similar type of psalm.
> Blessing.
> Note to the reader.

The Eucharistic liturgy proper of Waldegrave was essentially that of 1556, and was to follow on from the Morning service. As in the case of the Morning service, there are some variations of differing significance.

In the exhortation, "a singular medicine" was rendered "an excellent medicine", and the phrase "the true eatinge of his fleshe and drinkinge of his bloud" was altered to "the true and spiritual eating of his flesh and drinking of his blood".

The rubric after the Exhortation was considerably altered:

Waldegrave.	*1556.*
The exhortation ended, the Minister giveth thanks, either in these words followwing, or like in effect.	The exhortation ended, the minister commeth doune from the pulpit, and sitteth at the Table euery man and woman in likewise takinge their place as occasion best serueth, then he taketh bread and geueth thankes, either in these woordes followinge, or like in effect.

In Waldegrave the minister was to offer the Eucharistic Prayer in the pulpit, so that both the Institution Narrative and the Eucharistic Prayer could hardly be understood as consecrating the bread and wine in a localised sense; the Institution was addressed to the congregation, and the prayer to God; neither was spoken in association with the elements. It was only after the Eucharistic Prayer, that of 1556, that the minister came to the table, broke the bread and delivered it to the people with the words of delivery of Christ adapted for the congregation. Here was a strict interpretation of the action of the Eucharist — giving thanks, taking and giving, and the words of Institution as words of administration.

In the light of this, it is of little surprise that the rubric concerning the fraction and administration was rather different from that of 1556:

Waldegrave	1556
This done, the Minister, coming to the table (and the table being furnished), breaketh the bread, and delivereth it to the people, saying "Take and eat; this bread is the body of Christ that was broken for us"; who distribute and divide the same among themselves, according to our Saviour Christ's commandment. Likewise he giveth the cup, saying, "Drink ye all of this; this cup is the New Testament in the blood of Christ, which was shed for the sins of many: do this in remembrance of me".	This done, the Minister breaketh the breade and delyuereth it to the people, who distribute and deuide the same amongst theim selues, accordinge to our sauior Christes comandment, and in likewise geueth the cuppe.

Dr. Stephen Mayor is correct to point out that the change in the place of the recitation of the Eucharistic Prayer has necessitated the change in this rubric [109]. However, Mayor has failed to point out that the new rubric had the effect of heightening the fraction, for it was here that the action regarding the elements was concentrated. This may well have been deliberate policy on the part of the editors.

Already in Calvin's thought we find a stress on the words "broken" and "shed" in the Institution:

> We ought carefully to observe that the chief and almost the whole energy of the sacrament consists in these words, It is broken for you: It is shed for you. It would not be of much importance to us that the body and blood of the Lord are now distributed, had they not once been set forth for our redemption and salvation. Wherefore they are represented under bead and wine [110].

But Calvin himself made no textual liturgical use of the fraction. However, Thomas Cartwright, who may have been involved with the Waldegrave Book, certainly grasped the symbolism that could be associated with the fraction and delivery; commenting upon the Institution he wrote:

> When he had prayed thus, he broke the bread which he held in his hand (it was easier to break it than to cut it), with this intention, not

---

[109] S. MAYOR, op. cit., p. 11.
[110] *Institutes*, 4:17:3.

only to represent before their eyes the destruction of his most holy body, but also to distribute it when broken amongst them: after breaking it, he gave it to his disciples saying: This bread represents for you the whole man in me, body and soul together; the breaking of it is unto you my destruction, the distribution of it the communion I have with you: receive this bread in your hand and eat: it is my body in very faith. As often as you do this, keep it in your mind as a remembrance of my love for you and of my bitter death on the cross [111].

The same concern is found in Dudley Fenner:

In the first part the breaking of the bread commeth to be considered, which is so playnelie set forth as a worke, and hath relation to the tormentes of Christ on the crosse for us: for in that bread is broken, that it may be eaten it doeth liuelie set before us, that Christwas tormented for us and for our nourishment and as the Apostle saith from Christ, *my bodie* which was broken for you, although it be true that not a bone of Christ was broke, and so breaking is not here taken properlie, but by a similitude, for weeping, tormenting, &c. as he was pearced, crucified, and on the crosse made curse for us, & as the Prophet sayeth, *He was wounded for our transgressions, he was broken for our infirmities*: the chastisement of our peace was uppon him, and with his stripes we are healed, Esai 53.5. So then this is to be done playnlie in the sight of all, and all ought to give diligent heede and waightie consideration with the meditation of these thinges with us [112].

A similar concern for the symbolism of the fraction is to be found in another Puritan theologian, William Perkins. Observing that the minister's action in the Eucharist is four-fold — taking, blessing, breaking and distribution — Perkins commented:

The third, is the breaking of the bread, and pouring out of the wine; this doth seale the passion of Christ, by which he, verily upon the crosse was, both in soule and body, bruised for our transgressions [113].

In 1592, Lancelot Andrewes, later Bishop of Winchester, and a "Laudian" churchman, complained that the attention given to the fraction by the Puri-

---

[111] THOMAS CARTWRIGHT, *Harmonia Evangelica Commentario, Analytico, Metaphrastico, Practico*, Amsterdam, 1647, p. 891.
[112] DUDLEY FENNER, *The Whole doctrine of the Sacramentes, plainlie and fullie set downe and declared out of the word of God*, Middleburg, 1588, n.p.
[113] W. PERKINS, *A Golden Chaine: or, The Description of Theologie. Of the Lord's Supper*, in *The Works of William Perkins*, 3 Vols, 1626-31, Vol. 1, p. 75.

tans was transforming the eucharist into little more than an occasion for evoking mental images of the crucifixion, a trend wich he condemned as the "worshipping of imaginations" [114]. It could well be that the rubric was designed to bring out this symbolism of the fraction. It would certainly be well supported by the rubric (of 1556) which followed it:

> During the which time, some place of the Scriptures is read, which doth lively set forth the death of Christ, to the intent that ... our hearts and minds also may be fully fixed in the contemplation of the Lord's death, which is by this holy Sacrament represented.

The remainder of the liturgy was as in the 1556 *Genevan Service Book*

B. The Middleburg Book.

The Middleburg Book, editions of which appeared in 1586, 1587 and 1602, was a slightly revised edition of the Waldegrave Book. In the Morning service, the overall structure remained identical, except that the Apostles' Creed, Decalogue, and the Lord's Prayer after the Long Prayer were omitted. Only one change seems to be of any significance. Part of the Prayer for the Whole State of Christ's Church which prayed for the Queen was considerably expanded:

> especiallie, o Lorde, according to our bounded duetie, wee beseeche thee to maintaine and increase the prosperous estate of our moste noble Queene ELIZABETH: Who as thou has placed ouer vs in thy great mercie, & preserued her by thy mightie power: so wee beseeche thee, o Lorde, by the same mercie, to multiplie on her the excellent giftes of the holy Spirite: And by the same power as thou hast alvvayes preserued her, so to preserue her still. And as thou hast discouered the vnnaturall treasons, and vvicked practises, so to diascouer them still: that as for all other thy singular graces, so also for this great mercy, both Prince and people may reioyce & magnifie thy great Name. Also we pray thee for her Maiesties right Honorable Coucell, that thy good Spirite may furnishe euerie one of them with wisedome and strength, and other excellent giftes, fitte for their callinge. Furthermore, we pray thee for all other Magistrates, and for the whole Realme, that all men in their calling may be founde faithfull in seeking to set foorth thy glorie, & to procure the godlie peace and prosperitie of all the lande: And lette thy fatherlie fauour ... (as Waldegrave).

---

[114] LANCELOT ANDREWES, *Ninety-Six Sermons*, 5 Vols, Oxford, 1841-43, Vol. 5, p. 67.

This would appear to be a subtle declaration of loyalty, for it was obvious that the Queen was angered at attempts to remove the enacted *Book of Common Prayer*. The reference to "unnatural treasons" was in all probability an allusion to the Babington Plot of 1586, an attempt by certain Roman Catholics to assassinate Elizabeth and bring Mary Queen of Scots to the throne. The Puritans were never slow to improve their image by exploiting the political situation.

In "The Manner of Administering the Lord's Supper", the order is that of Waldegrave, with the exception of a few verbal alterations, and the recasting of one paragraph in the exhortation. Thus, for example, "Pastor" is used as an alternative for "Minister"; where the Waldegrave Book states the danger of unworthy reception as being "great", Middleburg has "exceeding great". Again, Middleburg adds after "the Lord his body" the clause "which is offered in the Sacrament to the worthy receiver".

The one alteration of significance is the paragraph in the exhortation concerning excommunication or the fencing of the table. The Waldegrave Book followed 1556, but in Middleburg it was expanded, and, to use Mayor's words, "becomes more severe" [115]. Mayor adds, "This was not at all the tone of Calvin's order" [116].

If the corresponding sections of Calvin and 1556 are compared, it will be seen that Mayor's second statement is incorrect; Calvin's excommunication is lenghtier and more severe than that of the *Genevan Service Book*. However, it is not Calvin who provides the source for the Middleburg paragraph, but it is the liturgy of Datheen [117].

Middleburg	*Datheen*
Therefore, if anie of you bee ignoraunt of GOD, a denier of the faith, an hereticke or scismatike an Idolatour, a worshipper of Angells, Saintes, or anie other creatures, a vvitch, sorcerour, southsayer, of suche as haue anie truste or confidence in them, a mainteyner of Images or mannes inuentions in the seruice of GOD, a neglecter, contemner, hinderer or slaunderer of God, his holye Worde, Sacramentes, and Discipline, a periured person, a prophaner of the Lords Sabboth: disobedient to parents, Magistrates, Mi-	Wherefore wee according to the commandement of Christ and the Apostle Paul, admonish all those, who are defiled with these following crimes, to keepe themselves from the Table of the Lord, and do declare unto them that they have no parte in the Kingdome of Christ: All Idolaters, all who invocate saints deceased, and angels, and other creatures, all who worship Images, all enchanters, diviners, charmers, and those who give credit to such enchantements. All despisers of God and his Worde, and his holy Sacra-

---

[115] MAYOR, *op. cit.*, p. 13.
[116] *Ibid.*
[117] Here we give a translation of 1732; the Dutch text is given in an appendix.

nisters, and other Superiours, or bee a murderer, or in malice and enuie, or bee mercylesse and cruell, or an oppressour, Vsurer, or fornicatour, adulterour, and incestuous person, buggerer, or bee a theefe, a false dealer in bargayninge, or anie the like matter: a slaunderour, backebyter, or false witnesse bearer, or in anie other grieuous crime, lament & bewayle your sinnes and iniquities, and presume not to come to this holie Table, least the Deuill enter into you, as hee entred into Iudas, and fill you full of all iniquities, and bringe you to destruction, both of bodie and soule.

ments: all blasphemers, all those who are given to make strife, sedition and mutiny in Church and commonwealth: all perjured persons, all disobedient to Parents or Magistrates, all murderers, contentious persons, who live in hatred and envy against their neighbour; all adulterers, whoremongers, drunkards, thieves, usurers, gamesters, coveteous and all who live a scandalous life. All these, so long as they continue in such sins, are to abstain from this meat (which Christ hath ordained only for the faithfull) lest their judgement and condemnation be made the heavier and encreased.

The editors of Middleburg seem to have filled out the paragraph of 1556 and Waldegrave with words from the Dutch liturgy, adding also a few words of their own for good measure.

The remainder of the rite follows Waldegrave. At the fraction and delivery the words are slighty altered:

> Take & eate, this bread is the body of Christ that was broken for us, Doo this in remembrance of him.
>
> Drinke ye all of this: This Cuppe is the newe Testament in the bloud of Christ, which was shedde for the sinnes of manie: Doo this in the remembrance of him.

In retrospect, the Puritans of the sixteenth and early seventeenth centuries provide rather a liturgical disappointment. The appeal to the Word of God produced only fickle arguments over the rubrics and phraseology of the *Book of Common Prayer* Eucharistic liturgy, resulting only in minor unofficial emendations, or the borrowing of someone else's liturgy, either the *Genevan Service Book*, or à Lasco's directory for worship, and pieces of Datheen's Dutch liturgy. The Puritans failed to produce an original alternative to the enacted rite. We may note that in appealing to the Stranger Churches and by issuing emended editions of the *Genevan Service Book*, the Puritans were perpetuating the liturgical division found in Calvin's rite, and maintained by à Lasco, which separated Word and Sacrament.

APPENDIX

Petrus Datheen's *Forme om het heylighe Avendtmael te houden. Part of the Exhortation.* Edition of 1611.

Daero wy oor nae den bevele Christi en des apost. Pauli, alle die hen met dese nabolgede lasteren besmet weten, vermanen va de tafel des heeren hen te onthouden, en vercondighen hen datse gee deel in Kijcke Christi hebbe. Als daer zijn alle afgodendienaers, alle die verstorvon heyligen, Engelen, oft andere Creaturen aenroepen. Alle die den Beelde eere aen doen, alle tooveraers en waerseggers, die vee ofte menschen, mitgaders ander dingen segenen, en die suleke segeninge geloove geve: alle verachters Gods, sijn Woorts, on dor H. Sacramenten: alle Gods lasteraers, alle die tweedratht, secte, en muyterie, in kercken, en wereltlicken Regimenten begeeren aen te richten: alle Mayneedighe: alle die haren ouderen en Overheyden ongehoorfaem zijn: alle Dootslagers, kijvers, en die in haet en nijt tegen hare nasten leven alle Echtbrekers, Koereerders, Dronckaertes, Diewen, Woeckeraers, Roovers, Tuysschers, Gierigaers, ende alle de gene die een ergerlick leven leyden. Dese allesoo lange sy in sulcken sonden blijven, sullen hen deser spijse (welcke Christus alleen sijnen geloovigen verordineert heeft) onthouden, op dathaer gherichte ende verdoemenisse niet dies te swarer werde.

CHAPTER 5

THE EUCHARISTIC LITURGY AMONG THE SEPARATISTS

The material available to us concerning the liturgical forms used by the Separatists is sparse. In the first place, their writings were mainly concerned with ecclesiology: their prime concern was the establishment and ordering of the Church in terms of covenanted believers, and their writings were mainly of a polemical nature, condemning the parochial system of the Church of England, and justifying from Scripture their own gathered congregational system. Again, as outlined above [1], they objected strongly to all forms of written prayer, and so were hardly likely to record the prayers uttered "in the Spirit" in their worship. The evidence and material is almost as fragmentary and scarce as that for the worship of the pre-Nicene Church, and indeed in many ways the Separatists found themselves in a similar position to the Church of those early years; being under the constant threat of arrest and imprisonment, they were hardly willing to divulge intimate information concerning their meetings. The material available to us consists of brief references in the writings of the Separatist leaders, and the descriptions found in some of the depositions made before ecclesiastical courts.

The Puritans demonstrated their dislike of the Prayer Book rites by a detailed analysis of the services; in contrast, since the Prayer Book was a written liturgy, the Separatists never subjected it to an analysis, for its very nature disqualified it from serious consideration. There are, however, a few passing references to it in the writings of the Separatist leaders.

Henry Barrow's contempt for the communion service of the Prayer Book is shown in a disapproving summary:

> Likewise in their sacrament of the Supper, their frivolous leitourgie stinting the priest when and how to stand at the north end of the table, what and when to saye and praye, when to kneele, when to tourne, when to glory God, etc. Also the vayne dialogue betwixt the priest, clarcke, and people. Their altering the wordes of Christ's institution, and delivering it after a popish maner. *The bodie of our Lord Jesus Christ, which was given for thee, preserve this thei bodie and soule unto everlasting life, etc.* and that kneeling, that they

---

[1] See Chapter 1.

might adore the bread, or at least retaine a taste of their former superstition in tyme of high poperie, etc [2].

As in the case of the Puritans, the Separatists detested the liturgical calendar:

> ... see how they abuse it to more accursed idolatry and abhominacion, as to their idol feastes both Jewish and popish, their fastes of all sortes, their holy daies [3].

> Well, and besides that you have receaved and derived these fastes from the church of Rome, let your special collects, upon your sainctes' Eaves, your bitter commination and special communion upon your Ash Wednesday, with your epistle out of Joel 2:12. *Tourne you unto me with all your heartes, with fasting, weeping, mourning, etc.,* your gospell out of Mathew 6:16: *When you fast be not sad as the hipocrites. etc.* Likewise your Collect and Gospell upon the first Sundaye of your Lent, making mention of Christ's forty dayes fast in the wildernes, desiring that your forty dayes fast may subdue the flesh, etc. Let this your apish, or rather popish counterfeighting, let your special communions in your passion weeke, your Maunday Thurs-daye, your Good Friday, etc., shewe how popishlie you keepe these your fastes [4].

Similarly, the Separatists disliked Saints' Days:

> Furder what wil you then say to your celebration of deade sainctes, keeping one solemne daye unto them all at once? And againe severallie to John Baptist, and to the apostles as they are allotted in their pageant. George also your St. patron must not be forgotten. A daye also is kept to the martyre Stephen, an other daye to the Innocents, with their daye, eave, fast, feast, cessation, special worship to everie one particularlie. What warrant can you shew for this out of the Bible? The patriarckes, prophets, godly kings were never so celebrated: neither have you anie commandment or president in all the Newe Testament thus to celebrate them. Paule and Peter whilest they were alive desired to be remembered and prayed for of the church, but never required anie such dutie being deade [5].

The Prayer Book lections for the Epistle and Gospel were also condemned:

---

[2] H. BARROW, *A Plaine Refutation*, in ed. LELAND H. CARLSON, *The Writings of Henry Barrow 1590-1591*, 1966, p. 85. Cf. JOHN GREENWOOD, *A Collection of Certaine Sclaunderous Articles*, in ed. LELAND H. CARLSON, *The Writings of John Greenwood 1587-1590*, 1962, pp. 167-8.

[3] BARROW, *A Brief Discoverie of the False Church*, in ed. CARLSON, *The Writings of Henry Barrow 1587-1590*, p. 383. Cf. GREENWOOD, *op. cit.*, p. 167; ROBERT BROWNE, *A Treatise of reformation without tarrying for anie*, ed. CARLSON and A. PEEL, *The Writings of Robert Harrison and Robert Browne*, 1953, p. 168.

[4] BARROW, *A Plaine Refutation*, in *op. cit.*, p. 69.

[5] *Ibid.*, pp. 72-73.

> I would moreover know of them, where they learned to hew out and dismember the Scriptures in this manner; to pluck them from the context with such violence, without al sense, order, or cause; ... I would also know of them, how their peeces of the prophecies became epistles? And where they learned to make thus many pistles and gospels [6]?

Henry Barrow also attacked the recitation of the Creed, complaining of

> their forged patcherie commonly caled the Apostles' Creed or symbole, Athanasius' Creed, the Nicene Creed, sometimes sayde in prose, sometimes songe in meter on their festivals [7]:

Barrow seems to have taken a particular dislike to the Preface in the communion service which mentioned angels and archangels. The latter are mentioned in Scripture twice only, I Thess. 4:16 and Jude 1:9. Apparently Barrow felt that this was not sufficient to warrant their mention at the communion service; writing in reply to the attack of George Gifford [8], he wrote:

> Nowe to help yout memorie a little furder, we woulde desire you to consider better of that glorious antheame you singe or saye in your publique communion, wherin "with angells and archangells and al the companie of heaven you laude and magnifie", etc. Wherin we will not demaunde of you howe, whilest you remaine in the flesh, you can have such familiar conversation with those heavenlie souldiours and elect spirits of the faithfull deceased, that you together with them can praise and laude God. Nether wil we presse you with the papistical and curious speculations in making digrees of angells, arch-angels, etc. But we would here knowe of you howe manie arch-angells you reade of and finde in the Scriptures, and whether you knowe anie more heades of angells than Christ himself. Except peradventure your church have some especial prerogative from the apostatical sea, to make arch-bisshops and arch-angells [9].

His reply to Gifford's rejoinder was more concerned with its liturgical origin:

> I hope you are not ignorant that the papists from whom you fet-

---

[6] BARROW, *A Brief Discoverie of the False Church*, in *op. cit.*, pp. 382-383; Cf. *A PLaine Refutation*, in *op. cit.*, p. 98; GREENWOOD, *A Collection of certaine sclaunderous articles*, in *op. cit.*, p. 167.
[7] BARROW, *A Brief Discoverie of the False Church*, in *op. cit.*, p. 382.
[8] George Gifford, Vicar of Maldon in Essex, attacked Barrow in *A Short Treatise against the Donatists of England, Whome We Call Brownists, 1590*, (print of MS of 1587/88) and *A Short Reply unto the Last Printed Books of Henry Barrow and John Greenwood, the cheafe Ringleaders of our Donatists in England, 1591*, in which he defended the *Book of Common Prayer*.
[9] BARROW, *A Plaine Refutation*, in *op. cit.*, pp. 91-92.

ched this glorious antheme (which thei used at their high masse and you at your solemn communion upon your high feasts) thought and taught that at that instant in that parte of their masse the angels and all the company of heaven, the spirits of men disceased, did worship and laude God with them. If you thincke not so and would not have others so to thincke, whie use you this popish anth in the same wordes, order, and (so my wordz be not to far inforced) action that thei do [10]?

It was almost certainly the *Book of Common Prayer* communion service which Browne described as "The Signe made mockerie and trifle":

> They take breade or a wafer cake and inchaunte it by reading a grace ouer it, and a number of other prayers: they reade it to be the bodye of Christ, which is but an Idole in stead therof, and they feede on it by their superstition, and growe into one wicked communion: so the priest doth eate of it himselfe, and carieth it rounde about vnto them, with a vayne babling ouer euery one, which receyue and eate it kneeling downe before him.
>
> Likewise also they take the cuppe, and inchaunte it, by reading a grace, or other prayers ouer it: then they reade it or by the booke pronounce it to be the bloud of Christ, which is but an Idole in steade thereof. And so he and they drinking it, doe euen drinke their iniquitie, and feede thereon.
>
> So are they imbouldned and further strengthned in their sinne [11].

The communion rite of the Prayer Book was superstitious and idolatrous; but wheras the Puritans turned to the liturgies of the Reformed Churches, the Separatist refused any written form of worship.

The Brownists.

According to *The Brownists Synagogue*, the normal worship of the congregation consisted of prayer, lasting half an hour and including a petition that God would be pleased to turn the hearts of those who had come to laugh and scoff. A sermon then followed, lasting and hour, followed by a commentary or explanation of the sermon by another member of the congregation [12]. More information is provided by Browne himself concerning his congrega-

---

[10] BARROW, *Barrow's Final Answer to Gifford*, in ed. LELAND H. CARLSON, *The Writings of John Greenwood and Henry Barrow 1591-1593*, London, 1970, pp. 155-156.

[11] BROWNE, *A Booke which sheweth the life and manners of all true Christians*, in op. cit., p. 284.

[12] *The Brownists Synagogue*, 1641, p. 5 f.

tion at Middleburg. The service included prayer, thanksgiving, reading of scripture, exhortation and edifying, with provision for discussion on subjects which were "doubtful & hard" [13].

Browne also provided directions for the celebration of the Eucharist. There must be adequate preparation beforehand:

> There must be a separation fro those which are none of the church, or be vnmeete to receaue, that the worthie may be onely receaued.
> All open offences and faultings must be redressed.
> All must proue and examine them selues, that their consciences be cleare by faith and repentance, before they receaue [14].

For the Eucharist to be rightly administered, the Word must be preached and the sign or sacrament rightly applied. Browne explained:

> By preaching the worde of communion we vnderstande not the blinde reading, or fruitlesse pratlinge therof at randome, but a teaching by lawful messengers, of the right vsing of the bodie and blood of Christ in one holie communion, and that with power [15].

This was qualified further:

> The death and tormentes of Christ, by breaking his bodie and sheading his bloud for our sinnes, must be shewed by the lawful preacher.
> Also he must shewe the spirituall vse of the bodie & bloud of Christ Iesus, by a spirituall feeding thereon, and growing into it, by one holie communion.
> Also our thankefulnes, and further profiting in godlines vnto life everlasting [16].

Then came the Eucharistic action:

> The preacher must take breade and blesse and geue thankes, and the must he breake it and pronunce it to be the body of Christ, which was broken for the, that by fayth they might feede thereon spirituallie & growe into one spiritual bodie of Christ, and so he eating therof himselfe, must bidd them take and eate it among them, & feede on Christ in their consciences.
> Likewise also must he take the cuppe and blesse and geue thankes,

---

[13] BROWNE, *A True and Short Declaration*, in *op. cit.*, p. 422.
[14] BROWNE, *A Booke which sheweth the life and manners*, in *op. cit.*, p. 280.
[15] *Ibid.*, p. 281.
[16] *Ibid.*, p. 282.

and so pronounce it to be the bloud of Christ in the newe Testament, which was shedd for remission of sinnes, that by faythe we might drinke it spirituallie, and so be ourished in one spirituall bodie of Christ, all sinne being clensed away, and then he drinking thereof himselfe must bydd them drinke thereof likewise and diuide it amog them, and feede on Christe in their consciences.
Then must they all giue thankes praying for their further profiting in godlines & vowing their obedience [17].

The Barrowists.

The little information we have describing Barrowist worship gives a picture not too dissimilar from that of the Brownists. We learn that meetings took place in private houses, or in some secluded place such as Islington woods [18]. From a certain Clement Gamble we learn that in summer they met in fields outside London, and sat down on a bank and "divers of them expound out of the Bible so long as they are there assembled" [19]. In winter they met in a house for prayer and exposition [20]. After a meal they made a collection to pay the expenses, and any that remained was taken to their members who were in prison [21]. One John Dove described their prayer thus:

> In there praier one speketh and the rest doe grone, or sob, or sigh, as if they wold wringe out teares, but saie not after hime that praieth, there praier is extemporall [22].

From a certain William Clark we learn that

> they prayed and exercised the word of God, and ther George Johnson used the exhortacon and prayer [23].

Only when Francis Johnson became pastor of the congregation did they begin to sing psalms [24].

Concerning the Eucharistic liturgy, Clement Gamble asserted that in

---

[17] *Ibid.*, p. 284.
[18] April 1593 Examinations before commissioners, Ellesmere Ms. 21 01, in *The Writings of John Greenwood and Henry Barrow 1591-1593*, p. 319.
[19] Certen wicked sects and opinions, March 1588-9, Harley Ms. 6848, in *The Writings of John Greenwood 1587-1590*, pp. 294-299.
[20] *Ibid.*
[21] *Ibid.*
[22] *Ibid.*
[23] Ellesmere Ms 2101, in *op. cit.*, p. 319.
[24] HENOCH CLAPHAM, *A Cronological Discourse*, 1609, p. 3, quoted in BURRAGE, Vol. 1, p. 157.

eighteen months as a regular attender, he had never seen the Supper celebrated [25].

Champlin Burrage suggested that the Supper was suspended while the Church was without a minister, though more recently Mayor has argued that Gamble saw no celebration because he was not regarded as a full member [26]. According Francis Johnson and William Denford, a schoolmaster, the Supper could be celebrated at any time of day or night [27].

A clear description was provided by Daniel Bucke:

> Beinge further demaunded the manner of the Lord's Supper administred emongst them, he saith that fyve whight loves or more were sett uppon the table and that the pastor did breake the bread and then delivered yt unto some of them, and the deacons delivered to the rest, some of the said congregacion sittinge and some stanginge aboute the table and that the pastor delivered the cupp unto one and he to an other, and soe from one to another till they had all dronken, usinge the words at the deliverye therof accordinge as it is sett downe in the eleventh of the Corinthes the xxiiiith verse [28].

And this description can be supplemented by Barrow's own brief directions:

> Unto the supper of the Lord are required the elements of bread and wine: which bread (after thankes giving) is to be broken and to be delivered with such wordes of exhortation as are therunto prescribed, and the cup to be delivered in like manner [29].

The Separatists believed that their services rested on Scripture alone: 1 Tim. 2:1ff required prayer; Romans 12:8, exhortation; 2 Cor. 1:12. 11:2, the sermon; and examination before communion, Matt. 18:15-18, 1 Cor. 5:3-5, 11, and 1 Cor. 11:27ff. A sermon before the sacrament which Browne insisted upon was warranted by Acts 20:27, and the Supper itself by the Synoptic Gospels and 1 Cor. 11:23ff. Certainly in the case of Browne [30], and probably in the directions given by Barrow also [31], there seems to have been a strict interpretation of the Words of Institution:

> Taking the bread.
> Blessing and giving thanks over it.

---

[25] Harley Mss. 6848 in *op. cit.*, p. 299.
[26] C. BURRAGE, *The Early English Dissenters*, Vol. I, p. 127; S. MAYOR, *The Lord's Supper in Early English Dissent*, p. 43. However, Burrage does suggest this in a footnote.
[27] April 1593, Ellesmere Mss. 2115 and 2117, in *The Writings of John Greenwood and Henry Barrow 1591-1593*, pp. 353-354; 363.
[28] Harley Mss. 6849, in *op. cit.*, p. 307.
[29] *A Brief Discoverie of the False Church*, in *op. cit.*, pp. 418-419.
[30] BROWNE, *A Booke which sheweth the life and manners*, in *op. cit.*, p. 284.
[31] BARROW, *A Brief Discoverie of the False Church*, in *op. cit.*, p. 418.

Breaking it.
Pronouncing it to be the Body of Christ.
Administration of the bread.
Taking the cup.
Blessing and giving thanks over it.
Pronouncing it to be the blood of Christ.
Administration of the cup.

However, the scriptural warrant was not followed to its logical conclusions; for example, some communicants sat, and others stood, but no one reclined as in the Gospels. Again, there was no restoration of a meal with the Eucharist. No Christian liturgy is a creation *ex nihilo*. Browne and his followers had been acquainted with the more extreme Puritans, and were no doubt familiar with the Puritan editions of the *Genevan Service Book*. The Brownist service of prayer, thanksgiving, lections and exhortation echo the *Genevan Service Book* as much as scriptural warrant. The preparation before the sacrament as given by Browne seems a very good summary of the exhortation with excommunication found in Calvin's rite and the *Genevan Service Book*. Also, according to the Gospel narratives, after the Supper the disciples sang a psalm; Browne recommended a prayer of thanksgiving, praying for "further profiting in godlines & vowing their obedience", which again recalls the Eucharist of Calvin and that of 1556. There is a strong suspicion here that the Separatist exegesis of scriptural worship was somewhat coloured by Calvinist liturgical usage.

One interesting fact which emerges from the Separatist accounts of worship is that the division between the service of Word and the Sacrament implicit in the Calvinist rites is now made explicit by the Separatists; the Eucharist was now an entirely separate service, and Clement Gamble could attend the ordinary worship for eighteen months withouth ever having seen the Eucharist celebrated.

Chapter 6

ENGLISH PURITANS IN THE NETHERLANDS

If the English Puritan tradition could not enjoy Reformed discipline and worship in England itself, then for some of its more extreme adherents the only course open was that of exile. Among the many possible places of exile, a high proportion of these Puritans chose the Dutch Netherlands. In the early years of the Reformation, England had provided a place of refuge for Dutch protestants who were oppressed by Habsburg Catholic rule. With the gradual advance of the Sea beggers in Zealand and Holland after 1572, the Dutch Reformed States in their turn provided an attractive retreat for dissident Puritan and Separatist ministers and their congregations.

In the late sixteenth and early seventeenth centuries two large groups of Englishmen were to be found in the Netherlands, each of whom were sympathetic to Puritan views, and who exercised a certain amount of independence from the hierarchy of the Church of England: the English Merchant Adventurers, who had a monopoly of trade with the Low Countries, and who appointed their own chaplains, and the regiments of English and Scottish soldiers who had been sent to the Dutch States at regular intervals from the 1580's to assist in the struggle of the northern states against the Spanish [1]. As the northern States and towns were liberated from Spanish hands, a swift change of local government followed. The Erasmian tolerance of the liberated States [2], together with a growth of Reformed discipline, meant that the English Puritans found some sympathy in the Netherlands; and it was in the Netherlands that Puritan theological tracts and works could be printed without hindrance from the authorities, and from there could be smuggled into England. The name of Richard Schilders, the printer to the States of Zealand, was notorious in this connection [3].

In such circumstances it is not surprising that many prominent Puritan

---

[1] PIETER GEYL, *The Revolt of the Netherlands*, London, 1958, passim. For the vascillating policy of Elizabeth I, see CHARLES WILSON, *Queen Elizabeth and the Revolt of the Netherlands*, London, 1970.
[2] GEYL, *op. cit.*, p. 52; WILSON, *op. cit.*, pp. 48, 96-97.
[3] A list of Puritan works printed by Schilders is to be found in, J. DOVER WILSON, "Richard Schilders and the English Puritans", in *Transactions of the Bibliographical Society*, Vol. 11, 1909-1911, pp. 65-134.

ministers sought refuge in the Netherlands [4]. Thomas Cartwright, Robert Browne and Henry Jacob were, successively, chaplains to the Merchant Adventures at Middleburg; John Forbes, the promoter of the congregational English Classis, was also chaplain to the Adventurers at Middleburg and Delft. In 1600 the Brownist congregation in Amsterdam chose Francis Johnson as pastor, and Henry Ainsworth as their doctor or teacher. John Robinson, whose congregation was later to sail to America, arrived in Amsterdam in about 1608. Dr. William Ames, a Fellow of Christ's College, Cambridge, was forced into exile, and became professor of theology at the University of Franeker (Friesland). And of no less significance, Hugh Peters, later chaplain to Cromwell, was minister of the English congregation at Rotterdam, aided by Jeremiah Burroughes, William Bridge and Sidrach Simpson; at Arhnem in 1633 there were to be found Philip Nye and Thomas Goodwin, leading Independents of the Westminster Assembly.

English and Scottish congregations were to be found at Amsterdam, Arnhem, Bergen op Zoom, 's-Hertogenbosch, Breda, Den Briel, Delf, Dordrecht, Vlissingen, Gorcum, Haarlem, 's-Gravenhage, Leiden, Middleburg, Rotterdam and Utrecht [5]. Professor R. P. Stearns has claimed that it was among these congregations that many of the "fathers of Congregationalism first found that freedom from English prelacy which enabled them to inaugurate and perfect their new polity without effective opposition" [6].

With such a medley of Puritan and Separatist ministers, liturgical usage was no doubt diverse, the precise forms of which would be a matter for speculation. However, some light is shed on the period 1628-1635 by information deriving from two interacting factors: first, the internal quarrels of the English Classis formed under the leadership of John Forbes, and secondly, the determined policy of Archbishop Laud "that over all provinces of him master a single rule should prevail" [7].

The Dutch States tolerated English congregations, but it was understood that the ministers would co-operate with and be subject to the Dutch Reformed Church, which was organised on the Presbyterian classis system. This was the position of John Paget, minister of the Begijnhof Church in Amsterdam. Paget had been a curate in Cheshire, and later served as chaplain to one of the English regiments in the Netherlands. On arrival in the Netherlands he subscribed to the Belgic Confession of Faith, and thus fitted himself to be

---

[4] KEITH L. SPRUNGER, *Dutch Puritanism. A History of English and Scottish Churches of the Netherlands in the Sixteenth and Seventeenth Centuries.*
[5] *Ibid.*
[6] R.P. STEARNS, *Congregationalism in the Dutch Netherlands*, p. 7.
[7] HUGH TREVOR ROPER, *Archbishop Laud*, second edition, 1962, p. 232.

called as minister to any congregation in the Dutch Reformed Church [8]. Samuel Blamford, minister at 's-Gravenhage from 1630, abandoned the English Classis for the Dutch, and used the latter as a shield from Laudian interference [9].

However, John Forbes, a chaplain to the Merchant Adventurers who had had considerable contact with Henry Jacob, was an Independent Puritan, and saw the best way of achieving fullest independency was by the formation of an English Classis. This classis would enjoy the best of both worlds; it would enjoy the privilege of other English congregations in the Netherlands as regards independence from the English hierarchy, and at the same time it would be quite independent of the Dutch Classis. It was able, in practice, to play one off against the other [10].

The formation of an English Classis in the Netherlands did in fact cause considerable friction, and various internal disputes arose [11]. The reports of various irregularities amounting to ecclesiastical anarchy encouraged Laud, or rather, provided him with an opportunity, to investigate the status of the English congregations in the Netherlands, and to bring them into full conformity with the mother Church. It is from the correspondence arising out of the reports of irregularities and Laud's investigations, mainly supplied by Sir Dudley Carleton and Sir William Boswell, ambassadors at 's-Gravenhage, that we learn something of the liturgical usage of the Puritan ministers.

Before 1628 there were rumours that the members of the English Classis were using new liturgies and set prayers; in a list of articles presented by Sir Dudley Carleton to the English Classis in May 1628, dealing with alleged irregularities, article 1 stated:

> It is his Majesties pleasure, that the said Ministers meddle not with the making or composing, much lesse ye publishing of any new Liturgie or sett forme of prayer for their congregations [12].

The ministers were swift to rebutt the charge:

> concerning the making or publishing of any new Liturgie. We are sorry, that our best intentions are so misconstrued, it never havinge

---

[8] A.C. CARTER, *The English Reformed Church in Amsterdam in the Seventeenth Century*, Amsterdam, 1964.

[9] KEITH L. SPRUNGER, "Archbishop Laud's Campaign Against Puritanism at The Hague", in *Church History*, 44 (1975), pp. 308-320. After dabbling in "Congregational" - style theology, Blamford returned to England in 1650 as a "Presbyterian".

[10] R.P. STEARNS, *op. cit.*, passim.

[11] *Ibid.*

[12] Articles exhibited & delivered unto the Synod of the English & Scottish Ministers in the Netherlands. Add Mss 6394 (Boswell Papers Vol. 1) fol. 41-44, ed. C. BURRAGE, *The Early English Dissenters*, Vol. 2.

> entred into our minds, to frame or publish any new Liturgie: or to oppose or condemne the Liturgies of any other Churches: but only to enlarge that allready extant (Wch by authority & command of the States we are enjoyned to observe:) by adding thereunto from other Liturgies; & among the rest from the Liturgie of England, so much as withouth offense or scandall in these Churches might be practised: wch foresaid Liturgie hath beene in continuall use in all Churches here, from the time of Q. Elizabeth of famous memory, whilst the Earle of Leicester did governe in these provinces; & agreed upon & practised in the Churches of the Brill & Vlissinghe, then absolutely depending upon ye authority of the Kings of England, & maintained by them. Such was the care of your Majesties royall predecessors to have all things among their subjects here residing to be done in conformity to the Churches of these lands, thereby to prevent all offense, & to maintaine the peace & unitie of the Church: wch course we trust assuredly, your Majestie intends we should follow; not purposing we should putt in practise any Liturgy never as yett authorized in these parts; or that we should leave every man to his owne liberty to use what Liturgie he pleaseth; seing thereby as great, if not greater confusion & disorder should raigne amongst us after order established, as was before the erection of our Synode [13].

The English ministers denied the charge of innovation, maintaining that it was their right and duty to use the liturgy of the Dutch Reformed Church. They claimed that they were allowed to make additions to this liturgy, providing that these did not cause offence — which meant providing the Reformed nature of the rite was not changed. This, they asserted, has been the position since the 1580's.

However, from a letter of 1633, written by Stephen Goffe, a pro-Laudian chaplain, we learn that the English ministers gave rather a liberal interpretation to their rights and duties in liturgical matters. Goffe tells of four liturgical uses among the English ministers:

> It is to be observed that of those Engl: Minister which use not the English forme (i.e. *Book of Common Prayer*)
>
> 1. Some use the Dutch translated, as M[r] Paine. but yet that mended much left out, and some things added, as may appeare by M[r] Paines booke.
>
> 2. Some use none at all as M[r] Forbes. but every time they administer the Sacraments a new. they doe not stand to one of their owne.
>
> 3. Some uss another English forme putt out at Midleborough 1586.

---

[13] A petition of English and Scottish ministers in the Netherlands to King Charles I of England against six articles exhibited by Sir D. Carleton, 4th June, 1628. Add Ms. 6394. ed. Burrage.

> This Mr Goodyer saith he vseth at Leyden. and Mr Peters saied to me that was the forme he found in his consistory. But whether he vse it or no I cannot tell, I believe he goes the Forbesian way.
>
> 4. Some vse our English forme in the sacraments but mangle them Leaving out and putting in whole sentences ... [14].

In the State Papers for Holland there is to be found what appears to be an expansion of the above synopsis [15].

These four liturgical uses outlined by Goffe will be considered further.

1. The Translation of the Dutch Reformed Liturgy.

Use of the Dutch liturgy was acknowledged by the ministers of the English Classis in their reply to the articles of 1628. Already in 1623 the English Synod had passed a resolution to follow the Dutch forms [16]. They appealed to the authority of the States General of the United Provinces, and to the precedent established in the 1580's. it seems that the English autorities were not altogether convinced by the reply, for in 1629 Sir Henry Vane was dispatched on a special embassy to Holland with intructions to consult the ministers in case "you find them ... framing new Liturgies, or translating the Dutch into English" [17]. The letter of Goffe refers specifically to Mr. Paine; apparently Paine used the Dutch forms as they had been translated by Captain Henry Hexham and written in the leaves of his Bible [18]. From the Boswell Papers we learn that in 1633 Mr. Paine was chaplain to the Scottish garrison at Bergen op zoom:

> Mr Paine was called from Schonehouen by ye Englishe classis to Bergen op Zone. after y^t by their Authority, they had depriued (i.e. the English Classis) one Mr Clarke the Scotch regiment Preacher to ye Earle of Bucklough [19].

In fact Paine had been deprived at Schonhoven for refusal to conform to the *Book of Common Prayer*, but Forbes was able to get him installed at Bergen. There he promptly proved his worth by persuading the Dutch ministers to lodge a strong protest at the use of the Anglican rite on an English ship [20].

---

[14] Add, Ms. 6394. fol. 168, ed. BURRAGE, *op. cit.*
[15] SP 16. Vol. 310, fol. 104. (Public Record Office). Cf. Boswell to Coke, SP 84, Vol. 146, fol. 195.
[16] SP 84. Vol. 112, fol. 4.
[17] King Charles to Sir Henry Vane, November 1629. SP 16. Vol. 152, fol. 74.
[18] SP 16. Vol. 310, fol. 103.
[19] Add. MS 6394, fol. 175, ed. BURRAGE, *op. cit.*
[20] HUGH TREVOR ROPER, *Archbishop Laud*, p. 248, citing State Papers 84. Vol. 147.

But according to Goffe, several ministers used a translation of the Dutch form, and since the States General expected them to conform with the Reformed nature of the Dutch Church, we may presume that most were acquainted with the Dutch liturgy.

The Dutch liturgy endorsed by the Synod of Dordt in 1619 was essentially that of Petrus Datheen of 1566, written for the Dutch congregation in the city of Frankenthal in the Palatinate. This work was in turn a translation and adaptation of the Pfalz liturgy of 1563, the work of Ursinus, a pupil of Melancthon, and Olevianus, whe had studied at Geneva. Its genesis would thus appear to be Lutheran and Genevan, without any apparent link with the Dutch liturgy of Micron. However, the 1563 Pfalz liturgy was itself based upon four other liturgies; the Lutheran Pfalz liturgy, 1557, the German editions of à Lasco and Micron, and the *Liturgia Sacra* of Poullain. Liturgically it was a mixture of Lutheran, Calvinist and pro-"Zwinglian" sources; but the rite itself was Reformed rather than Lutheran, and Zwinglian rather than Calvinist.

The Rhine-Palatinate, standing between Wittenberg and Switzerland, had been influenced by both Lutheran and Reformed theology, and it was in an attempt to end strife between the two Churches that the Elector Frederick had asked two of his court chaplains, Ursinus and Olevianus, to draft a new catechism (Heidelberg) and a liturgy [21]. Although the Lutheran Church seems to have conceded much liturgically, it should be remembered that the Lutheran rites of South and West Germany are grouped in a class described as "radical and mediating", and noted for their liturgical poverty [22]. The Lutheran Pfalz liturgy of 1557 was no exception to this rule; although affirming doctrinal loyalty to the Augsburg Confession, it commenced with the Calvinist votum "Our help is in the name of the Lord", it contained a confession which echoed that of Calvin's rite ("but also that I by nature, sinful and unclean, conceived and born in sin"), and before the Words of Institution it had an extremely lengthy exhortation [23]. Reformed liturgical features had already penetrated the Lutheran Church in the Palatinate, and thus less was conceded than may appear at first sight.

Petrus Datheen, the minister of the exiled Dutch congregation in Frankenthal, recognising the Elector's desire for harmony, very diplomatically translated and adapted the ecumenical Pfalz liturgy of 1563 for his own congregation. A leading Reformed minister in the early years of the struggle for

---

[21] Text in AE. L. RICHTER, *Die evangelischen Kirchenordnungen des sechszehnten Jahrhunderts*, 2 vols., Leipzig 1847, 1967 (reprint), vol 2, pp. 256-275; English text, Bard Thompson, "The Palatinate Liturgy Heidelberg, 1563", in *Theology and Life* 6 (1963), pp. 49-67.
[22] L.D. REED, *The Lutheran Liturgy*, Philadelphia, 1947, p. 90.
[23] Text in *Wolfgang's Kirchenordnung*, Nuremburg, 1570.

freedom in the northern provinces, it was Datheen's liturgy and not that of Micron which established itself as the official liturgical compilation of the Dutch Reformed Church. The actual textual provisions for the Morning worship in Datheen's liturgy were meagre — two prayers, one before the sermon and one after the sermon, and the Aaronic blessing. Of these two prayers, the first appears to have been his own composition, and the second was adapted from part of the prayer after the sermon of the Palatinate rite [24]. However, Datheen envisaged the use of other elements within the basic framework which he provided. Thus the order given in Austin Friars' 1571 edition envisaged the following:

> The reading or singing of the Decalogue.
> Confession.
> Words of Assurance.
> Warning to the impenitent and declaration of grace to the penitent.
> Prayer before the sermon, ending with.
> The Lord's Prayer.
> Creed.
> (Sermon).
> Prayer after the sermon, ending with.
> The Lord's Prayer.
> Aaronic Blessing.
> Commendation of the Poor.

We have previously suggested that Micron's liturgy was probably used in conjunction with the new prayers of Datheen, and a comparison of the above order with that of Micron gives strong weight to the suggestion. But Micron had also been used as a source for the 1563 Palatinate liturgy, and although in his Morning service Datheen's textual borrowing was slight, it would seem that some of the structuring of the German rite had influenced him. The 1563 rite envisaged the following:

> I Tim. 1:2
> Prayer before the sermon
> (Lections)
> Sermon
> Bidding to repentance (including Decalogue).
> Confession.
> Words of Pardon, with a warning to the impenitent.
> Invitation to confident prayer.
> Prayer after the sermon (thanksgiving and intercessions), ending with

---

[24] H. HAGEMAN, "The Liturgical Origins of the Reformed Churches", p. 127.

> The Lord's Prayer.
> Hymn.
> Aaronic blessing.

Whereas à Lasco-Micron and the Palatinate liturgy placed the Decalogue, confession and absolution after the sermon, Datheen placed these before the sermon. Further information regarding the structure of Datheen's Morning worship is provided by the resolutions of the Synod of Dordt, 1574 [25]. Resolutions 37-52 of the Synod relate to Morning worship: After a psalm, the minister commences with the Calvinist votum, "Our help is in the name of the Lord, who has made heaven and earth"; the sermon must be no more than an hour; the lections were to be taken from one book in succession, i.e. lectio continua; between the prayer before the sermon and the sermon itself the congregation sing *"O God die onse Vader bist"*, or some other hymn: the prayer after the semon may be shortened; the psalms of Datheen and other hymns could be sung; after the prayer following the sermon, the Creed was to be recited, and the Decalogue was transferred to the afternoon service; the congregation was free to read the psalms while they were being sung; the service concluded with the Aaronic blessing. It would appear that in some places in Holland the old Mass pericopes for the Epistle and Gospel were still used [26].

There would appear to have been considerable flexibility regarding the precise order of the Morning service, and Dr. H. Hageman has concluded that this was a deliberate policy to provide for both a Calvinist (Genevan) and a Zwinglian (Zurich) type of service [27]. What is significant is that much appeared to be left to the discretion of the minister, the liturgy being a type of directory.

Datheen's Eucharistic liturgy proper — which was to follow the Morning service — was an almost word for word translation of the Palatinate rite of 1563. it had the following structure:

> Institution narrative.
> Exhortation to examination, excommunication and reasons for the sacrament's institution.
> Eucharistic Prayer. Reference to the Holy Spirit: "thou wilt be pleased to work in our hearts through the Holy Ghost, that we may give ourselves more and more with true confidence to thy Son Jesus

---

[25] *De Kercken-Ordeninghen der Ghereformeerder Nederlandtscher kercken in de vier Nationale Synoden ghemaeckt ende ghearresteert. mitsgaders Eenige anderen in den Provincialen Synoden van Hollandt ende Zeelandt gheconcipieert ende besloten waerby noch anderen, in bysondere vergaderinghen goet-ghevonden, by ghevoeght zyn*, ed. I. Andriesz, Delft, 1622, p. 13 ff.
[26] H. HAGEMAN, "The Liturgical Origins of the Reformed Churches" in *op. cit.*, p. 120.
[27] *Ibid.*, p. 126.

Christ, that so our broken and burdened hearts may be fed and comforted throught the power of the Holy Spirit with his body and blood, yea with him true God and Man".
Lord's Prayer.
Apostles' Creed.
Reformed *Sursum corda.*
Fraction with Micron's words. During the administration a psalm may be sung, or reading on the Passion — Isaiah 53, John 13, 14, 15, 16, or 18.
Psalm 103.
Prayer of Thanksgiving.
Aaronic Blessing.

The use of Micron's words of administration, the *London aanhangsel*, was modified in the editions of 1568 and 1619, only the Pauline words being provided (1 Cor. 10:16). Furthermore, in Datheen's 1566 liturgy, Psalm 103 and the prayer of thanksgiving were alternatives.

The overall structure of Datheen's rite is not too dissimilar to that of Calvin/Poullain, and included the characteristic excommunication and Reformed *Sursum corda*. Of particular note is the reference to the Holy Spirit in the Eucharistic Prayer. It makes explicit the doctrine of Calvin that the communicant received the body and blood of Christ by faith and the power of the Spirit — a doctrine which Calvin himself failed to give adequate liturgical expression. As with à Lasco and Micron, the fraction is explicit. Yet in addition to the Calvinist elements in the rite, Zwinglian influence is also present; in particular the teaching of the exhortation, that the bread and wine are a sure remembrance and pledge that Jesus becomes to us meat and drink of eternal life on the cross, and that he satisfies our hunger — not in the eucharistic elements — but by his death on the cross.

2. *Extemporary or Free Prayer.*

Goffe's report regarding the use of free prayer is confirmed by a report of Edward Misselden, the Merchant Adventurers' Deputy at Delft. Misselden fell out with Forbes and reported him and his congregation for nonconformity, accusing them of using no forms of prayer, nor any liturgy [28]. According to Goffe, Hugh Peters also went the "Forbesian way".

We have already encountered Free Prayer with the Brownists and Barrowists. As with Browne, both Forbes and Peters had been Puritan minis-

---

[28] SP 16. Vol. 224, fol. 57. Cf. SP 16, Vol. 310, fol. 104; SP 84. Vol. 146, recto 202.

ters, and there is every reason to suppose that they were acquainted with the *Genevan Service Book*. Goffe confirms that Peters had access to the Middleburg Book. Possibly then, the type of order they used was very similar in outline to that in the Genevan and Dutch books, the ministers simply refusing to be bound by the texts provided. At Arnhem where Philip Nye and Thomas Goodwin were pastors we learn of the following type of service:

> They haue two Preachers, and this the discipline of theire Church: Vpon euery Sonday a Communion, a prayer before sermon & after, the like in the afternoone, The Communion Table stands in the lower end of the Church (which hath no Chancell) Altarwise, where the Chiefest sit & take notes, not a gentlewoman that thinkes her hand to faire to vse her pen & Inke, The Sermon, Prayer and psalme being ended, the greatest companie present their offeringes, ... [29].

The Eucharist here was celebrated weekly. It is interesting that prayers before and after the sermon correspond to the minimum textual provision in Datheen's rite. According to the "Dissenting Brethren", their services consisted of the same elements as their Reformed brethren [30].

3. The Genevan Service Book.

According to Goffe, Goodyer used the Middleburg edition of this rite at Leiden. It may also have been the liturgy used by John Paget at Amsterdam. A letter of Paget to Sir William Boswell of March 1636 stated:

> According to your desire I have sent vnto you this book of the forme of common prayers & administration of sacramentes printed at Midleburg this being the fourth edition. Some parts of it are translated out of the Dutch formulier; in some thinge it varies, Though I never accurately compared them together, yet I think vpon the view of some places, it had bene better if there had bene lesse variation. I can well misse it for twise so long a time as you mention; yet seing I have no more but this copy, neither know where they are to be got, I would willingly at your leasure receave it againe, when you have done with it [31].

Here Paget seems to have been referring to the fourth edition, 1602, of the

---

[29] Tanner Ms 65, fol. 24 (Bodleian), ed. BURRAGE, *op cit.*
[30] *An Apologeticall Narration*, p. 8.
[31] Add. Ms 6394 (Boswell Papers Vol. 1), folio 228, ed. BURRAGE, *op. cit.*

Waldegrave/Middleburg Book, where as we have observed above, certain material was incorporated from Datheen's rite.

Two things are of interest in Paget's letter. First, he did not know where to get another copy, suggesting that these Puritan liturgies were no longer in general circulation. Second, Paget was prepared to part with the book. Does this indicate that he used it merely as a guide or directory, and that during its absence, he went the "Forbesian way"? Or, could it indicate that in addition to this book he used the Dutch form? Since he was qualified to be a minister anywhere in the Dutch Church, it is logical to suppose that he was more than familiar with its liturgy [32].

4. The English Form.

As was the case in England, some Puritans in Holland simply made their own adaptations of the *Book of Common Prayer*. The report on the English Preachers in the Netherlands in the State Papers, which appears to be a fuller version of Goffe's report to Boswell, notes that some ministers use the English liturgy, "but mangle and pare, and purge it most spittifully" [33].

In exile in the Netherlands we find the same liturgical usages as amongst the Puritan extremists in England — the adaptation of the Prayer Book, the *Genevan Service Book* as printed at Middleburg, and Free Prayer. In addition, some ministers used the Dutch liturgy of Petrus Datheen, which in turn reflected the Calvinist - Zwinglian - Lutheran compromise of the Palatinate.

---

[32] Unless Paget did in fact use the Duth form, it is difficult to account for the claim of the Consistory of the Begijnhof Church that the liturgical forms of the Dutch Church "were first translated into English from the Latin and Dutch edition by Ministers of this Congregation". See the booklet, *The English Reformed Church Begijnhof Amsterdam*, p. 13.

[33] SP 84. Vol. 146 recto 202.

EPILOGUE

The purpose of this study has been to consider in some detail the origin and development of the liturgies which made up the English Reformed liturgical tradition of the sixteenth and early seventeenth centuries. While the reader may draw whatever lessons seem appropriate, the following points are offered for consideration.

1. On the whole previous studies have tended to give the impression that liturgically the English dissenting tradition of this period consisted of either the *Genevan Service Book*, or free prayer as practised by the Separatists. While undoubtedly both these elements are important — and the *Genevan Service Book* was to reappear as *The Service and Discipline* 1641 and 1643, and the *Settled Order*, 1644 — a wider variety of usages emerged during those early years: the *Book of Common Prayer* emended; the tradition of Geneva as mediated through Huycke, Poullain and Knox; the rites of à Lasco, Micron and Datheen; the free prayer of the Independent Puritans, as well as the Separatists. It is surprising that apparently, with the exception of Knox, the Puritans declined to compile an original or indiginous English Reformed rite. This may have been because in the face of the Royal Supremacy and the Act of Uniformity, it was more expedient to appeal to Scripture, and prestigious existing Continental rites. Rather than embark on work which would be their own private work, the Puritans appealed to what they believed had been handed down from the Lord, and the liturgies of "the best Reformed Churches", associated with the name of Calvin, Knox, à Lasco, or the Dutch States General. Not until 1645 were these Reformed Churchmen able to produce an indigenous English Reformed rite.

2. Under the influence of W. D. Maxwell, it has become usual to stress that the Reformed rites — at least, those of Bucer, Calvin and Knox — were derived from the Mass, and not from the Offices or *Pronaus*. However, while not directly based upon *Pronaus*, it does seem that the service did influence the Liturgy of the Word in the Reformed tradition, probably because it seemed more evangelical and didactic than the fore-mass. The influence seems to have been more than Maxwell would allow. In the case of the liturgies of à Lasco/Micron and Datheen, the influence is more discernable.

3. In previous studies, the use of the Dutch rite by some Puritans has been ignored, or passed over without further comment. Its influence is alrea-

dy to be seen in the Waldegrave and Middleburg Books. Many of the divines of the Westminster Assembly which met in 1644 had experience of exile in the Netherlands. It is perhaps not simply a coincidence that the Dutch rite of Datheen was used as a directory of worship, and that it was a directory for worship that the Westminster Assembly finally authorised for use. While there is no evidence that any of the subcommittee working on the *Westminster Directory* had direct knowledge of the Dutch rite, it may well be that this rite should be regarded as a factor in the making of the 1645 *Westminster Directory* [1].

---

[1] See BRYAN D. SPINKS, *Freedom or Order?*, Pittsburg, 1984.

APPENDICES

TEXT A

WILLIAM HUYCKE'S TRANSLATION OF CALVIN'S "LA FORME", 1550

THE FOURME
OF COMMON PRAYERS USED
IN THE CHURCHES OF GENEVA.

In the woorkyng dayes, the preacher maketh such exhortacion unto prayer, as seemeth unto hymselfe moste meete: applying or framyng the same, bothe to the tyme and matter whiche he entreateth of in hys sermon.
The Sundaye morning, immediately beafore the sermon, the preacher useth commonly a maner to prayee, as hereafter foloweth.

Our ayde and succour is in the name and power of GOD, whiche made bothe heaven and earth. So be it.

The Confession.

My brethren, se that every of you shew himselfe before the face of ye lord, acknowleging unto him, al your faultes & offences, thinkyng even from the botom of your hertes, ye wordes which I shal speake. LORD GOD everlastyng and almighty FATHER, we confesse and knowledge unfaynedly before thy blessed maiestye, that we are miserable synners, conceyved and borne in unrighteousnesse, and fylthe of synne, beyng naturally inclyned to doe wickedlye, beeyng also unapt and unhable to doe anything that is good, and that by the selfe same synne planted in us by nature, wee transgresse withoute all measure (never ceassynge from the same) thy moste holye and blessed commaundementes: wherein wee procure unto oure selves by thy ryghteouse iudgemente, confusyon and destruccyon. Yet moste mercyfull father and LORDE, for asmuche as wee are dyspleased with oureselves, in that wee have offended thy goodnesse: and seenynge wee condemne bothe oureselves and oure wyckednesse, beeynge truèlye repentaunte for the same, moste instauntelye desyrynge that thou of thy bountyfull goodnesse wylte helpe us in thys myserye: vouchesave nowe moste mercyfull GOOD and lovynge FATHER, to have pitie of us for thy only sonnes sake, for the merites (I say) of our LORDE Jesu Christ: not alonlye in puttyng awaye oure faultes and transgressyons, but also in gevynge unto us the gyftes of thy holye spirite, increasynge the same from tyme to tyme, to the ende that wee continuallye, even from the bottome of oure heartes, knowleging our own unrighteousnesse: may conceyve such a displeasure towardes sinne, as may bryng furth an unfained repentaunce, whereby we may both mortifye our synnefull inordinate affeccions, and also of an upryght conscience shew furth the fruites of righteousnes, whiche fruites (notwithstanding they bee polluted and imperfect through our naughty nature) thou dost accepte as perfecte, for JESU Christes sake, whiche liveth. &c.

> When the preacher hath on thys wise made his supplicacion, the whole multytude syngeth some Psalme in playnesong (the whiche thyng doone) the preacher begynneth to make hys prayer agayne, that God of hys grace would vouchesafe to sende downe hys holy spirite, as well that he may sette foorth the woord to the avauncement of Gods honoure and edifying of the people: as that the hearers maye also receyve it humbly with obedience due unto the same.
>
> The maner of prayer is referred to the dyscrecion of the preacher: Immediatly after the sermon, when the preacher hathe exhorted the people to praye, he begynneth on thys wyse.

O Almyghty GOD our heavenly Father, sithens thou hast fyrste promysed to fulfyll our requestes whiche we shall make unto thee in the name of our Lord Jesu Christ, thy welbeloved sonne: Secondarily, for so much as ye doctrine of Christ and hys Apostles doth teache us to make our common prayer in his name, promising that he will bee amonge us, and that he will make intercession for us unto thee; for the obtaining of al such thinges, as we shall Godly agree upon, here in earth: And thyrdly seeing thou hast geven us in commaundemente to praye, especiallye for suche as thou hast appoynted rulers and governours over us, and also for thynges nedefull to thy congregacion, and for all sortes of menne: wee conceyvynge a hardynesse, throughe thy holye woorde, leanynge assuredlye unto thy moste undoubted promesse, in so muche as wee are here gathered together beefore thy face in the name of thy onelye sonne oure Lorde JESUS: We therfore (I say) make our earnest supplicacion unto the, oure moste mercifull God and bountifull Father, that for Jesus Christes sake our savioure and onely mediatour, it maye please the of thy infinite mercy freely to pardon our offences, and in suche sort to drawe and lift up our hertes & affeccions towardes thee, that oure requestes maye bothe proceade of a fervent mynd, and also be agreeable unto thy most blessed will and pleassure, whiche is onely to be accepted.

We besech thee therefore our heavenlye FATHER, as touchinge all princes and rulers of the congregacion, unto whome thou hast commytted the administracion of thy justice, and namely, as touchyng the governours of this Citie, that it woulde please thee to graunte them thy holy spirite (the which onelye by righte is called the pryncipall spirite) & so to encrease the same from time to time in them, that they with a pure faythe knowledgyng Jesus Christe thy onelye sonne oure LORD, to bee the kyng of all kynges, and governour of all governours, even accordynge as thou hast geven al power unto him both in heaven and in y earth, may bende themselves with theyr whole indevour, to serve him, and to advance his kingdome and glorye in theyr dominyons, rulyng theyr subjectes, whiche bee thy creatures, and the shepe of thy pasture, even after thy good pleasure: wherby we beeyng mayntayned in peace and tranquillitie, bothe here & every where, may serve thee in all holines and vertue, so that wee beyng quytte and voyde from all feare of enemies, may render duelye unto the, laudes and praises during the tearme of our lyfe. We beseche thee also (most deare Father and savioure) for all pastours & curates of thy flocke, unto whom thou hast commited the charge of mens soules, & the ministery of thy holy gospel, ye it will please the likewise so to gyde them with thy holy sprite, that they may be found perfecte, faythfull and prayseworthy ministers of thy glory, directing alwayes their whole studies unto this end, that the poore shepe whiche be gone astraye oute of Christes flocke, may be sought out & broughte agayne unto the Lorde Jesu, which is the chiefe shepeheard, and head of all bishops, wherby they may from day to daye grow and increase in hym unto all righteousnes and holynesse. And on the other parte, that it maye please thee to delyver all thy congregacyons from the daunger of ravening wolfes, and from hyerlinges, who searche theyr owne ambicion and profyt, and not onelye the settynge foorthe of thy glorye, and the safegarde of thy flocke.

Moreover, we make our prayers unto thee (most mercifull & loving Father) for al menne in generall, that as thy will is that all the world knowledge thee to bee theyr saviour thorowe thy redempcyon made by thy onely sonne Jesu Christ: even so that such as have bene hitherto holden captyve in darkenesse and ignoraunce for lacke of the knowledge of thy Ghospell, maye throughe the preaching thereof, & the cleare lyghte of thy holye spirite, bee broughte into the ryght waye of healthe everlastyng, which is, to know that thou art onely very GOD, & that he whom thou hast sente is our saviour Christ. Lykewise ye they whome thou haste alreadye endued with thy grace, whose heartes thou hast lyghtened with the right knowledge of thy word, may continuallye encrease in godlynes, and bee plenteously enryched with spirituall benefites: so that we maye altogether in one accorde, both with hearte and mouthe render due honor and servyce unto Christ, who is oure onelye maister, kyng, and lawmaker.

In lyke maner (O LORD of all true coumforte) we commit unto thee in oure prayers all suche persones, as thou haste visited and chastened with the crosse of tribulation, all suche people as thou haste punished with pestilence, warre, or famyne, and all other persones afflicted with povertye, impriesonmente, syckenesse, or banyshment, or any lyke bodely adversitie, or hast otherwise troubled and afflycted in spirite: that it will please thee to make them perceyve thy tender Fatherly affeccions towardes them: that is, that these Crosses bee nothynge elles but Fatherly chastenynges to brynge them to amendment, whereby they may unfaynedlye and with all theyr heartes tourne unto thee, whereby they cleavynge unto thee and guyded by thy hande, may receave full coumforte and so bee cleane delivered from all maner of evyll.

    Finallye (O GOD most deare Father) we beseche the to graut us also, us (I saye) whiche bee here gathered together in the name of thy sonne Jesu, to heare hys woord preached (* and to celebrate hys holye Supper,) that wee maye knoweledge truely and upryghtelye without hipocrisye, and dissimulacion, in how miserable a state of perdicion wee are in by nature, & howe worthely we procure unto our selves everlasting damnacion, heapyng up fro time to time thy grievous punishmetes toward us, thorowe oure wicked and synnefull lyfe: whereby, seeyng that there remayneth no sparke of goodnesse in oure natures, & that there is nothyng in us as touchyng our fyrst creacion & ye which we receive of our paretes, mete to enjoy ye heritage of Gods kingdome, we may yelde & reder up ourselves with al our heartes (having a substancial and constant faythe) unto thy dearely beloved sonne JESU our LORD, our onelye savioure, and redemer: to the ende that he dwellyng in us maye mortifye our olde man (ye is to say) our sinneful affeccions, & that we may be regenerated in to a more godly lyfe: * wherby thy holy name (as it is worthy of all honour) may be advanced and magnifyed throughout the worlde and in all places: * so that whyles thou hast the tuicion and governaunce over us, we may learne dayly more and more to humble and submitte oureselves unto thy majesty: in such sorte that thou mayest bee counted Lorde and Kyng over all the worlde, guydyng thy people with the sceptre of thy woord, by the vertue of thy holy spirite, to the confusyon of all thyne enemyes through the might of thy truth and ryghteousnesse: so that by thys meanes all power and statelynesse withstandyng thy glory, may be continually throwen down and abolished, unto suche tyme, as the full and perfecte face of thy kyngdome shall appeare, when thou shalt shewe thy selfe in judgemente: Wherby also we with the rest of thy creatures, maye render unto thee perfect and due obedience, even as thy holy Aungels dooe applye them selves onelye to the perfourmyng of thy commandementes: so that thy onely will maye be accomplished and fulfylled without all repynynges, and that every man may bend hymselfe to serve and please thee, the contentacion of their own willes, and theyr proper desyres or affeccyons beeynge utterlye sette aparte. Graunte us also (good LORD) that wee thus walkyng in the love & dreade of thy holye name, maye bee fed and sustayned through thy goodnes, that we may receyve at thy handes al thinges expedyente and necessarye for us: wherby we may use thy giftes peaceablye and quyetelye, to thys ende that when wee see that thou haste regarde and care of us: wee maye the more affectuouslye knowledge the to bee oure FATHER, lookyng for all good giftes at thy hande: and by thys meanes we withdrawyng and pulling backe all oure vayne confydence from creatures, maye seeke thee and cleave onelye unto thee, puttyng oure whole truste in thy moste bountifull mercye, and for so muche as whyles wee continue here in thye transytorye lyfe, we are so myserable, so frayle, and so muche enclyned unto sinne, that wee fall contynuallye and swerve from the ryghte way of thy commaundementes. We beseche the pardon us our innumerable offences, by which we are woorthelye in daunger of thy judgement and condemnacion, and forgeve us so freely, that death and sinne, under whome we bee by nature holden in myserable captivitye, maye hereafter have no tytle, nor righte unto us: and that it may please the not to lay unto our charge, that evil & naughty roote or fountayne of sinne, which doth evermore remayne in us: in lyke maner as we forget the wronges or damages which other men doe unto us, and as we in the steade of seekyng vengeaunce, procure or purchase the welth of our enemies. Finallye, lette it bee thy good pleasure to ayde us, to holde up and sustayne oure weakenes, that hereafter the readines to synne whiche abydeth in us, doe not cause us to fall: and that where as we our selves be so frayle that we are not able to stand uprighte one minute of an houre: and where as on the other parte agayne, we are so belayde and affaulted evermore with such a multitude of so daungerous enemies, that the devil, the world, synne, and our owne concupiscence, dooe never leave of to wage battayle agaynste us, let it stand with thy good pleasure to strenghten us with thy holy spirite, and to dooe upon us, the sure armoure of thy grace, that therby we may bee able to withstande myghtelye all maner temptacyons, and to endure mannefuliye in this spirituall conflicte agaynste synne, until suche tyme as we shall wynne the fielde, that we maye once tryumphantelye rejoyce in thy kyngdome, with our captayne and governour our Lord Jesu Christ.

> What day they celebrate the supper of the Lorde, they use also to say thys that foloweth.

And accordyng as oure Lord Jesu thought it not sufficient only to offer up once his blessed body and bloud on the crosse to acquite us of all our sinnes: but doth vouchsafe also spirituallye, to deale and dystribute the selfe same unto us, for a sustenaunce to nouryshe us unto everlastynge lyfe: Even so maye it please thee to endue us with thy specyall grace, that with moste upryghte synglenesse of heart, and earneste ferventenesse of affeccyons, wee maye moste thankefullye receyve at hys hande so hygh a benefite, and so worthy (that is to say), that we may with a constante and assured faythe, receave bothe hys bodye and bloude, yea, verelye CHRIST hymselfe wholye, even as he, beeynge both verye GOD and manne, is moste woorthelye named to bee the holye breade of heaven, to quicken and refreshe oure soules: to the ende that from hencefoorthe wee maye cease to lyve in our selves, and after the course or inclinacion of our owne most corrupt and defyled nature: and that wee may lyve in hym, whiles we have hym also lyving in us, to conducte and guyde us unto the holy, most blessed and everlastynge lyfe. Graunte us also that in receyving the same, we become in verye deede partakers of the newe and everlastyng testament (that is to say) of the covenaunt of grace and mercy, being most certayn and assured, that thy good pleasure is to be our everlastyng mercifull Father, whyles thou layest not to our charge oure manifolde offences, and providest for us, as for thy dearely beloved chyldren and heyres, all thynges needefull as well for the body as for ye soule: so that we may without ceassing render laudes and thankes unto thee, evermore extollyng, and magnifyinge thy holye name both by worde and deede. And fynallye geve us grace so to celebrate thys day the holy remembraūce of thy blessed and dearelye beloved sonne, yea in such sorte to use and practyse oure selves therein, and so to shewe foorthe and declare the woorthy benefites of hys precious death: that we receiving thereby farther strengthe and more ample increase in faythe and all good thynges, maye with the lustier courage, and the more confidence prayse the our Father, rejoysyng and glorifying onely in thy name.

<blockquote>After the Supper of the Lorde is fynysshed, they use to geve thankes as it here foloweth, or after some other lyke maner.</blockquote>

We prayse the and thanke thee (oure moste mercyful FATHER) for that thou haste vouchesaved to graunte unto us miserable synners so excellente a benefyte, as to receyve us into the feloweshyp and companye of thy deare soonne Jesu Christe oure Lorde: fyrste delyverynge hym to a moste cruell deathe for oure sakes. Secondarilye, gevyng hym unto us as a necessarye foode and nouryshemente unto everlastynge life. Graunt to us (wee besuche thee) yet moreover, thys one requeste, that thou dooe never suffer us to beecome so unkynde, as to forgette so woorthye benefytes, but rather so imprinte them and fasten them in oure heartes, that wee maye grow and increase dayelye more and more in suche a ryghte faythe as doothe carefullye travayle, and is continuallye occupyed in all manner of good woorkes, and that in so doynge, wee maye leade foorthe and dyrecte our whole lyfe to the advauncemente of thy glory, and edifying of our neyghboures, thorough the merite of

Jesu Christ thy sonne, who in the unitie of the holye spirite lyveth one GOD with thee evermore. So be it.

> The blessynge whiche they use at the departure of the people, accordyng to the maner of Gods ordinaunce in the vi. Chapter of Numeri.

The LORD blesse you, and kepe you: The LORD make the beames of hys mercye and grace to shyne upon you: The Lorde shew a gentle mercifull and lovyng countenaunce towardes you, and maintain you in prosperous estate to hys pleasure. So be it.

> ### The maner of celebrating the supper of the Lord.
>
> It is to be noted fyrst that the sondaye nexte before the celebracion of the lordes supper, the preacher doth monyshe and exhorte the people that they prepare and dyspose themselves every one to receive it worthelye, and with such reverence as shal be semely. Secondarily that no man bring in thither any children, unles they be sufficiently instructed before, & such as have opēly professed their faith in ye church. Thirdly if there be any strangers yet rude, and lackyng farther instruccion herein, they may come, and offer themselves aparte to some pracher, thereby to be more exactly taught.
>
> The daye it selfe when the Sacramente is thus openlye minystred unto the people, the Preacher, eyther toucheth that matter in the ende of hys sermon, eyther if he shall thynke it good, he maye make hys whole sermon therof: Declaryng unto the people the meanyng of Christ, and for what purpose he dyd fyrst institute thys holye mistery, and howe it behoveth us to receyve the same.
>
> After the sermon whan he hathe sayde the common prayers, and made open confession of the christen faythe, to sygnifye in the behalfe of the whole multitude that they wil al live & dye in the doctrine and religion of Christ: the preacher saith with a loude voyce this that foloweth.

Let us marke and consider how Jesus Christe dyd ordaine unto us hys holye supper, according as S. Paule maketh rehearsal of the same in the xi. Chapter of hys fyrst Epistle to the Chorinthians.

I have receyved (sayeth he) of the LORD, that which I delyver unto you: to witte, that our Lord Jesus ye same hight, in whiche he was betrayed, tooke bread, and when he had geven thankes, he brake it, saying: take ye, eate ye, thys is my bodye, which is broken for you: do you this in the remembraunce of me. Lykewyse after supper, he toke the cup, saying: thys cup is the new testament or covenaunt in my bloud: doe ye this so oft as you shal drink therof, in remembrance of me. That is to say, so ofte as you shal eate of this bread or drink of thys cup, ye shall celebrate and shew furth the Lordes death untyll hys cumming. Wherefore, whosoever shall eate of thys breade, or drynke of thys cuppe unwoorthelye, he shall bee gyltye of the bodye and bloud of the Lord: than see that everye man prove & trye hymselfe, and so let him eate of this bread and drynke of this cup, for whosoever eateth or drynketh unworthely, he receyveth his condemnacion, for not having due regard or consideracion of the lordes body.

We have hearde (my brethren) in what sorte oure Lorde dydde celebrate hys Supper amongeste hys Dysciples: whereby we are also instructed that straungers, that is to say, suche as be not of the faythful congregacion, ought not by any meanes to be admitted therunto. Wherfore folowyng ye selfsame rule & order: In ye vertue & autoritie of our Lord Jesus Christ: I excomunicate & barre out al Idolaters, blasphemers, dispisers of God, heretiques, & al sortes of people ye bring in sectes, ye teache newe doctrine to breake ye unitie of Christes congregacion: al perjured persōs, al such as be disobediente to theyr father & mother, & to other their superiors or maisters, all sedicious persons, privy workers of dissencion, quarel pickers or fighters, skoulders, slaūderers, adulterers, whoremongers, theves drūkardes, gluttons, & finally al suche as leadeth a dyssolute lyfe to the slaunder or evyll exaumple of other, sygnifying unto them, that it is the parte of al such to absent themselves from thys table, & to conceyve thys reverent feare, not to pollute or defyle with theyr presence, those most holy and precious vitayles, which our Lord Jesus geveth to none but unto the faythfull of hys houshold. Therfore (accordyng to sainct Paules exhortacyon) see that every man enter into himselfe, and examyne duely hys owne conscience, to trye whether he have a true unfayned repentaunce for hys synnes, and an earnest dyspleasure agaynste hye owne faultes, most fervētlye myndynge and desyrynge from thys tyme forwarde, to lyve upryghtelye and in the lawe of GOD: and chiefely let every manne consider whether he have his assured confidence in Gods mercy, seeking everlastyng salvacion alonely in the merites and passiō of Jesu Christ, and whether havyng refused and forgotten all malyce and debate, he hath now a ful purpose and earnest desyre to lyve in brotherlye amitie and concorde with hys neyghboures.

Yf our heartes and consciences doe testifye unto us before GOD, that we are comen to thys poynte: we maye undoubtedlye thynke that he accepteth us for hys chyldren, & that our Lorde Jesus hath somoned and bydden us to hys table, there to receive that holye sacrament whiche he divyded among hys Disciples. And albeit wee feele in oure selves much frayltye, and wretchednes, as that we have not oure fayth so perfect & constaunt as we ought, beyng many tymes ready to dystrust Gods goodnes through our corrupte nature: And also that we are not so throughly geven to serve God, neither have so fervent a zeale to set foorth hys glory as our duety requireth, feelynge styll such rebellion in our selves, ye we have neede dayly to fyght agaynst the lustes of our flesh: yet nevertheles seing that our Lorde hath dealed thus mercifully with us, ye he hath printed hys gospel in our heartes, so that we are preserved from fallyng into desperacion, and misbeliefe, and seeyng also he hath indued us with a luste & desire to renounce & withstand our own affecciōs, with a longing for his righteousnes and the kepyng of hys commaundementes: we may be now right wel assured ye those defaultes & manifold imperfeccions in us, shal be no hynderance at all agaynst us, to cause hym not to accepte us, or accounte us as woorthye to come to hys spirituall table. For the ende of our cummynge thither is not to make protestacyon that we are upryght or just in ourselves: but contrary wyse we come to seke our life and perfeccion in Jesu Christ: acknowledgynge in the meane tyme that we of our selves be most miserablye the priesoners of deathe: Lette us consider than that thys sacramente is a synguler meadicine for all poore sycke creatures, a comfortable meane to weake soules, and that oure Lorde requireth no other woorthinesse of oure parte, but that we unfaynedlye knoweledge oure naughtines and imperfeccion: And that we be in dyspleasure and at defyance with the faultes wee have commytted, having our whole pleasure, joye and solace in hym alone. Fyrst then let us believe the promises which Christ being the most assured truth, hath in hys own person made unto us: that is to wete, that he will dystribute and geve unto us in dede, his very body, and his very bloud, to the ende that we maye have hym in our possession, & injoy him fully in such sort that both we may live in him & he in us. And albeit we se nothyng but verye bread & wyne, yet let us beleve undoubtedly ye he doth perfourme spiritually in oure soules, all that that he dooeth sygnifye by visible & outward sygnes unto oure sences: (to wete) that he is the breade of heaven, whiche feedeth & nourisheth us unto life everlastig. Evenso then let us geve diligente heede that wee bee not unthankefull to the infinite bounty of our saviour, who so lovingly bringeth and setteth before us in thys table, hys whole goodes & riches, to thintent to geve them & parte the amongeste us: for in that ye he geveth hymselfe unto us, he maketh evident declaraciō that whatsoever hw hath is oures. Therfore we receive thys Sacrament as a sure warrantyse or pledge ȳ the efficacye & vertue of his painful death, is reputed unto us, and coūted for our righteousnes, eve as verely as if we had suffered ye lyke passions in oure owne proper bodyes. Let us not then be so perverse & froward, as to withdraw & absent our selves from that banket, unto ye whiche Jesu Christ doth so lovingly bid us & allure us in his own mouth: but rather upon consideracion of ye worthines of so excellet a gift which he bestoweth upon us: let us presente & offre oure selves unto him in an earnest ferventnes of affeccion, that we may through hys goodnes be made metē to receive the same. And to ye end we may do thus, let us lift up oure heartes and mindes into heavē where Christ abideth in ye glory of his Father, & frõ whēce (our sure hope is,) he will come to shewe himselfe oure redemer. And let us not suffer our imaginacion to wander about the consideracion of these earthly and corruptyble thynges (which we see present to our eye, and feele with oure handes) to seeke Christ bodilye presente in them, as if he were inclosed in the breade or wine, or as if they wer transmuted & chaunged into hys substance. For the onely waye to dyspose our soules to receyve nourishment, reliefe, and quicknyng of hys substaunce: is to lyfte up our myndes by meanes of a ryght faythe, above all thynges worldly, and sensible, and thereby to enter into heaven, that we may fynd and receyve Christ where he dwelleth, undoubtedlye very God and very manne, in the incomprehensible glory of hys Father. So thē thys shalbe sufficiente to satisfye and content us: to take the bread and wine as sure signes and witnesses of Goddes promises adjoyned unto them: and therwithal to search spiritually the effect & substance of the same, there, where Gods woords dooeth say wee shall fynde it.

> Thys done and the people being advertysed to come peaceablye in ordre with al reverence, the ministers breake the breade, and geve the cuppe unto the people: and whyles that is a doing eyther they synge Psalmes meete for that tyme: eyther one of the preachers readeth some parte of the Scripture touching that matter.
> When all is doone they use to geve thankes, and to say the prayer set out here before.

We know ryght wel, that many have taken a greate occasion to bee offended at the alteracion whiche wee have made touchyng thys sacrament. For by meanes that the Masse hathe bene a long tyme had in suche reputacion, that the poore blynde people of the worlde did esteme and counte it as the chiefest poynte of our christen religion: it hath semed a very straūge case unto them, yt we have so utterly abolished it, & put it down: so that by occasion herof many rude (for lacke of right instruccion takyng the thyng amisse,) suppose yt we have utterly denyed and put away ye sacrament: but when men shal have wel wated, & sufficiently considered ye doctrine which we holde as touching this thing, they shall muche rather trye out, yt we have restored again this sacrament to his perfit integritie & ryght use. And to the intent to find my sayinges true, & pray you consider a litle what conformitie & agreablenes ther is betwene ye masse & the instituciō of our savior Christes supper: than surely ye shal perceyve it a thing most evident, yt they differ as much either frõ other, as ye daye varieth from the night. Albeit our purpose was not to discusse this mater touching the abolishment of the masse, here at length: yet mindyng to satisfy suche as thorow very symplicitie, myghte otherwyse be offended with us: we thought it not amisse thus lyghtly to touche it by the way, and in fewe woordes to shew for that cause we have fordon it.

When we sawe the sacramente of oure Lorde so horriblelye defyled, and corrupted with a number of erroures and abuses, that sundry persons had brought into it: As we minded the reformacion or amendment of the same, so we were of verye necessitie drieven to alter many thynges, whereof parte were of themselves naught, & naughtely put to, and an other parte (at the least) made naught thorow abuse & supersticion: & in conclusion to thintent to atchieve this interprise, yt is to say, to make a perfect reformacion: we coulde not devise a better way, neither a mean more fit, than to returne unto ȳ pure institucion of our savior Christ, ȳ which we folow symply without any patching, peecyng or adding to, as it is easy to be seene. And thys is the ryght way of reformacion, the whiche S. paule doeth also set foorth unto us.

The end of the maner of celebrating the Supper of the Lorde.

TEXT B

JOHN À LASCO'S "FORMA AC RATIO", 1555

Translated by D.G. Lane.

Concerning the form and order of ordinary services on Sundays and Festivals in the Churches of Foreigners in London.

It has been specifically laid down within the powers of the Ministers of the Word and the Elders of the Church that they should summon the congregation to a public meeting, whenever some need or other requirement of the Church seems to necessitate it. And always on such an occasion, whatever the meeting, some sermon, taken from the Scriptures, is delivered which seems to be of particular use for its purpose, and church services are never held at which the congregation is not taught something of the Word of God. But two ordinary services for the congregation are held on Sundayes and the chief Festivals, namely a morning service about 9.00 a.m. and an afternoon service at about 2.00 p.m. On other days each week, twice in the Church of the French — on Tuesdays and Thursdays —, and only once in the Church of the Germans because of the readings in Latin (about which later) — on Thursdays, Church meetings are held together with their services.

In the sermons the Scriptures are not explained bit by bit, as was the custom under the Pope, when sections of stories or portions of Scripture, sometimes without a beginning or an end, were set before the people in such a way that neither those parts which were set before them were sufficiently explained, but those parts which were not set before them were passed over indiscriminately and scarcely never mentioned before the people. Much less (frequently), however, sermons are put together from learned expositions, or treatises or the discourses of Philosophers, but some book of the Bible from the Old or New Testament is taken to be read from beginning to end, from which for individual sermons only as much is read as can conveniently be explained in common terms within the space of one hour, in such a way that everything can be easily understood and also remembered; it is on this that the success of all sermons to a very large extent depends.

Therefore on any Sunday the congregation assembles before 9.00 a.m.

and there at about 9.00 a.m. the Minister mounts the pulpit and first of all invites the congregation to pray with these or similar words:
"Now that you have assembled here like this for this purpose, beloved brothers in Christ, to be instructed for your salvation from the Word of God, first of all we must implore the grace of God, so that both I may teach nothing but the pure instruction of his word and that you too with his aid may hear it to your advantage".

Prayer before the Sermon

Our heavenly Father, whose law is unchanged, converting the soul, whose testimony is sure, supplying wisdom to the ignorant and enlightening the eyes of the humble, we humbly beseech you by your boundless mercy to deign to illumine our otherwise blind minds with the light or your Holy Spirit, that we may be able both to understand your sacred law aright and having understood it express it throughout all our lives. And because it has pleased you, Holy Father, to reveal to your childen in particular the mysteries of your divine will and to have regard chiefly to those who in humbleness of spirit and lack of faith in themselves seek your word alone, take pleasure in it and tremble respectfully at it like sons, grant us, we pray, your Holy Spirit that it may remove from our minds all trust in ourselves, and overcome within us all the wisdom of our flesh and also pride which is in itself opposed to you, and that it may gently bring us back once more into the whole truth when we have strayed and been out off by our sin from all beneficial acquaintance with the truth. Grant too that we may all worship you in holiness and righteousness all our lives, and truly and from our hearts confess in the sight of all that you are our true God, not only with our tongues, but also in the fruits of our lives. We ask this of you, most merciful Father, in the name of your beloved Son, Jesus Christ, in the very prayer which he himself gave us, saying: Our Father, who art in heaven, etc.

At the end of the Lord's Prayer at the bidding of the Minister those who have been specially chosen for the purpose so as to avoid disorderly singing begin a psalm, the whole congregation joining in immediately with the utmost sobriety and seriousness. When the psalm has finished, the Minister proceeds, where he had stood before, to continue with his reading from the Bible and reads as much in the text of the Scriptures as he thinks he can explain for the instruction of the congregation. The Minister moreover takes care, depending on the extent of his own gifts, not to wander too far from the explanation of the text, but after explaining all the teaching contained in the text chooses points to expound which seem particularly suitable for the edification of the congregation.

At the end of the sermon, which does not last more than one hour, before general prayers are offered, the Minister, if he has anything in particular which ought to be made known to the congregation or of which, as it happens, the congregation should be especially reminded, announces it in a few words and then begins the congregation's general prayers as follows:

Prayer after the Sermon

Lord God, our heavenly Father, since your son, Jesus Christ, teaches that only those will be blessed who not only hear your word, but also keep and observe it, — and none of us can keep it, unless it is written in our hearts by your Holy Spirit, — we humbly beseech you that you may be willing to keep Satan from us, so that he may in no way remove from us the teaching of your divine word which we have heard. Soften our stony hearts and gently moisten them with the dew of your Holy Spirit, so that the fruits of your divine word may not suddenly dry up as, through your good will, they increase in our hearts. Furthermore take from our minds the cares and worries of this world which by their nature choke your word in us like thorns, and make us a good and fertile soil in which your word may at length bring forth seed, fruits worthy of you, to the everlasting glory of your name. We ask this of you, most kindly Father, in the name of your only begotten Son, Jesus Christ, our Lord. Amen.

At the end of this prayer, but only on Sundays at the morning service, no at the afternoon one nor at services on other days, the Ten Commandments are read by the Minister from Exodus chapter 20, to hear which the Minister urges the people in the following words: "All of you, hear the law of the Lord our God".

(1) I am the Lord your God, who brought you out of the land of Egypt, from the house of bondage. You may have no other Gods before my face or in my presence.

(2) Do not make for yourself any statue nor any image from all the things that are in the heavens above, or on the earth under the heavens, or in the waters under the earth. Do not bow down before them or worship them, for I, the Lord your God, am powerful, impatient of insult, punishing the wickedness of the fathers on the sons of the third and fourth generation of those who hate me, and showing mercy on thousands of those who love me and keep my commandments.

(3) Do not take the name of the Lord your God rashly or in vain. For the

Lord will not regard as innocent the man who has taken his name rashly or in vain.

(4) Remember to keep the Sabbath holy. On six days will you labour and perform all your work, but on the seventh day is the Sabbath of the Lord your God. Then you will not do any work, neither you, your son, your daughter, your man-servant, your maidservant, your cattle and the stranger who is inside your gates. For in six days the Lord made the heaven, the earth, the sea and all that is in them, but on the seventh day he rested; for this reason the Lord blessed the Sabbath and made it holy.

(5) Honour your father and your mother so that your days may be long upon the earth which the Lord your God gives you.

(6) Do not kill.

(7) Do not be an adulterer.

(8) Do not steal.

(9) Do not witness falsely against your neighbour.

(10) Do not covet your neighbour's house. Do not covet your neighbour's wife, or his man-servant, or his maidservant, or his ox, or his ass, or anything in short that it your neighbour's.

When the Ten Commandments have been read, the Minister then takes the opportunity to remind the congregation of their sins and earnestly urges them to acknowledge them and to reproach themselves on this account and ask for divine pardon as follows:

By means of this divine law we perceive the dreadful corruption of our nature set before our eyes, as though a mirror of ourselves had been put before us. For those things, which through our nature we would not seek after, would be kept from us all in vain. Therefore, since by the evidence of this divine law which has been given to us, we are convicted of seeking after them all and being guilty of the these evils let us acknowledge our sins before the Lord and let us all reproach ourselves together on their account and humbly beg free pardon for them through Christ.

Prayer including the Confession

Almighty and everlasting God, merciful Father, we humbly prostrate ourselves before your divine majesty, against which we openly and without hypocrisy confess that we have sinned most grievously and also continually do sin from day to day, to such an extent that we are not worthy in the sight of your majesty, still less to be reckoned among your children. Indeed, but for the fact that we were conceived and born in sin, we are entirely destitute of all goodness and full of every wickedness and daily transgress your commandments in innumerable ways, while we do not worship you as we ought in proportion to the excellence of your divine majesty and your fatherly kindness towards us, and contrary to your commandment we deceive our neighbour in our duties towards him. And so by your just judgement it is proved that we are liable to eternal condemnation and that clearly it is all over for us, unless the boundless extent of your mercy prevails against the otherwise fair strictness of your judgement in a manner worthy of your forgiveness through your only begotten Son. In him without doubt you deigned to receive us, in such a way that of your own free will you come to meet all who are penitent, even though they may still be far away, with the full proof of your divine and fatherly kindness, and no more desire the death of a sinner, but rather that he may turn and live. On the contrary, you yourself would rush to embrace us and bring forth your ring and cloak as tokens of our union with you in your Son and of our right conduct in him. Trusting therefore in this your mercy, we fall down before your throne of grace, most merciful Father, and bewail our wretchedness before him and humbly beg your divine aid through the merit of your beloved son, that you may be willing to look on us no longer in ourselves, who are nothing but the slaves of sin and death, but in your beloved son who is our righteousness, and that you may grant us your Holy Spirit so that it may soften our hearts, which in themselves are otherwise hard as rock, with your divine breath and make them flesh so that your holy law may there be engraved and through its help be expressed throughout all our lives by us like sons dwelling in the newness of light and of life, to your glory and that of your son and your Holy Spirit and to the building up of your Church. Amen.

At the end of this prayer the Minister declares the remission or absolution of all their sins to the entire congregation through Christ and publicly announces it is follows:

We have a sure and certain promise in accordance with the everlasting and unchanging will of God because to all, who truly repent and who having acknowledged their sins and reproached themselves seek his grace in the name of Christ our Lord, he gives complete forgiveness of all their sins and effaces them and thereafter never wants to remember them at all. We have moreover the frightening sentence of divine judgement on all who prefer darkness to light and who spurn and despise the grace given (to us) in Christ, — for all such, I say, eternal damnation is appointed.

As many therefore of you as feel ashamed of your sins in consequence of the prayer made by us and who repent in the sight of God and having examined yourselves humbly seek forgiveness for them from God our heavenly Father, and who do not doubt that they are all freely and fully forgiven for you through Christ and the merit of his death, and have determined in your hearts that hereafter through the grace of God you want to destroy the old man in you with (all) his desires, that you may walk in newness of life instead of in weakness, — to all of you, I say, as feel thus, I declare trusting in the promises of Christ that all your sins are forgiven in every way in heaven by God our Father through our Lord and deliverer (who is) blessed for all time. Amen.

But to those who take such pleasure in their sins that they do not find fault with themselves so much as with divine strictness and make excuse for themselves, or to those who somehow acknowledge their sins but, having spurned the goodness of Christ our Lord through his death, invent other remedies of salvation for themselves, — to all these also I declare in accordance with the word of God that all their sins are confirmed in heaven, unless they come to their senses.

As by our prayers we have already clearly shown that we are completely alien from them, so we shall prove it much more so still by the following abbreviated confession of our faith:

I believe in one God, the Father almighty, maker of heaven and earth. And in Jesus Christ, his only begotten son, our Lord. Who was conceived by the Holy Spirit, born of the virgin Mary, suffered under Pontius Pilate, was crucified, dead and buried and went right down to hell. On the third day he rose from the dead. He ascended into heaven and sits at the right hand of God, his almighty Father. From there he will come one day to judge the living and the dead.

I believe in the Holy Spirit, the Holy Catholic Church, the communion of saints, the forgiveness of sins, the resurrection of our bodies and life everlasting. Amen.

At the end of this confession of (their) faith the Minister begins the general prayers for all the needs of the whole Church, while the congregation listens, as follows:
The general prayers for the needs of the Church.

Almighty and merciful Father, who on account of your boundless mercy deigned to free us from the darkness of our ignorance and the abyss of Roman idolatry, when the wholesome light was marvellously revealed to us in the gospel of your Son, we give you thanks on this account, most merciful Father, and we humbly beseech you that you may deign so to strengthen and fortify us with your Holy Spirit through your same beloved Son, that we may be able with his aid to keep the gift of our faith right to the end and somehow express it in newness of life.

We also pray you, most Holy Father, for the catholic Church of your

Son which is spread throughout the entire world, in which the true and wholesome teaching of your Son is taught and observed after the rejection of the abomination and idolatry of the Roman anti-Christ. Keep from it, we beg, all false pastors and teachers, harmful creatures, which destroy your vineyard and trample upon it, and direct into it devout, loyal and hardworking labourers as conscientious stewards of your ministry, who seek not their own, but only your glory and the building up your Church which was redeemed by the most innocent blood of your Son.

We especially pray you, most merciful Father, for the assemblies of this illustrious kingdom and all their ministers, in particular for our most gracious King Edward VI, whom, as up till now you have protected by your powerful hand from his and your enemies alike, so may you deign hereafter too to watch over and protect and guide and rule him with your Holy Spirit, that as your divine grace increases in him day by day as he grows older, so he may be able to govern his people under Christ, the leader of us all, so that by your aid we may be able to lead calm and peaceful lives under him in all piety and righteousness in accordance with your word.

In addition we pray you, most Holy Father, for the whole house and family of the same royal majesty, also for all chiefs and magistrates of his and the whole kingdom, especially for his most eminent Parliament. Bestow on them, we pray by your divine beneficence, the spirit of counsel, the spirit of courage and of perseverance that what they have already begun in abolishing the tyranny of Anti-Christ and in restoring true religion in this illustrious kingdom, they may pursue it right to the end with a determined and unbroken will. Grant to them, Lord, the spirit of unity and concord that they may with one mind follow what is right and promote and preserve peace and tranquillity in the State.

We further pray you for the entire people of this whole kingdom, almighty Father, that they may gladly embrace the teaching of your Son which has been handed down in the writings of the prophets and apostles and that they may daily increase in it more and more and continue steadfastly in lawful obedience to his royal majesty and the other magistrates to the well-being of the whole state and the building up of the Church.

We further pray your divine mercy for this city of London that you may deign to keep from it the common pestilences which we acquire daily and to preserve it in the pursuit of true godliness and peace and general tranquillity. And may you so guide its officials with your Holy Spirit that they may perform their duties faithfully and wisely and in fear of you.

In particular we pray you, most merciful Father, for our Foreigners' Churches here, that, as in your wonderful goodness you wanted them to be planted here, so too you may be willing to honour them with your divine favour so that through your ineffable power and mercy they may be free of all the tyranny of this world and all false teaching. We acknowledge your ineffable kindness in planting them and on this account we give you everlasting thanks. But because we know that whatever does not bear fruit is cut out, and this is a failing in us all — that we ourselves can of ourselves not even think of anything good, much less bear any fruit worthy of you — we humbly beseech you, almighty Father, that you yourself may deign to bring forth in us all through your Holy Spirit good fruits, worthy of that wonderful planting of your Churches here, — namely that our Churches planted here by your aid may have their continual increase in all godliness and true harmony of mind, to the glory of your honourable name and the comfort of the members of your Son exiled here and the building up of your catholic Church.

But we also pray your divine majesty for all other kings, princes and magistrates who, being hard pressed by anti-Christian tyranny, have still not been able to acknowledge the voice of your Son, Christ the Lord, and in ignorance have even persecuted the members of your Son, whom they do not know, like an enemy, that you may deign gradually to lead them and all others wherever they may be, who dwell in the darkness of ignorance or through weakness have somehow even been led astray, into the true light of your Son, so that we may all, gathered into his one fold, through your mercy freely given praise you as our true God Together and bend our knees before you in your same Son.

Finally we pray you, almighty and merciful Father, for all our brothers scattered throughout your holy Church who because of their true acknowledgement of your teaching and of your Son are in any way oppressed by anti-Christian tyranny under his cross. Comfort them, we beg, Lord, through your Holy Spirit who is the author of all true comfort, in their afflictions, and through their own troubles and your divine strength so strengthen their hearts from on high in true faith that they may be able to endure everything which you send upon them patiently, with great courage and thankfulness, and that they may have the strength fearlessly and continually to spread abroad in your Church your name and that of your Son as much in their lives as in their deaths; or may you deign in your grace to free them their wretchedness and afflictions and to mitigate their tribulations, if you think it in any way appropriate to the glory of your honourable name and the building up of your Church.

In particular we pray you most Holy Father, for the brothers of our Churches here, whether they be present or elsewhere away from home, whom you have deigned to visit and harass with your otherwise just judgement or with disease or even prison or want or exile or any hardship of body or soul. Do not abandon them in their afflictions but either in your fatherly kindness and pity lessen their troubles or give them strength and patience that they may endure everything which in your good pleasure you gently send upon them, so that they may realise that they are being proved by you, as by a most gentle father, in their afflictions for the sake of your love towards them. Without doubt you correct and harass those whom you love in this life even by means of alliction, so that thereafter they may appear better and more pure, made in themselves similar to your Son in his afflictions whom you in your eternal and altogether wonderful plan through suffering made immortal as the originator of salvation for us all.

We believe that we will gain this of you, our heavenly Father, by reason of your fatherly love and pity towards us, and in this hope we humbly call upon your holy name through your only beloved Son in the prayer appointed for us by him: Our Father, who art in heaven, etc.

At this point it should be noted that not infrequently other prayers too are inserted before the Lord's Prayer is said, especially if any particular needs of the Church chance to present themselves and seem to demand it in any way.

At the end of the Lord's Prayer, either a baptism is held if it happens that anyone is being presented for baptism, or the Lord's Supper is celebrated, if indeed it is to be celebrated at that time, or those seeking it are joined in matrimony. Or if anything of this kind occurs which ought to be carried out publicly before the congregation, it all takes place soon after the end of the Lord's Prayer. But if nome of these occurs, then those who are particularly appointed for it begin a psalm in the common tongue with great gravity, and soon the whole congregation joins with them like gravity, and whatever is sung by the whole congregation is sung with such restraint that everything which is being sung can be easily understood by all who only know the language.

Then when the psalm has been sung the whole congregation is dismissed by the minister with with peace, a commendation of the poor and the blessing, in these words: "Remember your poor and pray for each other in turn. And may God have mercy on you and bless you. May he shine upon you with the light of his divine countenance to the glory of his holy name and may he protect you in holy and health-giving peace. Amen."

While this is being said by the minister, the deacons in accordance with their position stand in line at the doors of the church and diligently collect alms at the doors of the church once the congregation has been dismissed and straightway write down in church whatever they have collected. This should be always be done at all other services of the church too.

Furthermore, the form of every other service on whatever day and at all meetings of the church is the same, except that the reading of the Ten Commandments, the prayer including the confession and absolution and the saying of the creed is omitted at all other services. But at the end of the service, as soon as the first prayer is finished, the Minister immediately starts the general prayers for the needs of the Church. And in this way when the Lord's Prayer has been added and the psalm sung the congregation is dismissed with the blessing written above: "Remember your poor etc.".

At afternoon sevices on Sundays the form of the service is just the same, but once the text of scripture read to the people has been explained (which should be for the space of one half hour only) the Minister commences the explanation of the greater Catechism which the children recite in the common tongue as is published in the church's books in their places where it had been finished at the previous service. More about this later, when there will be a special discussion about the practice of the Catechism.

Once the explanation of the Catechism is over, the service is ended with the prayers written above and the singing of a psalm, with the omission of the reading of the Ten Commandments and the prayer which includes the confession and absolution, and of the Creed, which is only used at morning services on Sundays.

Normally on Thursdays, however, public meetings of the congregation and public services are also held, unless a feast day falls upon the Wednesday or Friday next to it, the observance of which cannot yet have been ended. For on such an occasion the service is transferred to the feast day itself, not because of any distinction between the days, but so that the people, who do not then pursue their occupations, do not lose that day in leisure without hearing any admonishment from the word of God. Not infrequently too, however, it happens that a public service is held both on feast days, if they happen to occur in the week, and also notwithstanding on Thursdays as well, if it seems appropriate for the congregation.

And exactly the same form of service is observed on Thursdays too as is accustomed to be observed on other days during the week, except that at the end of the service when the general prayers of the Church have been said, before the psalm is sung, a public comparison of the scriptures in the common tongue is begun which we call Prophesying, in which the teaching of the previous services during the whole of that week is publicly examined and confirmed by means of a careful comparison of the places in scripture, and a unanimous agreement of the teaching is retained throughout the congregation. Such a Prophesying or examination of teaching lasts for an hour and then a psalm is sung. When it is finished, the congregation is dismissed in the manner described above with the blessing. But since we have two (different) practices of the Prophesying, one in the German, the other in the French Church, both of them of use to the Church and in agreement with the scriptures, we shall have to explain the procedure of them both. However, we shall first talk about the practice and procedure of the German Prophesying, then the French, when we have first explained the practice and examination of the catechism.

(The Lord's Supper)

Then the Minister begins the general prayers of the Church whose prescriben form is given above in connection with the ceremonies on an ordinary Sunday. At the end of the prayers, before the psalm is sung, he begins the rites of the (Lord's) Supper as follows.

First of all the ministers, elders and deacons all stand in front of the prepared table, with their faces turned towards the people, except for the Minister himself who is conducting the service. For he stays in the pulpit, and when the rest of the ministers, elders and deacons have taken their places in order in front of the table, as mentioned, first of all he reminds the congregation about all those who are to be prevented from enjoying the (Lord's) Supper.

First of all, if anyone in particular had been prevented from enjoying the Supper at the previous day's service, whether their name had been added or left out, in accordance with the measure of their blame, they are again prevented from coming to the Supper in the same way as before.

Then by public announcement all those in addition are prevented from enjoying the Supper, who have neither made confession of their faith either in public or at least before the ministers and elders of the Church, nor of their own free will have made themselves subject to the Church's teaching. For since they are unwilling to be counted among the members of our faith in the Church, so that they may acknowledge our ministry, neither can we count them among our sheep.

Finally, those too are prevented from enjoying the (Lord's) Supper who within fifteen days of the first announcement of the Supper have not once presented themselves to the ministers and elders, unless ill health has prevented them. For since they spurn the Church's ordination in our ministry, so that we can be sure about increases or decreases in the congregation and also so that we may fully examine the faith of everyone in the Church and, so far as is in us, remove hypocrites from the service, they declare themselves unworthy of being admitted to the Lord's Supper.

In general all those are rebuked as well who, after they have joined the Church, do not come for a while to the celebration of the Lord's Supper, even though they are not prevented by illness or any other pressing need, and the

Church teaches that all such people sin most grievously, first against Christ himself, the author of his Supper, who is despised in his own institution, and then too against the whole Church which is not respected in its public services and public ministry in accordance with the duties of each Christian.

At the conclusion of this brief preface, as it were, the Minister urges the congregation each to prepare themselves to approach the Lord's Supper in a worthy manner, and invites them all to pray with him and, as the whole congregation falls on its knees, prays in a loud voice from the pulpit as follows:

Almighty and everlasting God, merciful Father, behold we come here in the sight of your divine majesty to celebrate the Supper of your only begotten Son, Christ the Lord, in accordance with his instruction, so that we may celebrate the memory of his sacred body given up to death for us and of his most innocent blood poured also for our atonement, and that we may publicly and in the company of our Church bear witness to our sharing with him in the same body and blood. We therefore humbly beseech you, most Holy Father, that our hearts may be inspired by your Holy Spirit and that we may be able worthily to recognise for ourselves the great kindness of your Son towards us and practise our faith in him, and so through the increase of our faith and the strengthening of our hearts in our health-giving participation with him we may through your grace all be fed to life eternal which we do not doubt is prepared for us in him from everlasting in accordance with your ineffable mercy. We ask this of you, most merciful Father, in the name of your same Son, who alone is the true and only food of our spirits, so that we ourselves may be aware within ourselves by means of the evidence of our own conscience that you truly are God and our Father who hears us and that we in turn are your children and people, consecrated by the most precious blood of your Son, who lives and reigns with that same Son and Holy Spirit, ever one and three, God, worthy to be praised for ever. Amen.

At the end of this prayer the Minister urges the whole congregation to listen attentively to the institution of the Lord's Supper as recorded by St. Paul. Then in clear words he reads aloud the institution as follows:

This (is what) Paul the Apostle says concerning the institution of the Lord's Supper: he says, "I have received from the Lord what I have also handed on to you. Namely, that our Lord Jesus Christ on the very night in which he was betrayed took bread, and after giving thanks broke it and said, "This is my body, which is broken for you; do this in remembrance of me". Similarly, when he had eaten, he also (took) the cup, saying, "This cup is the new testament in my blood; do this as often as you drink, in remembrance of me. For as often as you eat this bread and drink this cup, you proclaim the death of the Lord, until he comes. Therefore whoever eats this bread or drinks this cup in a manner unworthy of the Lord will be guilty of the body and blood of the Lord. Let a man prove himself, however, and thus eat of this bread and drink of this cup. For he who eats and drinks unworthily, eats and drinks judgement for himself, by not distinguishing the body of the Lord".

When the institution of the Lord's Supper according to Paul has been read aloud in this way, the Minister briefly reminds the whole congregation once more about the dire threat in these words of Paul whereby those who partake unworthily in the bread and cup at the Lord's Supper are said to eat and drink judgment or damnation to themselves, in these words:

"You have heard, my brothers, how much peril an unworthy sharing of the bread and cup in this Supper brings with it, namely that it makes us guilty of the body and blood of Christ and that through such participation we are ourselves bringing eternal damnation upon ourselves. You have also heard where the blame for such an unworthy participation lies, namely in making no distinction in the body of the Lord. And you have heard in the same words of the Apostle Paul that this very distinction for the most part stems from a serous and diligent examination of ourselves. Indeed, those who do not distinguish between the body of the Lord share unworthily in the Lord's Supper as much as those who do not examine themselves. And again, if those who do distinguish share as worthily as do those who examine themselves, it is clear that the distinction in the body of the Lord in these words of Paul depends to a very large extent on a real and serious examination of ourselves. You have also heard on what an examination of ourselves in the main depends, namely in a real acquaintance with God and ourselves which somehow leads us to recognise the extent of his divine kindness to us in Christ and which in a marvellous way entrusts to us the worthiness of our sharing with Christ the Lord in his body and blood and causes us, once the worthiness of our sharing with Christ the Lord has been recognised, with the greatest reverence to distinguish the mystic food and drink of the Lord's Supper from all other food and drink and in like manner to distinguish too the body of the Lord in the exercise of the (Lords's) Supper, once our sharing with Christ in it has been considered by us.

Finally, you have heard how our sharing with Christ in his body and blood is represented and entrusted to the whole Church by the token of the Lord's Supper in its individual parts, and (you have heard) it under many names and considerations which are put before us in the individual parts of the token in the Supper as though before our eyes. Therefore now ponder all this yourselves in your hearts and turn it over in your minds and after begging the help of the Holy Spirit, lift up your hearts to perceive the effectual power and worthiness of our blessed and never to be interrupted sharing with Christ the Lord in his sacred body and blood. May our heavenly Father bestow this on us all through his Holy Spirit, with whom and his beloved Son he lives and reigns together, the true one and everlasting God, worthy of praise throughout all ages. Amen".

At the end of this admonishment the Minister comes down from the pulpit, while the whole congregation sits quietly, and comes to the other Ministers, Elders and deacons before the table prepared in the view of the whole congregation, as has already been mentioned, and sitting there in the midst of the Ministers, he reads aloud, facing the people, that joyful and salutary message from Paul to the whole congregation about that most innocent sacrifice for the whole world, Jesus Christ, who was offered up for our sins, in these words:

"See, beloved brothers. Christ, our Paschal Lamb, is sacrificed for us. Therefore let us keep the feast, not with the old leaven, nor with the leaven of malice and wickedness, but with unleavened bread, namely with sincerity and truth, through the same Jesus Christ, our Lord and Saviour. Amen".

After saying this the minister sits down at the centre of the table, his face turned towards the people, and on either side of him the other Ministers, Elders and deacons all take their places in order, and other people from the congregation until the whole table is full, but leaving an empty space in front of the Minister so that at all times he can be easily seen and heard by the whole congregation. When the whole table is full, with the exception of the space in front of the Minister, in the sight of the whole congregation the Minister takes bread into his hands from the larger plate which is full of bread, and in the sight and hearing of the whole congregation says in a loud voice and with clear words, "The bread which we break is a sharing in the body of Christ".

And at the same time as he says this, he breaks the bread which he has taken into his hands until he has filled both smaller plates, placed on either side of the larger plate piled (high) with bread, with the bread so broken, as much as is sufficient for one sitting at the table, so that each of those at the table can take a piece of bread from it. Meanwhile four cups, about which mention has already been made, are filled with wine and two are put on each side of the smaller plates. When all this has been arranged in this way, the Minister distributes one at a time the now broken bread, taken from the smaller plates, to those sitting next to him on either side, and while distributing it says, "Take, eat and remember that the body of our Lord Jesus Christ was for us given up to death upon the beam of the cross for the remission of all our sins".

At the same time the Minister himself too takes and eats a piece of bread and then passes the smaller plates with the broken bread to the ends of the table on either side, so that each person may take a piece of bread from it and eat it in memory of the body of Christ which was given up to death for him, until the plates reach the ends of the table via the others next to them and each of those at the table has taken bread from it to eat. When the Minister sees that all at the table have eaten of the bread, he takes a cup into his hand and then says in a loud voice, "The cup of blessing which we bless is a sharing in the blood of Christ".

Then giving two cups to either side, he says, "Take, drink and remember that the blood of our Lord Jesus Christ was for us poured out upon the beam of the cross for the remission of all our sins".

At the same time, in between giving the cups, the Minister himself drinks from one of them, and then all the others at the table, one giving the cup received from the Minister to another until everyone has drunk. When everyone at that sitting has drunk, all rise from the table, except only the Minister; for he sits at the centre of the table in his place to administer the Supper to all the rest of the congregation.

Certain Elders of the Church who have been specially allotted for it, bring back to the Minister at the centre of the table in their special order both the smaller plates which had been passed down to the ends of the table with the broken bread, and also the cups which are filled once more. Other Elders and deacons watch all those who want to come to the Lord's table, so that no unknown person may approach. And one of the Ministers goes up into the pulpit and in a loud voice and with clear words begins a sacred reading from the sixth chapter of John in which our spiritual participation in the body and blood of Christ is explained and commended to us. While this is being read, the congregation comes to the Lord's table from both sides of the church and from the ends of the table to its middle come up on either side of the table until the whole table is full, first the men in their due order, then the women. And when they have all sat down, the reader pauses for a time in his reading from the pulpit, so that the Minister sitting at the centre of the table may once more break the bread for those who have now sat down and together with the cup may procure as much as he thinks is sufficient for a whole new sitting. So, when the Minister sees that the whole table is full once more with the new sitting of brothers and the reader has ceased from his reading, then the Minister takes into his hands the bread, now broken, from the smaller plates, and, as he had done before, distributes it to those sitting next to him, adding the words written above at the first distribution of the bread. And so also, when he sees that all on both sides have taken and eaten the bread, he once more gives the cup on both sides to all who are at the table, adding the words already spoken when the cup was first held up. After these words when the cup is being displayed, the reader once more continues with his reading from the pulpit until those who were at the table rise again and others take their places in order, as has been mentioned. After each sitting the Elders appointed for the purpose take back in due order to the centre of the table the plates and the cups, once more filled by the deacons, and put them before the Minister, and he again breaks the bread taken from the larger plate (and puts it) on the smaller plates which have been put before him, as before, as much as he thinks is sufficient for each sitting. And in this way, while the other Elders and deacons continually watch the whole congregation, they come up in succession one after the other, as has been said, to the Lord's table in complete silence and with great dignity so that the sacred reading may in no way be interrupted. And when the men have shared in the Lord's Supper, then the women come up in order, as the men, to the Lord's table without any distinction of person, but as is convenient for each one, starting with those who were sitting further away than the rest in the company. At each sitting the reader breaks off his reading when he sees that the time has come for the Minister to display the bread and cup of the Supper to those who have taken their place (at the table), and when he has finished the sixth chapter of John, he continues his reading with the thirteenth, fourteenth and fifteenth chapters of the same evangelist and so on until the whole performance of the Supper is ended. Occasionally other readings are made from the scriptures as the Ministers of the Church judge it to be to the greater advantage of the congregation for its edification.

At the end of the entire performance of the Supper the reader ceases his reading from the pulpit and the Minister who administered the Supper or a Minister rises from the table and standing in the middle between the other Ministers and Elders before the table addresses the whole congregation with these words:

Be sure and do not doubt, all of you who have participated in this Lord's Supper and meditated on his divine mystery, that you have a sure and health-giving sharing with him in his body and blood to eternal life. Amen.

Then he invites the congregation to give general thanks with a preface of the following kind:

I think that there is none of you who on the evidence of this Supper do not realise within themselves the power and fruits of our sharing with the Christ the Lord in his body and blood, namely the peace and calm of your conscience because of the innocence, righteousness, recompense and victory of Christ the Lord, all of which we have witnessed are ours as a result of the practice of this Supper in accordance with the institution of Christ himself as surely as we know that we ourselves have shared in the bread and cup of the Supper with our own hands and mouths. I hope too that in coming to this table you have all perceived with the eyes of your faith that blessed reclining at table in the kingdom of God with Abraham, Isaac and Jacob, and that in your trust in the righteousness, recompense and victory of Christ the Lord in the sharing of which we have now been pledged you are as sure of this as we have surely taken our places together at this table of the Lord.

Moreover I do not doubt that you in turn feel some impulse in your hearts, on the Holy Spirit's instance, to give thanks for his divine favour for all these kindnesses bestowed upon us in Christ the Lord, and that every obligation of our thanks should be discharged so far as is in us, namely that we try to express in every way the righteousness, recompense and victory of Christ the Lord which has been given to us and God's great gifts to us and not mar them again by our own sins and drive them from us by our own wickedness. I believe that by means of the Holy Spirit you realise all this in your hearts, and therefore I think it right that, on account of all these gifts, we should fall on our knees and thank our God and Father and humbly beg that we may daily be strengthened in them more throughout all our life.

The Giving of Thanks after the administration of the Lord's Supper.

Lord God and our Heavenly Father, we thank your divine majesty through your Son, Jesus Christ, our Lord and Redeemer, that in that same Son you deigned to recall us from eternal death in which we had been confined through the expiation of all our sins in his death and the sharing given freely to us in his entire righteousness, recompense and victory, having observed which alone in itself in your eternal providence, you have chosen us, confined (though we were), for the body of your son for eternal life before the world was made. (We thank you) too that you have deigned to give him to us for food and our wholesome refreshment because of our inborn weakness which has no constant remedy in the administration, instituted by himself, of your divine word and sacrament in his Church, which we have now through your grace carried out. We acknowledge that all these are the free gifts of your ineffable divine goodness and mercy, bestowed upon us beyond all that we deserve. But we also acknowledge our own weakness and misery in ourselves, namely that of ourselves we can neither retain these your gifts nor express our thanks to you as we ought. Just as therefore we fall before your feet and thank you for these your kindnesses, most kindly Father, so too we humbly beg you through your same Son that you may deign to preserve in us to the very end this joining of us into one body with Christ which in your eternal providence and mercy you have long since undertaken and daily to strengthen us more and more through your Holy Spirit in his sure faith, so that, though we ourselves of ourselves can do nothing, nevertheless we may somehow be able to realise in our hearts the fruits of our faith both within ourselves through the renewal of our mind and of our affections and also declare them before your Church through the obligations of affection, so that your honourable name may be thus considered truly holy amongst us and be piously worshipped throughout the whole world, who alone in your divine Trinity are the one, true and eternal God, worthy to be praised above all (else). Amen.

At the end of this thanksgiving the Minister adds a brief reminder in which are explained the mysteries which proceed from a consideration of the elements of the Supper, the bread and the wine, and the congregation is reminded of its debt and obligation towards Christ for his kindnesses.

The theme of the reminder after the administration of the Lord's Supper.

The congregation is reminded, so that it may respect the mysteries in the very elements of the Supper, the bread and the wine, what in itself is unthinkable, that without thought they have invited Christ the Lord to its table and Supper. This can be easily understood from the words of Paul when he talks about the bread. Almost the same things can be noted upon consideration of the wine, as also in the bread, if only a few things are adapted in accordance with the nature of each, so that what is said of one can be seen to be said about both. And since Paul specifically mentions the mystery of the bread, it will be sufficient for us too if, following Paul's example, in considering only the bread we note those things which seem both in agreement with the word of God and also to lead more closely to the building up of the Church.

Therefore the congragation is taught that in the practice of the Lord's Supper through the element of the bread is signified for us, not the very substance of Christ's natural body when the substance of the bread has been removed, but rather the body of the Church which has assembled to share in the Supper. For thus Paul clearly teaches that we, who eat of one bread, are one bread. By these words of Paul is completely refuted the whole doctrine of transubstantiation of the Pope. For by the eating of it we are said to be that which we eat, indeed what we eat ought in reality to be that which we are said to be through eating it, if indeed the reasoning itself ought to make any advance. Otherwise, if in the Lord's Supper that which we eat *had* only been, but *is* no more bread, as the Papists idly think, by eating that which *is* not, but only *had* been bread we should without doubt not be able to be said to *be* bread now, but rather to *have* been. For us then the view of Paul alone is of more importance in this respect than that of all the transubstantial Papists, with whatever titles or insignia they may be adorned.

The congregation is also taught that the doctrine was not handed down to us by Paul to no purpose, that we are all one bread for this reason that we all alike partake of one bread in the (Lord's) Supper. Doubtless so that we may realise that, while we are all said to be one bread, all those things are required in us which it is agreed are characteristic of bread in itself in accordance with its nature. Moreover that there are many things which can be said about the characteristics of bread and adapted to our own consistution, but that there are certain special points which it is advantageous to be noted with profit and edification, which are briefly explained as follows:

(1) Just as bread cannot exist unless many grains have been collected together into one, so we must realise that we too cannot truly be the Lord's bread, which by the evidence of the (Lord's) Supper we profess that we are, unless we perceive that we are so gathered together in the Lord that we acknowledge that we acknowledge that we are members of one and the same body brought together under one head, Christ the Lord.

(2) Just as it is not sufficient that many grains are collected together to become bread unless they are ground equally on a mill-stone, so too we must realise that it is not sufficient that we are the bread of the Lord if we are gathered together into one, unless we all offer ourselves alike too with all the emotions of our flesh and all the counsels of our judgement, because it is of special importance for things divine, voluntarily to be ground upon the millstone of the divine word for the denial of ourselves and the endurance of the cross.

(3) Just as this too is not sufficient to become bread if grains collected together are ground, but when they have been ground, they have to be cleansed in order to become fine bread, so too we must realise that it is our duty and obligation that all the coarse bran amongst us, who still disgrace the ground grains in every way and do not allow themselves in any way to be cleansed by mutual correction in accordance with the word of God through the practice of the Church's teaching, should not be endured at all amongst us, if we want to be pure bread in the sight of Christ the Lord.

(4) Just as bread still cannot exist once all the grains from which bread ought to be made have been collected together, ground and cleansed, unless they are so bound together in one paste by the further addition of some water so that they cannot be further separated, so too we must realise that it is still not sufficient that we be the Lord's bread, if we seem to ourselves to have been gathered together, ground and cleansed, but that we ought still to have poured into us that life-giving water which only Christ the Lord can pour upon us in accordance with the will of his heavenly Father, I mean the Holy and honourable Spirit, by whose divine bond we are so united into one paste by an indissoluble link that there is one mind, one will and one faith of us all in Christ, whose bread we profess we are.

(5) Just as still not even then is bread complete when grains collected to-

gether, ground and cleansed are finally held bound together into one paste, but that paste has to be shaped into the form of the bread and then put into the furnace that has been lit so that it may be baked, so too we must realise that it is still not sufficient if we want to be the Lord's complete bread that we are gathered tother, ground, cleansed and then also made into one paste, but we should be shaped throughout our whole lives on the example of Christ who is the bread of our life, in such a way that his form can be seen in us, and that our afflictions and persecutions should be exposed to all the pressures of this life so that we may not refuse to be tried as though in a furnace and baked like bread, if indeed the Lord wants to entrust anything to us in accordance with the purpose of his will.

This is said in this way concerning the consideration of the bread in the reminder which is given after the administration of the Supper, so that everyone in the congregation may declare themselves to be the Lord's true bread in expressing these characteristics of bread, each in accordance with the measure of his gifts. Furthermore, all these reminders are extended or shortened as the situation and time seems to demand.

At the very end of this reminder a psalm is sung in the common tongue by the whole congregation. At the end of it the congregation is dismissed in the customary way with the commendation of the poor and the blessing of the whole congregation.

And the deacons, as has also been mentioned elsewhere, collect alms for the poor at the doors of the Church and distribute the residue of the bread and wine which remains from the celebration of the (Lord's) Supper to the poor of the congregation, as each has need, especially to the infirm or aged. So much for the ceremony of the Lord's Supper.

The fourme

of common prayers vsed in the churches of Geneua.

IN the woorkyng dayes, the preacher maketh such exhortacion vnto prayer, as seemeth vnto hymselfe moste meete: applying or framyng the same, bothe to the tyme and matter whiche he entreateth of in hys sermon.

The Sundaye morning, immediately beefore the sermon, the preacher vseth commonly a maner to praye, as hereafter foloweth.

OUr ayde and succour is in the name and power of GOD, whiche made bothe heauen and earth. So be it.

The Confession.

A.i.   My

Prayers.

My brethren, se that every one of you shew himselfe before the face of ye LORD, acknowlegyng vnto him al your faultes & offences, thinkyng euen from the botom of your hertes, ye wordes which I shal speake.

Lord God euerlastyng and almightye Father, wee confesse and knowledge vnfaynedly before thy blessed maiestye, that we are miserable sinners, conceyued and borne in vnrighteousnesse, and fylthe of synne, beyng naturally inclyned to doe wickedlye, beyng also vnapte and vnhable to doe any thing that is good, and that by the ssame synne planted in our selfe by nature, wee transgresse without all measure (neuer ceassyng

Prayers. Fol. ii.

ceassynge from the same) thy moste holye and blessed commaundementes: wherein wee procure vnto oure selues by thy ryghteouse iudgementes, confusyon and destructyon. Yet moste mercyfull Father and LORDE, for asmuche as wee are dyspleased with oure selues, in that wee haue offended thy goodnesse: and seeynge wee condemne bothe oure selues and oure wyckednesse, beyinge truelye repentaunte for the same, moste instauntelye desyrynge that thou of thy bountyfull goodnesse wylte helpe vs in this miserye: vouchsafe moste louynge FATHER, to haue pitie

A.ii.

Prayers.   Prayers.   Fol. iii.

pitie of vs for thy onely sonnes sake, for the merites (I say) of our LORDE Iesu Christ: not allonlye in puttyng awaye oure faultes and transgressyons, but also in geuynge vnto vs the gyftes of thy holye spirite, increasynge the same from tyme to tyme, to the ende that wee continuallye, euen from the bottome of oure heartes, knowleging our own vnrighteousnesse, may conceiue such a dyspleasure towardes sinne, as may bryng furth an vnfayned repentaunce, whereby we may both mortifye our sinnes, and also of an vpryght conscience shew furth the fruites of ryghteousnes, whiche fruites (not) withstandyng they bee polluted and imperfect through our naughty nature) yet thou doost accepte as perfecte, for IESV Christes sake, whiche lyueth. &c.

When the preacher hath on thys wyse made his supplication, the whole multitude syngeth some Psalme in playnesong (the whiche thyng doone) the preacher begynneth to make hys prayer agayne, that God of hys grace would vouchesafe to sendedowne hys holy spirite, as well that he may sette foorth the woord to the auauncement of Gods honoure and edifying of the people, as that the hearers made also accept it humbly with obedience vnto the same.

The manner of prayer is refferred to the dyscrecion of the preacher: Immeadyatly after the sermon, when the preacher hath exhorted the people to pray, he begynneth on thys wyse.

℞ A.iiii.

O Almighty GOD our heauenly Father, sithens thou hast fyrste promysed to fulfyll our requestes whiche we shall make vnto thee in the name of our Lord Iesu Christ, thy welbeloued sonne: Secondarily, for so much as ye Doctrine of Christ and hys Apostles doth teache vs to make our common prayer in his name, promisyng that he will bee amonge vs, and that he will make intercession for vs vnto thee, for the obtainyng of al such thinges, as we shall Godly agree vpon, here in earth: And thyrdly seeing thou hast geuen vs in commaundement to praye, especiallye for suche as thou hast appointed rulers and gouernours ouer vs,

Ioh.16.
Mat.18.
1.Tim.2.

vs, and also for thynges nedefull to thy congregacion, and for all sortes of menne: wee concidrynge a hardynesse, throughe thy holye woorde, leanynge assuredlye vnto thy moste vndoubted promesse, in so muche as wee are here gathered together beefore thy face in the name of thy onelye sonne oure Lorde IESVS: Wee therfore (I say) make our earnest supplication vnto thee, oure moste mercifull God and bountifull Father, that for Iesus Christes sake our sauioure and onely mediatour, it maye please thee of thy infinite mercy freely to pardon our offences, and in suche sort to drawe and lyft vp our hartes & affections to towardes thee, that oure requestes maye bothe procede of a feruent mynd, and also be agreeable vnto thy most blessed will and pleasure, whiche is onely to be accepted.

*We beseche thee therefore our heauenly FATHER, as touchinge all princes and rulers of the congregation, vnto whome thou hast committed the adminiftration of thy Iustice, and namely, as touchyng the gouernours of this Citie, that it woulde please thee to graunte them thy holy spirite (the which onely by righte is called the principall spirite) so to increase the same from time to time in them, that they (knowing aſſuredly and hauing a pure fayth knowyng Iesus Christe thy onely sonne oure LORD, to bee the kyng of all kynges, and gouernour of all gouernours, euen accordynge as thou hast general power vnto him both in heauen and in earth, maye bende themselues with theyr whole indeuour, to serue him, and to aduance his kingdome and glorye in theyr Dominions, rulyng theyr subiectes, whiche bee thy creatures, and the shepe of thy pasture, euen after thy good pleasure: wherefore euery where, may serue thee in all holines and vertue, and that wee beyng quyete and safe from all feare of ene-

*Psal.10.

1.Tim.6.
Act.17.1.
Mat.2.8.

mies, may tender duelye unto the, laudes and praises during the tearme of our lyfe. We beseche thee also (most deare Father and sauioure) for all pastours & curates of thy flocke, unto whom thou hast committed the charge of mens soules, & the ministery of thy holy gospel, p it wil please thee likewise to to gyve them with thy holy spite, that they may be founde perfecte, faythfull and prayse worthy ministers of thy glory, directing alwayes their whole studies unto this end, that the poore shepe whyche be gone astraye oute of Christes flocke, may be sought out & broughte agayne unto the Lorde Iesu, which is the chiefe shepeheard, and head of all bishops, whereby they may from day to daye grow and increase in hym unto all righteousnes and holynesse. And on the other parte, that it maye please thee to deliuer all thy congregacyons from the daunger of rauening wolfes, and from hyrelinges, who searche theyr owne ambicion and profyt, and not onelye the settynge foorthe of thy glorye, and the safegarde of thy flocke.

Moreouer, we make our prayers unto thee (most mercifull & louing Father) for al menne in generall, that as thy will is that all the worlde knowledge thee to bee theyr sauiour thorowe the redemption made

Prayers.

by thy onely sonne Iesu Christ: euen so that such as haue bene hitherto holden captyue in darkenesse and ignoraunce for lacke of the knowledge of thy Gospell, maye through the preaching thereof, & the cleare lyghte of thy holye spirite, bee broughte into the ryght waye of healthe euerlastyng, which is, to know that thou art onely very GOD, & that he whom thou hast sente is our sauiour Christ. Lykewise y^t they whome *Iohn.17.* thou haste alreadye endued with thy grace, whose heartes *Ephe.1.* thou hast lyghtened with the ryght knowledge of thy word, may continualiye encrease in godlynes, and bee plenteously endued with spirituall bene-

Prayers. Fol. vii.

fites: so that we maye altogether in one accorde, both with hearte and mouthe render due hono; and seruyce vnto Christ, who is oure onelye maister, kyng, and lawmaker.

In lyke maner (O LORD of all true coumforte) we committ vnto thee in oure prayers all suche persones, as thou hast visited and chastened with the crosse of tribulation, all suche people as thou haste punisshed with pestilence, warre, or famyne, and all other persones afflicted with pouertye, imprisonmente, sickenesse, or banyshment, or any lyke bodely aduersitie, or hast otherwise troubled and afflicted in spirite: that it will please thee to make

make them perceyue thy tender Fatherly affections towardes them: that is, that these
Crosses bee nothynge elles
but Fatherly chastenynges to
brynge them to amendment,
whereby they may be fashion-
ed and with all theyr heartes
tourne vnto thee, whereby
they cleauynge vnto thee and
receaue full coumforte and so
bee cleane deliuered from all
maner of euyll.

Finallye (O GOD most deare
Father) we beseche the to graunt
vs also, by (I saye) whiche
bee here gathered together
in the name of thy sonne Iesu,
to heare his word preached
(*and to celebrate bys holye Supper)
that

If the sacramente be mynistred.

that wee maye knowledge
truely and vnfaynedlye without hipocrisye, and dissimula-
tion, in how miserable a state
of perdicion wee are in by nature, & howe worthely we procure vnto our selues euerlastyng damnacion, heapyng vp
frō time to time thy grieuous
punishmētes towards vs, thorowe oure wicked and sinnes
full lyfe: whereby seeyng that
there remayneth no sparke of
goodnesse in oure natures, &
that there is nothyng in vs as
touchyng our fyrst creacion &
in which we receiue of our pa-
rētes, mete to enioy & heritage
of Gods kingdome, we may yelde
ouer vp our selues with alour
heartes (hauing a substancial
and

and constant fayth) vnto thy dearly beloued sonne IESV our LORD, our onely sauiour, and redemer: to the ende that he dwellyng in vs maye mortifye our olde man (þ is to say) our sinneful affections, & that we may be regenerated in

Halowed be thy name.

to a more godly lyfe: ✳whereby thy holy name (as it is worthy of all honour) may be aduaunced and magnifyed through out the worlde and in all pla-

Thy kingdō come

ces: ✳so that whyles thou hast the tuition and gouernaunce ouer vs, we may learne dayly more and more to humble and submitte our selues vnto thee in such sorte that thou mayest bee counted Lorde and Kyng ouer all the worlde, gui-

dyng thy people with the scep-tre of thy word, by the vertue of thy holy spirite, to the confusion of all thyne enemyes through the might of thy truth and ryghteousnesse: so that by thys meanes all power and statelynesse withstandyng thy glory, may be cōtinually thro-

Thy will be done.

wen down and abolished, vnto suche tyme, as the full and perfecte face of thy kyngdome shall appeare, when thou shalt shewe thy selfe in iudgemente: Whereby also we with the rest of thy creatures, may render obedience, euen as thy holy Aungels doe applye them selues onely to the perfourmyng of the commaundementes: so that

Prayers.   Fol.x.

affectuouslye knowledge the to bee oure FATHER, lokynge for all good giftes at thy hande: and by thys meanes we withdrawyng and pulling backe all oure affiaunce from creatures, made seeke thee and cleaue onelye vnto thee, puttyng oure whole trust in thy moste bountifull mercye, and for so muche as whyles wee continue here in this transitorye life, we are so myserable, so frayle, and so muche enclyned vnto sinne, that wee fall continualiye and swerue from the ryght way of thy commaundementes. Wee beseche thee pardon oure innumerable offences by thy passion

Prayers.

thy onely will maye be accomplished and fulfylled without all reppynges, and that euery man may bend hymselfe to serue and please thee, the contentacion of their own willes, and theyr proper desyres or affeccyons beeynge bitterlye sette aparte. Graunte vs also (good LORD) that wee thus walkyng in the loue & dreade of thy holye name, maye bee fed and sustayned through thy goodnes, that we may receaue at thy handes al thinges expedyente and necessarye for bodye, wherby we may lyue peaceablye and quietelye, beyng also mete & apt to receaue thy giftes to thys ende that when wee see that thou hast regarde and care for vs: we maye the more

We are woo(r)thelpe in daunger of thy iudgement and condemnacion, and forgeue vs so frely, that death and sinne, vnder whome we bee by nature holden in miserable captiuitye, maye hereafter haue no title, nor righte vnto vs: and that it may please the not to lay vnto our charge, that euil & naughty roote or fountayne of sinne, which doth euermore remayne in vs: in lyke maner as we forget the wronges or damages which other men doe vnto vs, and as we in the steade of seking vengeaunce, procure or purchase the welth of our enemies. Finallye, lette it bee thy good pleasure to ayde vs, to

Mat.6. *And lead vs not into temptacion.* holde vp and sustayne oure weaknes, that hereafter the readines to synne whiche abydeth in vs, doe not cause vs to fall: and that where as we our selues be so frayle that we are not able to stand vprighte one minute of an houre: and where as on the other parte agayne, we are so belayde and assaulted euermore with such a multitude of so daungerous enemies, that the deuil, the world, sinne, and our owne concupiscence, dooe neuer leaue of to wage battayle agaynste vs, let it stand with thy good pleasure to strengthen vs with thy holy spirite, and to dooe vpon vs, the sure armoure of thy grace, that thereby we maye bee able to withstande mightelye all

Prayers. Fol.xii.

crosse vs vnto euerlastynge lyfe: Euen so mape it please thee to endue vs with thy spe=cyall grace, that with moste bryghte syngleneße of heart, and earneste feruentenesse of affeccyons, wee maye moste thankefullye receyue at thys hande so hygh a benefite, and so worthy, (that is to say) that we may with a constante and assured faythe, receaue bothe hys bodye and bloude, yea, bothe CHRIST hymselfe wholye, euen as he, beeynge both verye GOD and manne, is moste woorthye named to bee the holye bread of hea-uen, to quicken and refreshe oure soules: to the ende that from henceforthe wee maye

Prayers.

all maner temptacyons, and to endure manfullye in this spirituall conflicte agaynste synne, vntyll suche tyme as we shall wynne the feilde, that we maye once tryumphantelye re-ioyce in thy kyngdome, with our captayne and gouernour our Lord Iesu Christ.

What day they celebrate the sup-per of the Lorde, they vse also to saye thys that foloweth.

AND accordyng as oure Lord Iesu thought it not sufficient only to offer vp once his blessed body and bloud on the crosse to acquite vs of all our sinnes: but doth vouchsafe also spiritually, to deale and dystribute the selfe same into vs, as for a contynuaunce

Prayers.

cease to lyue in our selues, and after the course or inclinacion of our owne most corrupt and defyled nature: and that we may lyue in hym, whiles we haue hym also lyuing in vs, to conducte and guyde vs vnto the holy, most blessed and euerlastynge lyfe. Graunte vs also that in receyuing the same, we become in verye deede partakers of the newe and euerlastyng testament (that is to say) of the couenaunt of grace and mercy, being most certayn and assured, that thy good pleasure is to be our euerlasting merciful Father, whyle thou layest not to our charge our manyfolde offences, and promisest for vs as thy dearely beloued

Prayers. Fol.lxiii.

ned chyldren and heyres, all thynges needefull as well for the body as for ye soule, so that we may without ceassing render laudes and thankes vnto thee, euermore extollyng, and magnifyinge thy holye name both by worde and deede. And fynally, geue vs grace so to celebrate this day the holy remembraūce of thy blessed and dearelye beloued sonne, yea in suche sorte to vse and practyse our selues therein, and so to shewe forth and declare thy worthy benefites of this pretious Death: that we receiuing thereby farther strengthe and more ample increase in fayth and all good thynges, that with the inwarde courage, and

Prayers. Fol.xliii.

foode and nouryshemente vnto euerlastynge life. Graunt to vs (wee beseche thee) yet moreouer, thys one requeste, that thou doe neuer suffer vs to become so vnkynde, as to forgette so worthye benefytes, but rather so imprinte them and fasten them in oure heartes, that wee maye growe and increase dayly more and more in suche a ryghte faythe as doothe carefullye trauayle, and is continuallye occupyed in all manner of good woorkes, and that in so doynge, wee maye leade oure whole lyfe to the aduauncemente of thy glory, and edifying of our neyghbours, thorough thy Sonne Iesus Christe oure lorde. Amen.

Prayers.

the more confidence prayse the our FATHER, reioysyng and glorifying onely in thy name.

After the Supper of the Lorde is fynyshed, they vse to geue thankes as it here foloweth, or after some other the lyke maner.

WE prayse the and thanke thee (oure moste mercyful FATHER,) for that thou haste bouchesaued to graunte vnto vs miserable synners so excellente a benefyte, as to receaue vs into the felowshyp and companye of thy deare soonne Iesu Christe oure Lorde: fyrste delyueryng hym to a moste cruell deathe for oure sakes. Secondaryle, geuyng vs hym vnto vs as a necessarye foode

merits of Iesu Christ thy sonne, who in the unitie of the holye spirite lyueth one GOD with thee euermore. So be it.

The blessynge whiche they vse at the departure of the people, according to the maner of Gods ordinaunce in the .vi. Chapter of Numeri.

The LORD blesse you, and kepe you: The LORD make the beames of hys mercye and grace to shyne vpon you: The Lorde shew a gentle mercifull and louyng countenaunce towardes you, and maintain you in prosperous estate to thy pleasure. So be it.

For so muche as the Scripture teacheth vs, that pestilence, warre, and otherlyke aduersities, be sent by Gods visitation, to punyshe oure synnes: whensoeuer we feare suche plages, it behoueth vs to consider that GOD is angry with vs, and thereupon also (if we wil bee of the noumber of hys children) it shalbe our partes to knowlege oure faultes, and in thys behalfe to bee earnestlye dyspleased with our selues, and so to retourne vnto our LORD with true repentance, amendyng our lyues, and moste humbly beseching hym that he wil freely pardon vs all our faultes.

Wherefore if we shall see at any tyme any lykelyhode of plage whiche we may count to be a threatning of Gods father punyshmét, to the end that we prouoke not euermore Gods longe sufferaunce, but rather that we maye pictuere his punyshmente, which he times it se otherwyse to see alreadye hangyng ouer our heades: it shalbe conuenient also to haue some seuerall dayes weekly appoynted, that the people therfore comming together, may haue those preceding thynges vttered vnto them, and maye also make they common prayers and generall supplications.

Fol.xxxvi.

The maner of celebratīg the supper of the Lord.

IT is to be noted first, that the souper haue neither before the celebration of the lordes supper, the preacher doth exhorte the people that they prepare, and dyspose themselues euery one to receiue it worthylie, and with such reuerence as that be semeth.

Secondarily that no man beyng in this feare any childe, unles they be sufficiently instructed before, & such as haue openly professed their faythe in churche.

Thirdly if there be any strangers yet rude, and lackyng farther instruction herein, they may come, and offer them selues aparte to some practised teachers, to be more exactly taught.

These things when the Sacrament is, thus openlye mynystred vnto the people, the preacher expouncheth that matter in the ende of hys sermon, eyther of that shall ...

The Supper

wholesome signification thereof: bringing into the peoples the meaning of Christ, and for what purpose he did first institute the holye ministery, and how it behoveth vs to receive the same.

¶ After the sermon (which he hathe saying the common prayers, and made open confession of the Christen fayth, to pray (even in the behalfe of the whole congregation) that they wil allure & open the doctrine and religion of Christ: the preacher saith with a loude voyce his followship...

¶ Let vs marke and consider how Jesus Christ did ordaine vnto vs his holye supper, according as S. Paule maketh rehearsall of the same in the xi. Chapter of his first Epistle to the Corinthians.

Ye that I haue receyued (sayth he) of the Lord, that which I

of the Lord.

delyuer vnto you: to witte, that our Lord Jesus ÿ same night in whiche he was betrayed tooke bread, and when he had geuen thankes, he brake it, saying: take ye, eate ye, this is my body, which is broken for you: Do you this in the remembraunce of me. Lykewyse after supper, he toke the cup, saying: this cup is the new testament or couenaunt in my bloud: Doe ye this so oft as you shal drink thereof, in remembrance of me. That is to say, so oft as you shal eate of this bread or drink of this cup, ye shall celebrate and shew furth the Lordes death vntyll his cumming. Wheras this bread is broken, or eate of this

The Supper of the Lord. Fol.xxxvii.

supper vnworthely, he shall bee gylty of the bodye and bloud of the Lord, than see that euery man proue & trye hym selfe, and so let hym eate of this bread, and drynke of this cuppe: for whosoeuer eateth or drynketh vnworthely, he eateth & drynketh his condemnacion, for not discerning ouer regard or consideration amongest ye Disciples indigo or receyueth this Supper celebrated as it ought to be amongest the faythful congregation, of suche as are of one fayth, suche straungers, that is to saye, such as neither haue hearde (vn¶les then) in what sorte our Lorde Iesus celebrated this Supper amongest hys Disciples: nor are also instructed to discerne ye Lordes body, haue no parte (my brethren) in this doctrine, nor are they meete to be admitted to the Supper of the Lorde: In y⁴ vertue & autoritie of our Lord Iesu Christ: I excomunicate & barre out al Idolaters, blasphemers, Dispisers of God, heretiques, & al sortes of people ye bryng in sectes, ye teache newe doctrine to breake ye vnitie of Christes congregacion, al periured persōs, al such as bedisobedient to theyr father & mother, & to other their superiours or maisters, all (odious) persones, quarrel pickers or fighters, shoulders, slaunderers, aduouterers, whormongers, theues, drunkardes, gluttons, & finally al suche as leade a diffolute lyfe, to auoyde ye suffring and to accomplyshe the commaundement

The supper

vnto them, that it is the parte of al suche to absent themselues from thys table, & to conceyue thys reuerent feare, not to pollute or defyle with theyr presence, those hitaples, which our Lord Jesus geueth to none but vnto the faythfull of hys houshold. Therfore (accordyng to saynct Paules exhortacyon) see that euery main enter into himselfe, and examyne duely hys owne conscience, to trye whether he haue a true vnfayned repentaunce for hys synnes, and an earnest displeasure agaynste hys other faultes, most feruẽtly myndynge and despysynge from this tyme forwarde, to

of the Lord.   Fol.xxxix.

lawe of GOD: and chiefely let euery manne consider whether he haue his assured confidence in Gods mercy, seeking euerlastyng saluacion alonely in the merites and passiõ of Jesu Christ, and whether hauyng refused and forgotten all malyce and debate, he hath now a fulful purpose and earnest desyre to lyue in brotherlye amitie and conscorde with hys neyghbours. Yf our heartes and consciences doe testifye vnto vs before GOD, that we are comen to thys poynte: we maye vndoubtedlye thinke that he accepteth vs for hys chyldren, & that our Lorde Jesus hath sõmoned and bydden vs to hys table, there to receaue hys holde sacrament whiche he stupped among hys Disciples. And albeit wee feele in oure selues muche frayltye, and wretchednes, as that we haue not oure fayth so perfect & constaunt as we ought, beyng many tymes ready to dystruſt Gods goodnes through our corrupte nature: And also that we are not so throughly geuen to serue God, neither haue so feruent a zeale to set foorth hys glory as our duety requireth, feelynge styll such rebellion in our selues, ꝑ we haue neede dayly to fyght agaynst the lustes of our fleſh: yet neuertheles seing that our Lorde hath dealed thus mercifully with vs, ꝑ he hath printed hys gospell in our heartes, so that we are preserued from fallyng into desperacion, and misbeliefe, and seeyng also he hath induced vs with a luste & desire to renounce & withstand out own affeccios̄, with a longing for hys righteousnes and the keepyng of hys commaundementes: we may be now right wel assured ꝑ those defaultes & manifold imperfeccions in vs, shall be no hynderance at all agaynst vs, to cause hym not to accepte vs, or accounte vs as woorthye to come to hys spirituall table. For, the ende of our cummynge thither is not to make protestacyon that we are bryght or just in ourselues; but contrary wyse we come to seke our life and perfeccion in Jesꝰ

The supper

Jesu Christ: acknowledgynge in the meane tyme that we of our selues be most miserable the prisoners of deathe: Lette vs consider than that thys Sacramente is a syngular medicine for all poore sycke creatures, a comfortable meane to weake soules, and that oure Lorde requiteth no other worthinesse of oure parte, but that we vnfaynedly knowelege oure naughtines and imperfection: And that we be in dyspleasure and at defyance with the faultes wee haue commytted, hatyng our whole pleasure, ioye and solace in hym alone. Fyrst then let vs beleue the promisses which Christ being the moste assured truth, hath in hys own persone

of the Lord. Fol. xli.

person made vnto vs: that is to wete, that he wyll dystribute and geue vnto vs in dede, his very body, and his very bloud, to theende that we maye haue hym in our possession, & inioy him fully in such sort that both we may liue in him & he in vs. And albeit we se nothyng but bare bread & wyne, yet let vs beleue vndoubtedly that he doth perfourme spiritually in oure foules, all that that he doeth signifye by the visible & outward sygnes vnto oure senses (to wete) that he is the breade of heauen, whiche feedeth & nourisheth vs vnto life euerlastyng. Euenso then let vs geue diligente heede that wee bee not vnthankefull to the infinite bountye

F.i.

bounty of our sauiour, who so louingly bringeth and setteth before vs in thys table, hys whole goodes & riches, to thintent to geue them & parte thē amongeste vs: for in that ꝑ he geueth hymselfe vnto vs , he maketh euidēt declaraciō that whatsoeuer he hath is oures. Wherfore we receiue thys Sacrament as a sure warrantyse or pledge ꝑ the efficacye & vertue of his painful death, is reputed vnto vs, and coūted for our righteousnes, euē as verely as if we had suffered ꝑ lyke passions in oure owne proper bodyes. Let vs not then be so peruerse & frowarde, as to with drawe & absent our selues from that banket, vnto ꝑ whiche Iesu Christ

Christ doth so louingly bid vs & allure vs in his own mouth: but rather vpon consideraciō of ꝑ worthines of so excellēt a gift which he bestoweth vpō vs: let vs presente & offre oure selues vnto him w an earnest feruētnes of affection, that we may through hys goodnes be made mete to receiue the same. And to ꝑ end we may do thus, let vs lift vp oure heartes and mindes into heauē, where Christ abideth in ꝑ glory of his Father, & frō whēce (our sure hope is,) he will come to shewe himselfe oure redemer. And let vs not suffer our imagination to wā der about the consideraciō of these earthly and corruptible thynges (which we see present to to our eye, and feele with oure handes) to seeke Christ bodily presente in them, as if he were inclosed in the breade or wine, or as if they wer transmuted & chaunged into hys substance. For the onely waye to dyspose our soules to receyue nourishment, reliefe, and quickenyng of hys substaunce: is to lyfte vp our myndes by meanes of a ryght faythe, aboue all thynges worldly, and sensible, and thereby to enter into heauen, that we may fynd and receyue Christ where he dwelleth, vndoubtedly very God and very manne, in the incomprehensible glory of hys Father. So thē thys shalbe sufficiente to satisfye and content vs: to take the bread and wine as sure signes and witnesses of Goddes promisses adioyned vnto them: and therwithal to searche spiritually the effect & substance of the same, there, where Gods woorde dooeth saye wee shall fyndett.

Thys done and the people being aduertised to come peaceablye in ordre with al reuerence, the minister breake the breade, and geue the cuppe vnto the people, and whyles that is a doing eyther they synge Psalmes meete for that tyme: eyther one of the preachers readeth some parte of the Scripture touching that matter.

¶ When all is doon: they giue life to giue thankes, and to say the prayer set out here before.

¶ We knowe right wel, that many haue taken a greate occasion to bee offended at the alteration whiche wee haue made touchyng thys sacrament. For by meanes that the Masse hathe bene

of the Lord.   Fol. xliiii.

to discusse this mater touching the a=
bolishment of the masse, were at length:
yet mindyng to satisfye suche as tho=
row very symplicitie, myght be other=
wyse be offended with vs: we thought
it not amisse thus lightly to touche it
by the waye, and in fewe wordes to
shew for what cause we haue forborn.

When we sawe the sacrament of
our Lorde so horribly despised, and
corrupted with a number of errours
and abuses, that suche persons had
brought into it: Iohan Calvyn (at the
least) made naught those disorders, &
so he were of verye necessitie driven
to alter many thynges, whereof parte
perteyned to the institution of Christ, &
parte but to the fonde invention of me,
to achieve this intent. And first (to say
make a perfect reformation of cir=
cumstaunces of the action, and chaunge
not deuised or estableshed by the first
institucion of our sauiour Christe, ra=
more fit, than certaine ceremonies

The supper

bene a long tyme had in suche reputa=
tion, that the poore blynde people of
the worlde dyd esteme, and counte it as
the chiefest poynte of our christen reli=
gion: hath semed a very straunge case
vnto them, & we haue so briefly case
layed it, & put it down, to that the occa=
sion of many rude (for lacke of right
instruction takyng the thyng amisse)
suppose we haue utterly denyed and
put awaye y sacrament: but when men
that haue had ware & sufficient con=
sidered our doctrine, which we haue of=
fered herevnto they shall muche
touching this thing, they shall muche
rather iudge out of us, & haue restored a=
gaine this sacrament to his prestine pu=
ritie & dignitie. And to y intent to con=
firme a little what conformitie y agre=
me we haue of our last supper, we haue
blessed the supper of our lorde: we have
signifying of our saviour Christes supper:
that they had dronke a thing
more common, as they dyd drinke from
the cuppe: as, as a day haueth from
the one other, as a day haueth from
the nyght: Albeit in the way that is
not much abhorred our purpose was

BIBLIOGRAPHY

UNPUBLISHED

The Seconde Parte of a Register, Morrice Collection A, B, C, Dr. Williams's Library, London. Harleian Mss 787.
Add. Ms. 6394 Boswell Papers, British Museum, 2 Vols. (Some of the papers are published in C. BURRAGE, *The Early English Dissenters*, 2 Vols., Cambridge 1912, and R.P. STEARNS, *Congregationalism in the Dutch Netherlands*, Chicago, 1940).
State Papers for Holland, Public Record Office London, 84 Vol. 146; 16 Vol. 310.
Correspondence with Dr. A.C. Honders, Groningen University; the Archivists of Amsterdam, Bergen, Rotterdam and Arnhem.
E.P. WINTER, "The Theory and Practice of the Lord's Supper, Among the Early Separatists, Independents and Baptists, From A.D. 1580 to A.D. 1700", B. Litt. Thesis, University of Oxford, 1953.

PUBLISHED WORKS

ANONYMOUS, *An abridgment of that Booke which the Ministers of Lincoln Diocess delivered to his Maiestie upon the first of December last*, London, 1605.
The Brownists Synagogue, London 1622.
The Confession of faith, of the Reformed Churches in the Netherlands. With the formes which they use in the administration of the Sacraments, Amsterdam, 1732.
A Parte of a Register, Middleburg, 1593.
A Survey of the Booke of Common Prayer, By way of 197 queres grounded upon 58 places, London 1606.
G.W.O. ADDLESHAW, *The High Church Tradition*, London, 1941.
WILLIAM AMES, *The Marrow of Sacred Divinity*, London 1642.
— *Conscience with the Power and Cases Thereof. Divided into 5 Books*, London, 1643.
LANCELOT ANDREWES, *Ninety-Six Sermons*, 5 Vols., Oxford 1841-43, Vol. 1.
Ed. I. ANDRIESZ, *De Kercken-Ordeninghen der Ghereformeerder Nederlandtscher Kercken in de vier Nationale Synoden ghemaeckt ende ghearresteert. mitsgaders Eenige anderd in den Provincialen Synoden van Hollandt ende Zeelandt gheconcipieert ende besloten waerby noch anderen, in bysondere vergaderinghen goet-ghevonden, by ghevoeght zyn*, Delft, 1622.
Ed. E. ARBER, *A Brief Discourse of the Troubles at Frankfort, 1554-1558 A.D.*, London, 1908.
J.M. BARKLEY, *The Worship of the Reformed Church*, London, 1966.
Ed. J.G. BAUM, *La Maniere et fasson* (G. Farel), Strasbourg, 1859.
W. BRADSHAWE, *English Puritanism*, London, 1605.
F.E. BRIGHTMAN, *The English Rite*, 2 Vols., 1915.
Y. BRILIOTH, *Eucharistic Faith and Practice Evangelical and Catholic*, ET A.G. HEBERT, London, 1930.
P.N. BROOKS, *Thomas Cranmer's Doctrine of the Eucharist*, London, 1964.
C.O. BUCHANAN, *What did Cranmer Think he was Doing?*, Grove Liturgical Study 7, Bramcote 1982 (2nd edition).
L. BUCHSENSCHUTZ, *Histoire des liturgies en langue allemande dans l'église de Strasbourg au XVIe siècle*, Cahors, 1900.
G.B. BURNET, *The Holy Communion in the Reformed Church of Scotland 1560-1960*, Edinburgh, 1960.
C. BURRAGE, *The Early English Dissenters*, 2 Vols., Cambridge, 1912.
— *The True Story of Robert Browne*, Oxford, 1906.
C.C. BUTTERWORTH, *The English Primers (1529-1545)*, Philadelphia, 1963.

BIBLIOGRAPHY

JOHN CALVIN, *Commentary on a harmony of the Evangelists*, ET W. Pringle, 3 Vols., Edinburgh, 1846.
— *Commentary on the Epistles of Paul the Apostle to the Corinthians*, ET J. Pringle, 2 Vols., Edinburgh, 1848.
— *Institutes of the Christian Religion*, trans. H. Beveridge, 2 Vols., London, 1962.
CALVINI OPERA, *Corpus Reformatorum*.
DOUGLAS CAMPBELL, *The Puritans in Holland, England and America*, 2 Vols., London, 1892.
Ed. E. CARDWELL, *A History of Conferences and other Proceedings*, Oxford, 1841.
Ed. LELAND H. CARLSON, *The Writings of John Greenwood 1587-1590*, London, 1962.
— *The Writings of John Greenwood and Henry Barrow 1591-1593*, London, 1970.
ALICE CLARE CARTER, *The English Reformed Church in Amsterdam in the Seventeenth Century*, Amsterdam, 1964.
THOMAS CARTWRIGHT, *A Confutation of the Rheimists Translation, Glosses and Annotations on the New Testament*, Leiden, 1618.
— *Harmonia Evangelica Commentario, Analytico, Metaphrastico, Practico*, Amsterdam, 1647.
HENOCH CLAPHAM, *A Cronological Discourse*, London, 1609.
P. COLLINSON, *The Elizabethan Puritan Movement*, London, 1967.
J. COSIN, *Notes on the Book of Common Prayer*, in ed. J. Barrow, Works, 5 Vols.
T. CRANMER, *On the Lord's Supper*, Parker Society, London, 1844.
G.J. CUMING, *A History of Anglican Liturgy*, London, 1969.
— *The Durham Book*, Oxford, 1961.
Ed. W.F. DANKBAAR, *Marten Micron, De Christlicke Ordinancien der Nederlantscher Ghemeinten te Londen (1554)*, Kerkhistorische Studien Deel VII, 's-Gravenhage, 1956.
H. DAVIES, *The Worship of the English Puritans*, Oxford, 1948.
G. DIX, *The Apostolic Tradition*, London 1937.
— *The Shape of the Liturgy*, London, 1945.
G. DONALDSON, *The Making of the Scottish Prayer Book of 1637*, Edinburgh, 1954.
HASTINGS EELLS, *Martin Bucer*, New Haven, 1931.
F.G. EMMISON, *Elizabethan Life: Morals and the Church Courts*, Chelmsford (Essex County Council), 1973.
DUDLEY FENNER, *The whole doctrine of the Sacramentes, plainlie and fullie set downe and declared out of the word of God*, Middleburg, 1588.
JOSEPH FOSTER, *Alumni Oxonienses, 1500 - 1714*, Oxford, 1891, Vol. 1.
Ed. W.H. FRERE and C.E. DOUGLAS, *Puritan Manifestoes*, London, 1907.
WILLIAM FULKE, *The Text of the New Testament of Jesus Christ translated out of the vulgar Latine by the Papistes of the traiterous Seminarie at Rheims... with a confutation*, London, 1589.
NICOLAS DE GALLARS, *Polite et Discipline Ecclesiastique observee en L'eglise Des Estrangiers Francois A Londres*, 1561.
H. GEE and W.J. HARDY, *Documents illustrative of English Church History*, London, 1896.
J.F. GERRARD, *Notable Editions of the Prayer Book*, Wigan, 1949.
PETER GEYL, *The Revolt of the Netherlands*, London, 1958.
T. GOODWIN, et al, *An Apologeticall Narration*, London, 1643.
RICHARD GREENHAM, *Workes*, London, 1601.
JOHN GREENWOOD, *The Writings of John Greenwood and Henry Barrow 1591-1593*, ed. Leland H. Carlson, London, 1970.
C.H.D. GRIMES, *The English Church at Utrecht*, Chambery, 1930.
W. JARDINE GRISBROOKE, *Anglican Liturgies of the Seventeenth and Eighteenth Centuries*, AC London, 1958.
B. GUSTAFSSON, *The Five Dissenting Brethren*, Lund, 1955.
BASIL HALL, *John à Lasco 1499-1560. A Pole in Reformation England*. Dr. Williams's Trust, London, 1971.
C. HILL, *Society and Puritanism in Pre-Revolutionary England*, Panther edition, London, 1969.
E. BROOKS HOLIFIELD, *The Covenant Sealed: The Development of Puritan Sacramental Theology, in Old and New England, 1570-1720*, New Haven and London, 1974.
A.C. HONDERS, *Valerandus Pollanus Liturgia Sacra (1551-1555)*, Kerkhistorische Bijdragen 1, Leiden, 1970.
W. HUYCKE, *Geneva: The Forme of common praiers used in the churches of Geneva: The mynystracion of the sacramentes, of Baptisme and the Lordes supper: The vysitacion of the sycke: And the Cathechisme of Geneva: made by master John Calvyne*.

In the ende are certaine other Godly prayers privately to be used: translated out of frenche into Englyshe. London, 1550.
J.A. JUNGMANN, *The Mass of the Roman Rite,* 2 Vols., New York, 1951-55.
Ed. A. KUYPER, *Kerkeraads-Protocollen Der Hollandsche Gemeente te Londen 1569-71,* Utrecht, 1870.
— *Joannis a Lasco Opera,* 2 Vols., Amsterdam, 1866.
JOHN à LASCO, *Forma ac Ratio Ecclesiastici ministerii in peregrinorum positissimum vero Germanorum Ecclesia instituta Londinii in Anglia,* in ed. A KUYPER, *Joannis a Lasco Opera,* vol. 2, Amsterdam, 1866.
— *Toute La forme & maniere du Ministere Ecclesiastique, en l'Eglise des estrangers, dresse a Londres en Angleterre, par le Prince tres fidele dudit pays, le Roy Edouard IV: de ce nom: L'an apres l'incarnation de Christ, 1550 avec le privilege de sa Majeste a la fin du livre.* Frankfurt, 1556.
— *La forma delle publiche orationi, et della cofessione, & assolutione, la qual si usa nella chiesse de forestieri, che è nuouamente stata instituita in Londra (per gratia di Dio) con l'autorita & cosentimento del Re.* London, 1551?
J.W. LEGG, *Cranmer's Liturgical Projects,* HBS, London, 1915.
J. LINDEBOOM, *Austin Friars. History of the Dutch Reformed Church in London 1550-1950,* The Hague, 1950.
P. LORRIMER, *John Knox and the Church of England,* London, 1875.
R. MARCHANT, *The Puritans and the Church Courts in the Diocese of York 1560-1642,* London, 1960.
WALTER MARSHALL, *The Gospel Mystery of Sanctification,* London, 1692.
W.D. MAXWELL, *The Liturgical Portions of the Genevan Service Book,* Edinburgh, 1931, and London, 1965.
S. MAYOR, *The Lord's Supper in Early English Dissent,* London, 1972.
KILIAN MCDONNELL, *John Calvin, the Church, and the Eucharist,* Princeton, 1967.
MAARTEN MICRON, *De Christlicke Ordinancien der Nederlantscher Ghemeinten te Londen,* editions of 1554 and 1582, Austin Friars Library.
H.O. OLD, *The Patristic Roots of Reformed Worship,* Zurich, 1975.
— *Original Letters relative to the English Reformation,* Parker Society, 2 Vols., London, 1846-47.
T.H.L. PARKER, *John Calvin: A Biography,* London, 1975.
Ed. A. PEEL and L.H. CARLSON, *The Writings of Robert Harrison and Robert Browne,* London, 1953.
Ed. A. PEEL, *The Seconde Parte of a Register,* 2 Vols., London, 1915.
WILLIAM PERKINS, *The Works of William Perkins,* 3 Vols., London, 1628-31.
— *Puritanism in Tudor England,* London 1970.
F.J. POWICKE, *Robert Browne Pioneer of Modern Congregationalism,* London, 1910.
F. PROCTER and W.H. FRERE, *A New History of the Book of Common Prayer,* London, 1901.
W. PRYNNE, *A Briefe Survey and Censure of Mr. Cozens His Couzening Devotions,* London, 1628.
M. RAMSEY et al, *The English Prayer Book 1549-1662,* AC London, 1966.
L.D. REED, *The Lutheran Liturgy,* Philadelphia, 1947.
Ed. J.K. REID, *Calvin Theological Treatises,* Library of Christian Classics Vol. 22, London 1954.
C.C. RICHARDSON, *Zwingli and Cranmer on the Eucharist,* Illinois, 1949.
AE.L. RICHTER, *Die evangelischen Kirchenordnungen des sechszehnten Jahrhunderts,* 2. Vols., Leipzig, 1846 (1967 reprint). Vol. 2.
JOHN ROBINSON, *The Works of John Robinson,* ed. R. Ashton, London, 1851.
HUGH TREVOR ROPER, *Archbishop Laud,* 2nd edition, London, 1962.
F. SCHMIDT-CLAUSING, *Zwingli als Liturgiker,* Gottingen, 1952.
M.A. SIMPSON, *John Knox and the Troubles Begun at Frankfurt,* West Linton, Tweedale, 1975.
C.H. SMYTH, *Cranmer & The Reformation under Edward IV,* Cambridge, 1926.
ANNELIESE SRENGLER-RUPPENTHAL, *Mysterium und Riten nach der Londoner Kirchenordnung der Niederlander.* Koln, 1967.
KEITH L. SRUNGER, *Dutch Puritanism. A History of English and Scottish Churches of the Netherlands in the Sixteenth and Seventeenth Centuries,* Leiden, 1982.
R.P. STEARNS, *Congregationalism in the Dutch Netherlands,* Chicago, 1940.
W. STEVEN, *The History of the Scottish Church at Rotterdam,* Edinburgh, 1832.
J. STRYPE, *Life of Parker,* 3 Vols., 1821.
— *Life of Grindal,* Oxford, 1821.

JEREMY TAYLOR, *A Collection of Offices*, 1658.
BARD THOMPSON, *Liturgies of the Western Church*, New York, 1962.
P. TOON, *Hyper-Calvinism*, London, 1967.
— *Puritans and Calvinism*, Swengel, Pennsylvania, 1973.
L.J. TRINTERUD, *Elizabethan Puritanism*, New York, 1971.
JAN UTENHOVE, *De Psalmen Davidis, in Nederlandischen sangs-ryme; ddor Ian Wtenhove van Ghendtt*, 1551.
G.J. VAN DE POLL, *Martin Bucer's Liturgical Ideas*, Assen, 1954.
R.S. WALLACE, *Calvin's Doctrine of the Word and Sacrament*, Edinburgh, 1953.
E.C. WHITAKER, *Martin Bucer and the Book of Common Prayer*, AC London, 1974.
B.R. WHITE, *The English Separatist Tradition from the Marian Martyrs to the Pilgrim Fathers*, Oxford, 1971.
C.E. WHITING, *Studies in English Puritanism*, London, 1931.
G.G. WILLIS, *Essays in Early Roman Liturgy*, AC London, 1964.
C. WILSON, *Queen Elizabeth and the Revolt of the Netherlands*, London, 1970.
H.A. WILSON, *The Order of the Communion*, 1548, HBS London, 1908.
WOLFFGANG, *Wolffgang's Kirchenordnung*, Nuremburg, 1570.
C. WORDSWORTH and H. LITTLEHALES, *The Old Service-Books of the English Church*, London, 1904.
H.J. WOTHERSOIIN and G.W. SPROTT, *The Liturgy of Compromise used in the English Congregation at Frankfort*, Edinburg, 1905.

ARTICLES AND ESSAYS

J.M. BARKLEY, "Pleading His Eternal Sacrifice in the Reformed Liturgy", in Bryan D. SPINKS (ed.), *The Sacrifice of Praise*, C.L.V. Rome, 1981, pp. 123-140.
J. CADIER, "La Prière Eucharistique de Calvin", in *Eucharisties d'Orient et d'Occident*, Lex Orandi 47, ed. B. Botte, Paris, 1970, pp. 171-180.
P. COLLINSON, "The Authorship of A Brieff Discours off the Troubles Begonne at Franckford", in *JEH* 9 (1958), pp. 188-208.
P. COLLINSON, "The Elizabethan Puritans and the Foreign Reformed Churches in London", in *Proceedings of the Huguenot Society of London*, 20 (1958-64), pp. 528-555.
A.H. COURATIN, "The Holy Communion 1549", in *CQR* 164 (1963), pp. 148-159.
— "The Service of Holy Communion 1552-1662", in *CQR* 163 (1962), pp. 431-442.
— and the late E.C. RATCLIFF, "The Early Roman Canon Missae" in *JEH* 20 (1969), pp. 211-224.
H.J. COWELL, "Valerand Poullain. A Precursor of Congregationalism?", in *CHST* 12 (1933-36), pp. 112-119.
G.J. CUMING, "John Knox and the Book of Common Prayer: a short note", in *LR* 10 (1980), pp. 80-81.
G. DIX, "Dixit Cranmer et non Timuit" in *CQR* 145 (1947-8), pp. 145-176; 146 (1948), pp. 44-60.
D.N. GRIFFITHS, "The French Translations of the English Book of Common Prayer", in *Proceedings of the Huguenot Society of London*, 22 (1972), pp. 90-114.
H. HAGEMAN, "The Liturgical Origins of the Reformed Churches', in *The Heritage of John Calvin*, ed. J.H. Bratt, Grand Rapids, Michigan, 1973.
RALPH A. KEIFER, "The Unity of the Roman Canon: An Examination of Its Unique Structure", in *SL* 11 (1976), pp. 39-58.
S. MAYOR, "The Lord's Supper in Separatists' Teaching", in *CHST* 19 (1956), pp. 212-221.
E.C. RATCLIFF, "Christian Worship and Liturgy", in K.E. KIRK, *The Study of Theology*, London, 1939.
— "The Institution Narrative of the Roman Canon Missae; Its Beginnings and Early Background", in *Studia Patristica* II, pp. 64-82, *Texte und Untersuchungen* 64, Berlin, 1957.
— "The Liturgical Work of Archbishop Cranmer", in *JEH* 7 (1956), pp. 189-203.
— "The English Usage of Eucharistic Consecration, 1548-1662", I and II, in *Theology*, 60 (1957), pp. 229-236, 273-280.
— "Puritan Alternatives to the Prayer Book", in *The English Prayer Book 1549-1662*, M. Ramsey et al., AC London, 1963, pp. 56-81.
KEITH L. SPRUNGER, "Archbishop Laud's Campaign Against Puritanism at The Hague", in *Church History* 44 (1975), pp. 308-320.

V. THALHOFER, "Vom Pronaus, speciell von den an die Pfarrpredigt sich anschlissenden Gebeten und Verkundigungen", in *Theol. prakisch Quartalschrift* 38 (1885), pp. 25-42.
BARD THOMPSON, "The Palatinate Liturgy Heidelberg 1563", in *Theology and Life* 6 (1963), pp. 49-67.
G.B. TIMMS, "Dixit Cranmer" in *CQR* 143 (1946-7), pp. 217-234; 144 (1947), pp. 33-51.
J. DOVER WILSON, "Richard Schilders and the English Puritans" in *Transactions fo the Bibliographical Society* 11 (1909-1911), pp. 65-134.
H.G. WOOD, "Puritanism and Capitalism", in *Congregational Quarterly* 29 (1951), pp. 104-114.

INDEX OF LITURGIES

Book of Common Prayer 17-27; 37-46
Dutch Reformed Rite (Datheen) 115, 117; 135-139
Forma ac Ratio 100-113
Fome des prieres 46-47; 55-83
Forme of Common Praiers 55-83
Form und Gstalt wie das Herren Nachtmal 49
Genevan Service Book 76-83
Knox's Liturgy for Berwick on Tweed 89-94

Liturgia Sacra 103-107
Liturgy of Compromise 70-76
Maniere et fasson 49; 60-62
Middleburg 76-77; 119-121
Order of the Communion 17-19; 40-41
Psalter mit aller Kirchenubing 50-54; 56-60
Separatists (Brown and Barrow) 28-32
Waldegrave 114-119
Western Rite (The Mass) 8; 37-47

INDEX OF NAMES

Addleshaw G.W. 34
À Lasco J. 14, 42, 46-47, 78, 96-98, 100-102, 105, 107-110, 112-113, 121, 138-139, 143
Alcuin 37
Ambrose 37, 39
Ames W. 15, 32, 132
Andrews L. 118-119
Andriesz I. 138
Arber E. 20, 70
Ashton R. 32
Augustine 81, 95

Barker Ch. 27
Barrow H. 12-13, 29-31, 123-126, 129
Baum J.G. 50
Baynes P. 15
Beamund S. 28
Beza 9, 86
Blamford S. 133
Blarer 55
Bonner E. 19
Boswell W. 132, 140-141
Bourroughes J. 15, 132
Bouyer L. 79-80
Bowler R. 26
Bradshaw W. 13, 22
Bratt J.H. 105
Bridge W. 15, 132
Brightman F.E. 18, 35, 40-43, 48, 52-53
Brilioth Y. 44, 62
Broke Th. 46
Brooks Holifield E. 85, 113
Brooks P. 44

Broughton H. 15
Browne R. 12-13, 29, 124, 126-127, 129-130, 132, 139
Brully 103
Bucer M. 7, 20, 42, 46, 50-54, 56, 59-60, 65, 81-82, 107, 110, 115, 143
Buchanan C.O. 43
Büchsenschütz L. 52
Bucke D. 129
Bullinger H. 7, 9, 19, 48, 86, 97, 110
Burcher J. 9
Burrage Ch. 10-14, 32, 99, 128-129, 133, 135, 140
Butterworth C.C. 17

Cadier J. 56
Calvin J. 7-9, 11, 31, 48-50, 54-56, 58-67, 69, 73, 76-79, 81-83, 107, 109-116, 120, 139, 143
Capito 48, 55
Cardwell E. 24
Carleton D. 133-134
Carlson L.H. 12-13, 30, 124, 126
Carter A.C. 133
Cartwright Th. 10-11, 15, 28, 88, 90, 95, 113, 115, 117-118, 132
Charlemagne 37
Chrysostom J. 81, 86
Clapham H. 128
Clark W. 128
Cole T. 72, 76
Cole W. 28
Collinson P. 10, 26, 28, 70, 94-95, 99

INDEX OF NAMES

Cope A. 28, 113
Cosin J. 35
Cotton J. 14-15, 33
Couratin A.H. 42
Coverdale M. 9
Cowell H.J. 103
Cox 76, 93
Cranmer Th. 17-20, 31, 37, 42-43, 85, 87, 97
Crespin J. 76
Cuming G.J. 17, 34, 37-38, 44, 70, 77
Cyprian 37, 81

Dankbaar W.F. 101, 103
Datheen P. 102-103, 115, 120, 122, 136-137, 141, 143
Davenport J. 15
Davies H. 23, 28, 62, 78
Denford W. 129
De Poll (Van) G.J. 51-52, 56, 59, 62
Dering E. 88
Dionysius of Alex. 86
Dix G. 37, 44, 81-82
Donne J. 7
Douglas C.E. 22, 24, 99
Dove J. 128
Dover W.J. 131
Dugmore C.W. 42, 44

Edwine J. 87
Eells H. 51
Elliston J. 26
Emmison F.C. 28
Erasmus 97

Farel G. 48-49, 55, 60-62, 65-66, 69, 81, 83, 107
Funner D. 15, 113, 118
Field J. 24, 29, 86, 93, 113
Fitz R. 11
Forbes J. 15, 132-133, 135, 139
Foster J. 46
Fox 76
Frere W.H. 22, 24, 26, 99
Fulke W. 10, 23, 88, 95

Gallars (Des) N. 105
Gallus R. 97
Gamble C. 128, 130
Gardiner 19, 42
Gee H. 17
Geiler 55
Gerrard J.F. 26
Geyl P. 131
Gifford G. 125
Gilby A. 72, 76, 87-88
Goffe S. 134-136, 139, 140-141
Goodyer 140
Goodwin Th. 15, 34, 132, 140

Grafton R. 47
Greenham R. 12
Greenwood J. 12-13, 29-31, 124-125
Griffiths D.N. 98
Grindal 27-28
Grisbrooke W.J. 35, 37
Guillaume Th. 66
Gustafsson B. 16

Hadrian (Pope) 37
Hageman H. 104, 137-138
Hall B. 97, 110
Hardy W.J. 17
Harrison R. 12
Hermann 40
Hesbert A.G. 62
Hill C. 7
Hippolytus 37
Holmes M. 15
Honders A.C. 82, 103-104
Hooper J. 8-9, 19, 42
Huray (Le) P. 45
Huycke W. 45-47, 55-56, 58, 70, 76, 81, 143

Irenaeus 39

Jacob H. 13-15, 99, 132
Jacobs E. 50
Jasper R.C.D. 37
Jenkynson W. 94
Johnson F. 13, 15, 95, 128-129, 132
Jungmann J.A. 37
Justin (Martyr) 37-38

Karlstadt 110
Keifer R.A. 39
Kirk K.E. 39
Knox J. 42, 46, 65, 67-69, 71-72, 76, 78-81, 143
Kuyper A. 105-106

Lane D.G. 106
Laud W. 35-36, 96, 132-133
Legg J.W. 17
Leonus W. 97
Lever Th. 9, 71
Lindeboom J. 14, 97, 100, 102
Littlehales H. 17
Lorimer P. 66, 69, 77
Luther M. 7, 55, 69

Marchant R. 26, 94
Marot 55
Mayor S. 59, 82, 117, 120, 129
Maxwell W.D. 47, 50-52, 58-59, 62, 71, 77-80, 114, 143

INDEX OF NAMES

McDonnel K. 64
Melanchton Ph. 7, 138
Mensinga J.A. 100-101
Micron M. 96-98, 101-103, 112-113, 136-137, '139, 143
Misselden E. 139
Munster S. 48

Neal D. 21
Nichols J. 94
Nuttall G.F. 16
Nye Ph. 15, 132, 140

Oecolampadius 49, 51, 55, 61, 66, 81, 97, 107, 110
Old, H.O. 55, 81
Olevianus 138
Oliphant H. (Old) 81
Owen J. 15

Paget E. 25-27
Paget J. 15, 132, 140-141
Paine 134-135
Parker R. 15
Parker T.H.L. 48, 50
Parker T.M. 18
Parry 72
Peaston A.E. 26, 75, 96
Peel A. 12-13, 28, 113, 124
Penry J. 12-13
Perkins W. 29, 118
Peters H. 15, 132, 140
Porter H.C. 27-28
Potts L. 15
Poullain V. 14, 46-47, 70, 96-98, 103-105, 109-112, 139, 143
Pringle W. 62-63
Proctor 26
Prynne W. 35

Quinn C.U. 80

Ramsey M. 18, 42
Ratcliffe E.C. 39, 42, 95-96
Reed L. D. 136
Reid J.K.S. 63
Richardson C.C. 44
Richter Ae. L. 136
Riverius F. 97
Robinson J. 13, 15, 32-33, 132
Ruper H.T. 132, 135

Sampson Th. 9
Scambler 94
Schilders R. 28, 114, 131

Schmidt-Clausing F. 49
Schwarz D. 51, 55
Sehling Th. 33
Simpson M.A. 70, 73
Simpson S. 15, 132
Smyth C.H. 97, 110
Spinks B.D. 36, 59, 69, 82, 144
Sprengler-Ruppenthal A. 108-109, 111-112
Sprott G.W. 27, 73
Sprunger K.L. 15, 28, 132-133
Stearns R.P. 96, 132-133
Strype J. 25-27
Surgant J.U. 48, 55
Sutton E. 70

Taylor J. 34
Thalhofer V. 48
Thompson B. 49-50, 60-61, 83, 115
Timms G.B. 44
Toon P. 8-9
Travers W. 113
Trinterud L.J. 7-8, 23-25
Trust W. 97
Tunstall G. 67
Turner P. 28, 113
Turrianus F. 35

Ursinus 136
Utenhove J. 97-98, 101-102

Vadian 110
Vane H. 135
Vanville R. 104-105
Vergerio P.P. 102
Vermigli P. (Martyr) 7, 45

Waldegrave R. 113, 116-117, 121
Watson Th. 8, 22-23, 36
Wentworth P. 28, 113
Whitaker E.C. 42
White B.R. 10-12
Whitchurche E. 46-47, 55
Whittingham W. 9, 26, 70, 72, 76-77
Wilcox 24, 29, 86, 113
Williams W. 70
Willis G.G. 37-39
Wilson H.A. 19, 40, 45, 131
Wingen (Van) G. 103, 113
Wishart G. 66
Wood Th. 70
Wordsworth C. 17
Wotherspoon H.J. 27, 73
Wriothesley C. 45

Zwick 55
Zwingli 49, 65, 97, 107, 110, 113

CONTENTS

	Pag.
Preface (Bryan D. Spinks)	5
Abbreviations	6
INTRODUCTION: PURITANISM AND SEPARATISM	7
CHAPTER 1: PURITANS, SEPARATISTS, AND LITURGICAL FORMS	17
The Book of Common Prayer	17
Puritans and Liturgical Criteria	22
The Separatists and Liturgy	28
Independent Puritans	32
Laudianism	34
CHAPTER 2: THE OFFICIAL EUCHARISTIC LITURGY: THE DERIVATION OF THE COMMUNION SERVICE OF THE BOOK OF COMMON PRAYER 1559 AND 1604	37
CHAPTER 3: EARLY PURITAN EUCHARISTIC LITURGIES	45
1. William Huycke's Translation of Calvin's «La Forme», 1550	46
2. John Knox's Liturgy from Berwick on Tweed, 1550	66
3. The Liturgy of Compromise, 1555	70
4. The Genevan Service Book, 1556	76
Appendix: A Comparison between the Exhortations of Calvin and Farel	83
CHAPTER 4: PURITANISM AND THE EUCHARISTIC LITURGY IN ENGLAND: THE SIXTEENTH AND EARLY SEVENTEENTH CENTURIES	85
A. The Antecommunion	89
B. The Eucharist Proper	92
1. Adaptations of Prayer Book Communion Service	94

2. The Stranger Churches: The Liturgies of Vareland Poullain,
   John à Lasco and Maarten Micron 96
3. Editions of the Genevan Service Book 113
   A. The Waldegrave Book, 1584 114
   B. The Middleburg Book 119

CHAPTER 5: THE EUCHARISTIC LITURGY AMONG THE SEPARATISTS 123

The Brownists 126
The Burrowists 128

CHAPTER 6: ENGLISH PURITANS IN THE NETHERLANDS 131

1. The Translation of the Dutch Reformed Liturgy 135
2. Extemporary of Free Prayer 139
3. The Genevan Service Book 140
4. The English Form 141

EPILOGUE 143

Text A: William Huycke's Translation of Calvin's «La Forme» 145
Text B: John à Lasco's «Forma ac Ratio», 1555 157

BIBLIOGRAPHY 201

INDEX OF LITURGIES 207

INDEX OF NAMES 207

BIBLIOTHECA EPHEMERIDES LITURGICAE
COLLECTIO « SUBSIDIA »

C.L.V. - Edizioni Liturgiche — 00192 Roma
Via Pompeo Magno, 21
Tel. (06) 353.114 — C/CP. 56307002 Edizioni Liturgiche

---

1. CONFÉRENCES ST. SERGE, 1974, *La maladie et la mort du chrétien dans la liturgie*, 1975. In 8°, 468 pp.   L. 14.000

2. J. PINELL, O.S.B., *Las oraciones del Salterio « per annum » en el nuevo libro de la Liturgia de Las Horas*, 1974. In 8°, 100 pp. L. 4.000

3. CONFÉRENCES ST. SERGE, 1973, *Liturgie et rémission des péchés*, 1975. In 8°, 294 pp.   L. 12.000

4. A. CUVA, S.D.B., *La Liturgia delle Ore. Note teologiche e pastorali*. 1975. In 8°, 158 pp.   L. 4.000

5. F. GASTALDELLI, *Boezio*, 1974. In 8°, 64 pp.   L. 2.000

6. G. LANDOTTI, C.M., *Le traduzioni del Messale in lingua italiana anteriori al movimento liturgico moderno*, 1975. In 8°, 248 pp.   L. 8.000

7. CONFÉRENCES ST. SERGE, 1975, *Liturgie de l'Église particulière et liturgie de l'Église universelle*, 1976. In 8°, 410 pp.   L. 15.000

8. CONFÉRENCES ST. SERGE, 1969, *Le Saint-Esprit dans la liturgie*, 1977. In 8°, 182 pp.   L. 10.000

9. CONFÉRENCES ST. SERGE, 1976, *L'assemblée liturgique et les différents rôles dans l'assemblée*, 1977. In 8°, 350 pp.   L. 14.000

10. J. GILBERT Y TARRUELL, *Festum Resurrectionis. El significado de la expresión « Pascha » en la liturgia hispánica*, 1977. In 8°, XXIV + 46 pp.   L. 4.000

11. B. NEUNHEUSER, O.S.B., *Storia della liturgia attraverso le epoche culturali*, 2ª ediz. riveduta e ampliata, 1983. In 8°, 160 pp.   L. 10.500

12. M. PATERNOSTER, *L'imposizione delle mani nella Chiesa primitiva. Rassegna delle testimonianze bibliche, patristiche e liturgiche fino al sec. V*, 1977 (2ª ristampa 1983). In 8°, XXIV + 50 pp.   L. 5.000

13. E. CATTANEO, *Il culto cristiano in Occidente. Note storiche*, 2ª ediz. (con appendice di F. BRÓVELLI, *L'eucologia*), 1984. In 8°, 658 pp.   L. 32.000

14. CONFÉRENCES ST. SERGE, 1977, *Gestes et paroles dans les diverses familles liturgiques*, 1978. In 8°, 352 pp.   16.000

15. E. LODI, *Enchiridion euchologicum fontium liturgicorum*. 1979. In 8°, XXXII + 1866 pp.   L. 120.000

16. CONFÉRENCES ST. SERGE, 1978, *La liturgie expression de la foi*. 1979. In 8°, 378 pp.   L. 18.000

17. E. COSTA jr, *Tropes et séquences dans le cadre de la vie liturgique au moyen âge*, 1979. In 8º, XVI + 96 pp.   L. 6.000

18. CONFÉRENCES ST. SERGE, 1979, *L'Eglise dans la liturgie*, 1980. In 8º, 410 pp.   L. 20.000

19. BRYAN D. SPINKS (ed.), *The sacrifice of praise. Studies on the themes of thanksgiving and redemption in the central prayer of the Eucharistic and baptismal liturgies in honour of Arthur Hubert Couratin*, 1981. In 8º, 272 pp.   L. 20.000

20. CONFÉRENCES ST. SERGE, 1980. *Le Christ dans la liturgie*, 1981. In 8º, 376 pp.   L. 20.000

21. P. TIROT, O.S.B., *Un « Ordo Missae » monastique: Cluny, Cîteaux, La Chartreuse*, 1981. In 8º, 81 pp.   L. 4.000

22. F. BROVELLI, *Per uno studio de « L'Année Liturgique » di P. Guéranger, Contributo alla storia del movimento liturgico*, 1981. In 8º, 81 pp.   L. 4.000

23. P. BARBERI, *La celebrazione del Matrimonio cristiano. Il tema negli ultimi decenni della teologia cattolica*, 1982. In 8º, LIV + 549 pp. L. 30.000

24. A.G. MARTIMORT, *Les diaconesses. Essai historique*, 1982. In 8º, 277 pp.   L. 22.000

25. CONFÉRENCES ST. SERGE, 1970, *L'économie du salut dans la liturgie*, 1982. In 8º, 286 pp.   L. 20.000

26. R. KACZYNSKI - G. PASQUALETTI - Ph. JOUNEL (edd.), *Liturgia, opera divina e umana. Studi sulla riforma liturgica offerti a S.E. Mons. Annibale Bugnini*, 1982. In 8º, 715 pp.   L. 40.000

27. CONFÉRENCES ST. SERGE 1981, *La liturgie: son sens, son esprit, sa méthode*. In 8º, 386 pp.   L. 28.000

28. P.F. BEATRICE, *La lavanda dei piedi. Contributo alla storia delle antiche liturgie cristiane*. 1983. In 8º, 250 pp.   L. 28.000

29. CONFÉRENCES ST. SERGE 1982, *Liturgie, spiritualité, cultures*, 1983. In 8º, 420 pp.   L. 32.000

30. A. BUGNINI, *La riforma liturgica (1948-1975)*, 1983. In 8º, 930 pp. L. 65.000

31. R. FRATTALLONE, *Musica e liturgia. Analisi dell'espressione musicale nella celebrazione liturgica*, 1984. In 8º, 94 pp.   L. 10.000

32. CONFÉRENCES ST SERGE, 1983, *Trinité et liturgie*, 1984. In 8º, 458 pp.   L. 40.000

33. B.D. SPINKS, *From the Lord and « The Best Reformed Churches ». A Study of the Eucharistic Liturgy in the English Puritan and Separatist Traditions (1550-1633)*, Vol. I, 1984. In 8º, 212 pp.
Il II Volume, con lo stesso titolo ma comprendente il periodo 1645-1974, edito dalle « Pikwich Publications », 4137 Timberlane Drive, Allison Park, Pennsylvania 15101 - U.S.A., si può acquistare anche presso le nostre Edizioni.

34. P. TIROT, *Histoire des prières d'offertoire dans la liturgie romaine du VIIè au XVIè siècle*, 1985. In 8º, 125 pp.

35. In preparazione: CONFÉRENCES ST. SERGE 1984, *Eschatologie et liturgie*.

Finito di stampare nel mese di aprile 1985
presso La Casa della Stampa, Tivoli (Roma) -
Tel. (0774) 25766